The story of Metlakahtla

Henry S. Wellcome

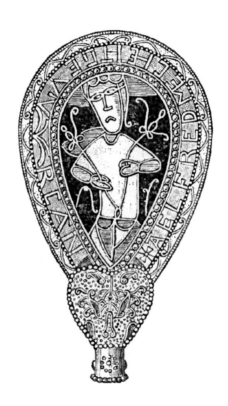

Publishers' Mark

THE STORY

OF

Metlakahtla

BY

HENRY S. WELLCOME

ILLUSTRATED

ADVANCE COPY FOR REVIEW,
With the Publisher's Compliments,
Price, $1.50.

Kindly send copy of Journal, containing review, to
SAXON & CO., 39 CHAMBERS ST.. NEW YORK.
To be issued to the trade Monday, June 13th, 1887.

LONDON AND NEW YORK
1887

THE STORY

OF

Metlakahtla

BY

HENRY S. WELLCOME

ILLUSTRATED

"Materials for another Evangeline."—*N. Y. Sun.*

"The case is one of great interest and involves a story of peculiar cruelty."
—*N. Y. Herald.*

"Tired of British rule."—*N. Y. World.*

"They have decided to try to get the protection of Uncle Sam."
—*N. Y. Tribune.*

"A story of outrage upon, and cruelty to, a civilized Indian community on the part of the Dominion of Canada."—*Providence Journal.*

"The community is on the point of disorganization, and the work of thirty years is threatened with destruction."—*Springfield Republican.*

"The victims have decided to go to Alaska if they can be assured that under American laws they will be protected in what they produce."—*N. Y. Times.*

"At Columbia, on the coast of the Pacific, a practical missionary genius named William Duncan, has succeeded in civilizing a body of Indians, degraded by cannibalism, and, at his Metlakahtla mission, stands at the head of a community of some thousand persons, which has a larger church than is to be found between there and San Francisco. Testimony to the value of the results was borne in 1876 by Lord Dufferin, then Governor-General of Canada, who declared that he could hardly find words to express his astonishment at what he witnessed."—*Encyclopædia Britannica.*

PUBLISHED BY

SAXON & CO.

OF

LONDON AND NEW YORK

1887

TROW'S
PRINTING AND BOOKBINDING COMPANY,
NEW YORK

DEDICATED

TO THE CAUSE

OF

JUSTICE, TRUTH, AND HUMANITY.

" Once in an ancient city, a brazen statue of Justice
  Stood in the public square, upholding the scales in its left hand,
  And in its right a sword, as an emblem that justice presided
  Over the laws of the land and the hearts and homes of the people.
  Even the birds had built their nests in the scales of the balance,
  Having no fear of the sword that flashed in the sunshine above them.
  But in the course of time the laws of the land were corrupted ,
  Might took the place of right, and the weak were oppressed, and the mighty
  Ruled with an iron rod   Then it chanced in a nobleman's palace
  That a necklace of pearls was lost, and ere long a suspicion
  Fell on an orphan girl who lived as maid in the household.
  She, after form of trial, condemned to die on the scaffold,
  Patiently met her doom at the foot of the statue of Justice.
  As to her Father in heaven her innocent spirit ascended,
  Lo ' o'er the city a tempest rose , and the bolts of the thunder
  Smote the statue of bronze, and hurled in wrath from its left hand
  Down on the pavement below the clattering scales of the balance,
  And in the hollow thereof was found the nest of a magpie,
  Into whose clay-built walls the necklace of pearls was inwoven."

                                                    —*Evangeline.*

INTRODUCTION.

A CIVILIZED Christian community of native British Columbians, is now seeking refuge under the American flag from gross, and malicious persecution, of Church and State. This people, only thirty years since, consisted of some of the most ferocious Indian tribes of this continent, given up to constant warfare, notorious for treachery, cannibalism, and other hideous practices. Although incurring great personal risk, and several times narrowly escaping assassination, Mr. William Duncan, with rare fortitude, and genius, began single-handed a mission among them : he educated them, and taught them Christianity, in the simplest possible manner ; at the same time gradually introducing peaceful industries ; and by these means he wrought in a single generation a marvellous transformation. A work that stands absolutely without parallel in the history of missions. Where blood had flowed continually he founded the model, self-supporting village of Metlakahtla,—now consisting of a community of one thousand souls,—that will compare favorably with almost any village of its size in England or America, for intelligence, morality, and industrial thrift. There are also several thousand other civilized Indians, of nearly the same standard, in the outlying missions under his influence ; who, aggravated by similar causes, will doubtless follow the Metlakahtlans.

This successful work is now threatened with utter destruction. In spite of Mr. Duncan's protests, the Church of England Missionary Society through its bigoted Bishop, has attempted to force these simple-minded Christians, to adopt its elaborate rites, and ceremonies. The Indians resent this, and reject the Bishop. The Society in its efforts to destroy the independence of the Metlakahtlans, and compel them to surrender to its dictation, has through its representatives resorted to all manner of intrigues, intimidations, and even schemes to cripple them by impoverishment. Failing to crush them by these measures, the Society's emissaries through great Church influence, have succeeded in inducing the Government to seize a portion of the Metlakahtlans' land without compensation, or treaty, and hand it over to the Society.

All appeals of the Metlakahtlans to the Dominion and Provincial Governments, have been treated with evasion or contempt. In contradiction to all precedents in British and American usage, and the repeated declarations of Earl Dufferin,—while Governor-General of Canada ;—the authorities have proclaimed, that the Indians of British Columbia, are, but beggars, and have no rights whatsoever to the land, and that all *their* land belongs to the Crown. Recently the government authorities have sent men-of-war, and taken active coercive measures, to enforce their decision to despoil the peaceful, and law-abiding, Metlakahtlans; and in consequence of urging their rights by simple protests, without violence, several of the Metlakahtlans have been arrested, and conveyed like criminals, six hundred miles from their homes, and thrown into prison.

Despairing of justice in their own country, and preferring a peaceful solution of their grievances, rather than avenging themselves by warfare, they have unanimously empowered Mr. Duncan, to treat with the Government at Washington for homestead land in Alaska (the boundary of which is but thirty miles distant from their present abode) whence they may remove, and re-erect their build-

ings, re-establish their industries, and secure to
their children full right, and title, to their possessions. These sorely oppressed people, naturally turn
to the United States of America, which has ever
been looked to as the refuge for all those who have
been persecuted by Church or State. Mr. Duncan, comes to this country bearing the following
letter, signed by several of the most distinguished
residents of British Columbia :

"Victoria, B C., November 16, 1886

"To the Lovers of Civil and Religious
        Liberty in America.

" The bearer, Mr. William Duncan, for thirty
years a devoted missionary of religion and civilization, in North British America, and during the
whole of that period well known to the undersigned, is on his way to Washington, deputed by
the native Christian brethren of Metlakahtla, to confer with the United States authorities, on matters
affecting their interest and desires.

" Like the Pilgrim Fathers of old, this afflicted but
prospering and thrifty flock seek a refuge from grievous wrongs, and hope to find it under the American
flag.

"They prefer abandoning the home of their fathers, and the precious fruits of their industry, to submitting to the violent seizure of their land, and the intolerable stings of religious greed, and interference.

"We therefore, most respectfully commend Mr. Duncan, and his mission, to such brothers and friends in our sister country—the land of the free— as may be disposed to use their influence, in aid of the oppressed.

[Signed]

" E. CRIDGE,
    BISHOP, R.E.C.   Resident since 1854.

" B. W. PEARSE,
    Formerly Surveyor General, Vancouver Island; also Chief Commissioner Lands and Works, British Columbia; also Resident Engineer, P. W. Department, Canada.   Resident since 1851.

" W. J. MACDONALD,
    Life Senator of the Dominion Parliament of Canada from British Columbia.   Resident since 1850

" TURNER, BEETON & CO.,
    Merchants, British Columbia.

" J. H. TURNER,"
    Member Provincial Parliament, Victoria, B. C.

The touching appeal of these people, ought to stir the heart, of every liberty-loving American citizen. And it is to be hoped that Congress will secure to them the small area of homestead-land, which they require, out of the many million wild acres in Alaska. Our Government would thereby gain several thousand, industrious, self-supporting, thrifty settlers, as a powerful civilizing nucleus, whose influence upon the yet wild, and savage tribes of the great Arctic State, would be most beneficial.

My first acquaintance with this subject, dates from a visit to the North Pacific in 1878, when I learned much of Mr. Duncan's remarkable civilizing work. From that time, I have kept myself well informed in regard to his progress, and the element of discord which now so seriously threatens to destroy his prosperous community.

In writing THE STORY OF METLAKAHTLA, I have drawn information from official and other reports of the North Pacific, dating from the time of Captain Cook's voyages to the present. Many of the facts have been recounted to me personally by recent travellers and explorers.

I have also had access to the Metlakahtlans' correspondence with the Governments, and, with the Church of England Missionary Society; and, to various State documents bearing upon the sub-ject.

The chief object of this volume, is not to panegy-rize either Mr. Duncan, or the Metlakahtlans, or to make a tirade upon imaginary foes; but more is the pity of it, it is, but, to place the story of the indubit-able wrongs, of the Metlakahtlans before the Ameri-can people, and enlist public sympathy. I have assumed the task voluntarily, and solely, at my own cost, and risk, and I hold myself responsible for the statements I place before my readers; and chal-lenge refutation.

I have no interest to serve, save that of humanity. If the book should meet with sufficient success, to yield a profit above the absolute cost of publication, and distribution of a certain number of free copies, every penny of such net profit to me, shall go to the public fund of the Metlakahtlan community.

In upholding the cause of the Metlakahtlans, I have endeavored to urge upon my readers, a humane consideration of all Aboriginal peoples; and I shall feel more than repaid for my efforts, if my words should in any measure, result in promoting a better understanding of their capacities, and a recognition of what is due them as fellow-men.

To my critics, it is but just to myself to say, that

in holding the chief object of the book in view, I have been compelled to subjugate literary effect too often to the recordance of heterogeneous facts.

Mr. Duncan has not come to the United States begging for money, but merely seeks to secure to these people actual homesteads, with suitable fishing and hunting grounds. However, it will cost upwards of $50,000 to move their houses and effects, to a suitable location on the Alaskan coast. Could some means be devised by which the burthen, of this heavy outlay could be lifted from their shoulders, it would measurably relieve the Metlakahtlans from one of the greatest hardships in being forced to abandon the homes of their forefathers.

It rests with our country, with its " government of the people—by the people, and for the people " to save this stricken community from desperation, and perhaps, from bloodshed.

HENRY S. WELLCOME.

LOTOS CLUB,
New York, May 10, 1887.

OBLIGATIONS.

To those to whom I am indebted for information, and for illustrations I extend my cordial appreciation and thanks. Among these I must particularly mention :

Mr. William Duncan for having at my solicitation placed at my disposal requisite evidences and documents.

Mr. Robert Gordon Hardie for sketches from drawings, photographs and prints.

Dr. Sheldon Jackson for information and photographs, and also for illustrations from his book "*Alaska and the Missions of the North Pacific Coast.*"

Col. Vincent Colyer for use of drawings made during his visit to the North Pacific Coast.

Miss Alice Fletcher for valuable information on Indian laws and legislation.

E. Ruhamah Scidmore for illustrations from "*Journeys in Alaska.*"

Julia McNair Wright for an illustration from "*Among the Alaskans.*"

Rev. J. J. Halcombe for an illustration from "*Stranger than Fiction.*"

In quoting from authors I have given credit in the text.

EXPLANATION.

Metlakahtla is pronounced Met-lā-kāht-lā.

Tsimshean is pronounced T'sim-she-an.

CAPITALS and *Italics* in quotations, I have frequently taken the liberty of using at my own discretion.   H. S. W.

CONTENTS.

- - - - - - - -

APPENDIX.

———

ILLUSTRATIONS.

NATIVE HOUSE WITH CARVED TOTEM POLE.

THE STORY OF METLAKAHTLA.

CHAPTER I.

DAYS OF PERIL.

A CIVILIZING work without parallel, alike remarkable for the original thought and genius displayed, and for the heroic courage in execution; is
that conceived and carried out by William Duncan,
in British Columbia, on the North Pacific coast,
near Alaska.

Captain (now Admiral) Prevost, returning to
England from a cruise in the North Pacific, excited
great public interest by his account of the terrible
state of barbarism that prevailed there. Mr. Duncan, sacrificed a highly lucrative position in a business house and started out for this field under the
auspices of the Church Missionary Society, taking
passage in a Hudson's Bay Company's sailing vessel,
which rounded Cape Horn. On reaching Vancouver Island, Sir James Douglas, then the governor
of the Hudson's Bay Company, urged in the strong-

est possible terms the folly of his attempting to civilize the murderous hordes of the North Pacific; asserting that it would be a fruitless sacrifice of his life. Notwithstanding this, Mr. Duncan, persisted in his determination to go on, and he was taken to Fort Simpson, a fortified trading post of the Hudson's Bay Company. This post was protected by palisades of heavy timbers, massive gates, and flanked by four bastions, with galleries on which cannon were mounted, and strongly garrisoned with riflemen. Sentinels kept watch night and day. So fearful were the commanding officers of the treachery of the natives, that only two or three were allowed to enter the stockade at a time; and these were admitted only through a narrow angular passage to the great store-room window, where they might pass in their furs in barter for store-goods; also, great care was taken not to display too many fine goods, to excite their cupidity. During a siege it was sometimes necessary to keep the gates constantly closed and barricaded for months at a time.

The walls of the fort, and roofs of the houses within showed many marks of bullets of the Indians, fired while fighting among themselves or in attacking the post. Fort Simpson was the centre of an Indian settlement, consisting of nine Tsimshean tribes, notorious on the whole coast for their cruel, bloodthirsty savagery—given up to dark superstitions and atrocious habits of cannibalism—constantly waging merciless war upon the neighboring tribes.

Their warfare was carried on with revolting cruelty, and in taking captives they enslaved the women, and children, and beheaded the men. As they did not take scalps, the heads of their victims served as their trophies of war, which—after the manner of our own highly civilized ancestors in the last century—were borne home on the points of their spears; to afterward dangle from their girdles during their hideous devil dances.

Despite their atrocious barbarity, these people showed evidence of superior intellectual capacity. Their language, abounding in metaphors, is copious and expressive, and with few exceptions the sounds are soft, sweet, and flowing.

In front of every hut was erected a totem-pole, elaborately carved with the figures of birds, or animals, or other objects designating the crest of the clan to which the occupant belonged. Sometimes the entire front of the hut was carved and stained to represent the head and face of an animal or bird, the mouth or beak of which served as a door-way. Every article, whether canoe, fish-spear, war-club, or spoon, served as examples of their skill in carving.

Among their various occupations; they wrought and exquisitely engraved bracelets and other ornaments of gold, silver, and copper; and made baskets and pouches, of a peculiar grass so closely woven as to hold water, all embellished with unique heraldic designs.

A stranger on visiting a village, could always claim, and was always certain, to receive entertainment at the hands of those of his own clan.

Before white men's customs were adopted they produced fire by friction, by twirling rapidly between their hands a pointed stick resting on the edge of a split, against which was heaped a pinch of tinder-bark teased into a fibre. They also boiled water and cooked their food in wooden bowls by placing into them super-heated stones.

The sea, rivers, and forest supplied them with food and raiment. Elk, deer, bear, mountain goat, salmon, herring spawn, oolachan, clams, and clakkass, a ribbon-like seaweed similar to dulse pressed into cakes, and berries; were their principal food. The oolachan, or candle-fish, is rich in a butter-like fat much prized and very nutritious; this fish is so inflammable when dried that when touched with a flame it burns, and is used as a torch.

The coast is as rugged and fierce as the natives who inhabit it. Battling the elements in their struggle for life the savages actually seem to partake of the character of their surroundings. A warm current from Japan setting in against their coast moderates the temperature for a few leagues inland —the season however is too short to ripen cereals.

The Tsimsheans' beliefs and superstitions, are mainly based upon their rich fund of legendary lore. They have a version of the creation, and of the flood; they believe in a good and evil genius, and in special deities who control the sea, the storms, etc. They believe that the world was once wrapped in utter darkness and inhabited only by frogs. The frogs refusing to supply the devil with oolachan, to be avenged he sneaked into heaven and stole daylight, which was kept there in the form of a ball, and broke it over their heads, and, thus gave light to the world. The devil's chief traits were lying and stealing. The world was at one time very close to heaven, so very close, that, the people in heaven, could hear the voices of those on the earth, and, the people on earth, could hear the voices of those in heaven;—the children of the earth made such a clamour, that they disturbed the great Shimanyet Lakkah, and he shoved the earth a long way off. In the next world the good will have the best quality of fish and game, while the wicked will receive only that caught out of season and of poorest quality.

The medicine-man, claiming direct intercourse with the spirit-world, held great influence over the people. He arranged himself, in the skin of a bear or wolf, the head and muzzle of which formed a helmet, the tushes falling about his temples; and a hideously carved mask covered his face, armlets and anklets of repulsive design encircled his shrivelled limbs. To add to the ferocity of his appearance, the exposed parts of his body were daubed with red and black paint, and he was covered with pending charms, such as dried skunk-skins, distended fish-bladders,

tails of animals, feathers, rare shells, highly polished
little horns, eagles' claws, engraved bones and teeth,
which dangled about him as he advanced into the
room with a series of postures and jerks. Armed
with a mystic wand and a huge wooden rattle,
fashioned in the form of an eagle, with a demon
carved on its back pulling out a man's tongue with
its teeth, he proceeds aggressively, to overpower
and frighten away the evil spirit by giving vent to
a series of unearthly wailing and guttural sounds,
vehemently brandishing and marking time with the
rattle. However, if not successful in frightening
away the evil one by these noises, he begins to hack
the ailing part and suck or burn it out. The Shaman received a liberal retainer, in view of securing
his cleverest arts, in exorcising the invading demon.
This evil spirit was supposed to be sent by some
designing enemy; who if discovered was killed by
relatives of the afflicted. If the patient recovered
the Shaman received an additional fee, but, if he
died the fees must be forthwith returned, and sometimes, he also suffered death as a penalty for his
" bad medicine ! "

One of the most marked characteristics of these
people is their inordinate personal pride and vanity—in fact, this is true of all the North Pacific
tribes. Because of a slight taunt or insult a man
will sometimes kill a slave or destroy all his property, believing thereby he wipes out the disgrace.
Some years ago an officer in charge of a division of

DOG-EATERS' RELIGIOUS ORGIES.

an Arctic search expedition; indiscreetly gave out that he was about to *send* for a certain prominent chief. Word of which reached the ears of the chief in question, who was in the habit of *being waited* upon, or the *honor* of his presence *requested*, so, when the officer's emissaries arrived, they were carved, and grilled, and eaten by the affronted chief and his council—this to wipe out the insult.

It was the ambition of every Indian to accumulate as much property as possible. Even depriving himself and his family for many years, of the ordinary comforts of life in his hoarding, in order some day to hold a great feast which should outrival in display those given by his neighbors. On such an occasion he gave away all his property, consisting mainly of blankets—a common form of currency. In doing this, he secured recognition as being a great man in his tribe and thenceforth, took a certain prominent rank.

It is their custom to confine for one month in an isolated cabin girls when attaining the age of puberty, usually their thirteenth year. No one is allowed to see them during this time, and it is supposed that they are away on a voyage to the moon, or to some other celestial abode; and at the end of the month they return to their people amid great feasting and rejoicing. It is on the occasion of a feast accompanying the Potlach, or giving away, or destroying of property; or, the return of a maiden, or the initiating of youth into the

mysteries of Shamanism, that dog-eating and cannibalism, devil-dancing and other wild revelries, occur.

Shortly after Mr. Duncan's arrival he witnessed,
while standing on the gallery of one of the bastions, a most sickening sight: a party of hideously
painted and bedecked cannibals, tearing limb from
limb, the body of a woman who had just been
foully murdered by a chief, each struggling for a
morsel of the human flesh, which they devoured,
accompanying their fiendish orgies with unearthly
howls, and weird beat of their medicine-drums.
Bespattered with the blood of their victim, mad-
dened with rum, frenzied by their hysterical enthusiasm in these superstitious rites, they wrought
themselves into a wild and furious delirium, imi-
tating ravenous wolves in their ferocity. These
ceremonies continued during the night, and were
followed by debaucheries lasting for several days,
during which most terrible atrocities were perpetrated, several of their number being slain, just
without the gates of the fort.

Such scenes as these well might quail the stout-
est heart—but, on the contrary, to Mr. Duncan, they
proved a stimulus to his intrepid determination to
rescue them, from their benighted state.

In one of his letters he writes:—"To attempt to
describe their condition would be but to produce a
dark, revolting picture of human depravity. The
dark mantle of degrading superstition envelopes
them all, and their savage spirits, swayed by pride,

jealousy, and revenge, were ever hurrying them on to deeds of blood. Their history is little else than a chapter of crime and misery." Without a moment's delay he secured the services of Clah, one of the most intelligent Tsimshean natives, to assist him in learning their language in his quarters within the walls of the fort. No white man having yet mastered their tongue, all intercourse with these people had been through the medium of the Chinook jargon, and, a sign language common to the coast. The jargon, however, was too incomplete for teaching purposes, hence, Mr. Duncan, saw that to reach the inner life of the people, he must gain a thorough knowledge of the language, in which they formulated their thoughts.

With great patience and rare ingenuity, by means of signs, gestures, and objects, Mr. Duncan soon secured from Clah a fair vocabulary of Tsimshean words, which he wrote down phonetically, and as soon as possible began to construct sentences. At the end of several months he was able to write out a simple address, explanatory of his mission among them. However, in the meantime, through Clah, he had already conveyed to the Indians, the information that a white man had come, not, to barter, or get gain, but to bring them a message from the white man's God, and to teach them the knowledge of those things in which the white man, was superior to the red man. This naturally excited the curiosity of the Indians, and finally, when Mr. Duncan,

ventured out among them, in spite of the warning
of the officers of the fort, he was warmly received
by the chiefs and people, who regarded him, as some
supernatural being.

In deference to their tribal customs, Mr. Duncan,
found it necessary to speak to the people of each
of the nine Tsimshean tribes, at the houses of their
respective chiefs, during the same day. In some
instances, when Mr. Duncan, saw that the people
gave more attention to his buttons, or the cut of
his garments, than to his words; he repeated his
address until they did listen and comprehend his
message.

Mr. Duncan, had not ventured to address them
until he felt certain he could make himself clearly
understood. He had made it a special study to
acquire their picturesque and expressive figures of
speech. Literal translations into Indian tongues
are very barren, and often extremely droll. One
dignitary of the Church, who began his address to
a coast tribe—" Children of the forest "—was not a
little confused when he found that his interpreter
could only render it, in the Chinook jargon, *Tanass
man cupah hyyu stick*—signifying, little men among
many sticks or stumps.

In the simplest possible manner, after their own
method framing his speech in that peculiar figurative language that appealed most directly to their
understanding, Mr. Duncan, told them the story of
the Bible, and the Saviour, Jesus Christ ; and

pointed out to them the grave sin of taking human life; and the abomination of their present heathenish practices; and pictured to them the benefits of a true Christian life.

Mr. Duncan, opened a school at the house of one of the chiefs. This school was eagerly attended both by children and adults. Finding the Indians so responsive, he, with the assistance of a few of his most zealous followers, erected a log schoolhouse. In this new building his work prospered. Soon he had an attendance of about two hundred pupils, including children and adults, among the latter being numbered several chiefs. There was evidently a general desire for instruction, and a strong feeling prevailed that the white man, possessed some grand secret about eternal things which, even if it involved the overthrow of their most cherished superstitions, they were intensely anxious to know.

By frequent visitation to the houses of the people of all classes, and by searching out and ministering to the sick, he gained a fair insight into their lives, familiarized himself with their customs, and unlocked a special entrance to their hearts.

> "———— He who would gain
> A fond, full heart, ...
> Should seek it when 'tis sore, allay its pain,
> With balm by pity prest : 'tis all his own so held."
> —ZOPHIËL.

The Shamans, or medicine-chiefs, saw in Mr. Duncan's teachings the utter destruction of their craft, for with education and enlightenment ultimately the people would cease to believe in their empty sorceries; therefore, they determined to thwart him. One day he received notice from Legaic, the *head chief* of *all* the tribes, to stop his school for a month during the season of the Medicine Feast. Recognizing that compliance would be regarded as a surrender, he firmly refused to close his school so long as pupils came to be taught. Legaic threatened the lives of Mr. Duncan and his pupils if he did not yield.

Mr. Duncan, fearlessly continued his work, and that day struck the steel which served as a bell to call the children together as usual. Finding he was not to be intimidated by threats, Legaic, followed by a party of medicine-men, all hideously painted, and decked in feathers and charms, rushed into the school. The scholars fled from fear, but Mr. Duncan, met Legaic face to face, and believing that they expected to overcome him by their numbers and frightful appearance, he spoke in a calm and conciliatory tone; pointing out the evil of their ways, urging them to accept his teachings—at the same time assuring them that their threats would be without avail. Legaic, who was fired with drink, and in a furious passion savagely gesticulating, replied that he himself, and his companions were murderers, and the white man's teachings could do them no good. Mr. Duncan, continued to address them pacifically. At one moment, Legaic, appeared

LEGAIC, CHIEF OF ALL THE TSIMSHEAN CHIEFS, ATTACKING MR. DUNCAN

to weaken, but one of his confederates taunted him; and demanded, if he had valor, then, to cut off the white man's head, and he would kick it on the beach. Legaic's pride was stung by this and he drew his knife, and was about to make a thrust, when suddenly his arm fell as if smitten with paralysis, and he cowed and slunk away.

Unknown to Mr. Duncan, Clah, his faithful pupil-teacher,—who had himself been a murderer previous to his conversion,—hearing of Legaic's designs, had armed himself with a revolver and crept quietly into the school-house; just at the moment Legaic lifted his knife to strike, Clah stepped behind Mr. Duncan, and it was the sight of this defender that repulsed the would-be assassin.

One day while addressing his congregation, Mr. Duncan, noticed that the renowned warrior Cushwaht, suddenly rose, gave him a fierce look, and dashed out of the house as if in a rage. After, the service he learned that Cushwaht, was mortally offended at a portion of his sermon, and was "*talking bad*" saying; that Mr. Duncan, had told all the people about *his* bad ways. In reality Mr. Duncan, had only been enumerating and condemning the wrong-doings of *all* those who still continued their heathen practices. Cushwaht's own pricked conscience had accepted the moral challenge.

It was this savage warrior who had incited Legaic, by his demand for Mr. Duncan's head, and later on had sought to kill Mr. Duncan, and failing in his attempt, he vented his wrath by wantonly smashing all the windows of the school-house. While on a trading trip to Victoria he committed some violent deed, for which he was publicly whipped, and then imprisoned. Mr. Duncan, being in Victoria at the time, Cushwaht sent entreating him to come to him. The clement man went, and found the desperado in a cell, pale and haggard; completely crushed now, contritely suing for his intercession—he said:—

" You did not punish me, when I attempted your life, and did you great wrongs; but, God has punished me bitterly:—forgive me:—and I will be good:—you have great influence with the white chief:—pity me:—ask him to free me:—let me go home:—the white chief, will surely do what you ask."

Mr. Duncan pleaded for the release of this penitent miscreant, and vouched for his deportment. The government acceded immediately; placing him in the custody of Mr. Duncan, who sent him forthwith to Fort Simpson; where after living a better life, for some months he was stricken down with small-pox. The contagiousness of his malady, necessitated his sequestration; and he was sheltered in a tent on the beach. As the fear of contagion, would prevent the celebration of his death, with the usual pomp and ceremony for one of his distinction; it was his dying request that his death should be marked by the firing of a cannon; and, the hoisting of a flag over his tent. The Tsimsheans faithfully carried out the behest, of this once cruel and merciless warrior, whose name had been a terror in all that region.

During the first few years of Mr. Duncan's work among the Tsimsheans, he witnessed many scenes of violence and bloodshed: their recounting would alone fill a volume; however, it is not my purpose to chronicle these events, only insomuch as they go to illustrate the character of the people, and the dangers he encountered. On several occasions he narrowly escaped assassination, but by his fearlessness and earnest, unselfish devotion to their welfare, he gradually won their confidence and drew about him a goodly band of faithful followers.

In striving to induce these people to abandon their barbarous customs, Mr. Duncan, perceived he must show them evidence of material advantages to be gained in adopting the new life. He recognized a fact which has, unfortunately, been so little appreciated in the past by those attempting to civilize heathen people; hence, the comparatively few marked successes.

Mr. Henry M. Stanley, one of the greatest students of the savage mind, and one whose vast practical experience enables him to speak with authority, is fully alive to this point. In his book "*Through the Dark Continent*," he says:—

"It is strange how British philanthropists, clerical and lay, persist in the delusion that the Africans can be satisfied with spiritual improvement only. They should endeavor to impress themselves with the undeniable fact that man—white, yellow, red or black—has also material wants which crave to be understood and supplied. A barbarous man is a pure materialist. He is full of cravings for possessing something that he cannot describe. He is like a child which has not yet acquired the faculty of articulation. The missionary discovers the barbarian almost stupefied with brutish ignorance with the instincts of the man in him, but yet living the life of a beast. Instead of attempting to develop the qualities of this practical human being, he instantly attempts his transformation by expounding to him the dogmas of the Christian faith, the doctrine of transubstantiation, and other difficult subjects, before the barbarian has had time to articulate his necessities and to explain to him that he is a frail creature, requiring to be fed with bread, and not with a stone.

" My experience and study of the pagan proves to me, however, that if the missionary can show the poor materialist that religion is allied with substantial benefits and improvements of his degraded condition, the task to which he is about to devote himself will be rendered comparatively easy. For the African once brought in contact with the European becomes docile enough ; he is awed by a consciousness of his own immense inferiority, and imbued with a vague hope that he may also rise in time to the level of this superior being who has so challenged his admiration. It is the story of Caliban and Stefano over again. He comes to him with a desire to be taught, and seized with an ambition to aspire to a higher life, becomes docile and tractable; but to his surprise, he perceives himself mocked by this being, who talks to him about matters that he despairs of ever understanding, and therefore, with abashed face and a still deeper sense of his inferiority, he retires to his den, cavern, or hut, with a dogged determination to be contented with the brutish life he was born in.

" It is not the mere preacher that is wanted here. The Bishops of Great Britain, collected with all the classic youth of Oxford and Cambridge, would effect nothing, by mere talk with the intelligent people of Uganda. It is the practical Christian tutor who can teach people how to become Christians, cure their diseases, construct dwellings, understand and exemplify agriculture, and turn his hand to anything, like a sailor—this is the man who is wanted. Such an one, if he can be found, would become the saviour of Africa. He must be tied to no church or sect, but profess God and his Son and the moral law, and live a blameless Christian, inspired by liberal principles, charity to all men and devout faith in Heaven. He must belong to no nation in particular, but to the entire white race."

Of the missionaries who went to Central Africa, disregarding Mr. Stanley's warnings, several have been brutally murdered, and others are now held captive, while nations ripe for practical missionary work, first, became confused by the theogonies which, were injudiciously urged upon them by missionaries of rival sects, and of rival nations ; then, out of this discord was bred suspicion, which has developed into absolute hostility.

The plan which Mr. Stanley, recommended for Central Africa is practically the same as that inaugurated by Mr. Duncan, in 1857 among the Tsimsheans.

Mr. Duncan, found these people extremely filthy in their persons and in their homes. With *the well-known precept* in view, he secured an abatement in the price of soap, and, after removal to Metlakahtla, he taught them the art of soap-making—Formerly they had been obliged to pay one mink-skin, valued at about one dollar, for a piece of common bar-soap the thickness of one finger ; whereas, he produced a whole large bar for a sixpence. This little industry, though very simple, had a marked effect upon the minds of the people. However, this was but the beginning of the introduction of many other peaceful industries, for it was evident to Mr. Duncan, that in elevating these people and introducing civilized habits of life he was imposing increased expenditures, and in consequence they must find new sources of income ; furthermore, he realized that idleness was always a source of danger.

However, the Hudson's Bay Company, saw in

these industries an interference with their traffic with the Indians, and began to offer opposition.

At the end of four years Mr. Duncan, found, as the result of his devoted labors, that he could muster a fair number of sincere converts; but these were subject to the temptations incident to a trading post, especially as regards drunkenness. Also, he deplored the retrograding influence of constant intercourse with those natives who continued their heathenish rites, and who sought in every possible way to destroy the work of the Christian white man. It is not fair to presuppose that these Indians, with their immature intellects, would be less susceptible to temptations than their more enlightened white brethren.

One of the most serious difficulties in reforming the women lay in the practice of the parents selling their daughters, and that the men hired out their wives and slaves to white men for prostitution. In holding slaves as their concubines, not unfrequently the white traders left children of their own blood in slavery.

In consideration of these obstacles Mr. Duncan, resolved to remove his followers from their pernicious surroundings, and establish an isolated model community. He selected for this purpose a place called Metlakahtla, about twenty miles from Fort Simpson, the site of one of the ancient Tsimshean villages, which had been abandoned by the natives some years before, to join the trading settlement at Fort

Simpson. Metlakahtla presented the advantages of good and convenient fishing and hunting grounds, a good harbor, and a suitable soil for gardening— besides, Nature had modelled its surroundings on a plan of remarkable beauty and grandeur.

For more than a year before the time fixed upon for removing to the new location Mr. Duncan, circulated among the people a set of rules, announcing that he should require all those who joined him to subscribe to them.

These rules are as follows :

1. To give up their " Ahlied," or Indian deviltry.

2. To cease calling in "Shamans," or medicine-men, when sick.

3. To cease gambling.

4. To cease giving away their property for display.

5. To cease painting their faces.

6. To cease indulging in intoxicating drinks.

7. To rest on the Sabbath.

8. To attend religious instruction.

9. To send their children to school.

10. To be cleanly.

11. To be industrious.

12. To be peaceful.

13. To be liberal and honest in trade.

14. To build neat houses.

15. To pay the village tax.

On the day appointed for the removal, fifty souls—men, women, and children —were ready to start, and others promised soon to follow. Mr. Duncan, had pulled down his school-house, and formed the materials into a raft to be navigated to Metlakahtla harbor. He, describes as extremely solemn and impressive the embarkation of his little flock in their six canoes, freighted with their belongings, while the whole population turned out to witness their departure and say farewells. Some earnest in their protestations that they too would soon join them, others faltering with indecision, many predicting failure and return, and not a few, headed by the Shamans, were openly hostile to the movement.

Thus, firm in their adherence to the leadership of their good master, they set sail for their *New Home.*

CHAPTER II.

THE ARCADIAN VILLAGE.

On landing at Metlakahtla, Mr. Duncan, and his Indian converts began immediately to erect huts and a school-house, which also served as a church.

Mr. Duncan, was greatly encouraged and strengthened in his cherished project; when within a week after their arrival, a fleet of thirty canoes came from Fort Simpson, bringing recruits to the number of nearly three hundred, including two chiefs.

The difficulties experienced in organizing and governing a new community, composed of such crude material, were very great. Mr. Duncan, wisely began by placing upon the people themselves much of the responsibility. So closely was their purity and integrity guarded, that every candidate for membership to the community, must be acceptable to all, and subscribe to the rules in public assembly. He organized a village council of twelve including three chiefs who had joined him; and, a native constabulary force.

The council was consulted on all important matters relating to the welfare of the village, however, Mr. Duncan, sometimes found it necessary to act arbitrarily and disregard their opinions, as their clannish prejudices, inconsistencies, and oblique ideas of justice, often made their sitting in judgment very anomalous, especially in passing upon the offences of their own people. With time and experience, under the careful guidance of so just a man; they gradually imbibed ideas of equity, and as their sense of justice expanded greater reliance was reposed in them.

Various public works were required and consequently a tax was necessary. This was fixed at one blanket, valued at $2.50, for each male adult, and one shirt, valued at $1, for such as were approaching manhood. The first assessment yielded to the exchequer the following unique returns:—One green, one blue, and ninety-four white blankets; one pair white trousers, one dressed elk-skin, seventeen shirts, and seven dollars.

Their public works consisted in digging drains, making roads, fixing rests and slides for their canoes to serve all tides; erecting two large houses for the accommodation of strange Indians who came to trade, thus avoiding too intimate mingling of his people with their uncleansed and barbarous visitors. They dug wells and formed a public common and play-ground.

Their instructor seemed mindful of all their natural wants, regarding evil as frequently but nature perverted, hence in displacing gambling and other objectionable games, which had previously served as a pastime among them, he introduced and encouraged cheerful and rational amusements, especially among the young, such as games of foot-ball, marbles, gymnastic-bars, swings, etc.

In carrying out the public works Mr. Duncan, had in view not only the material comforts of his people, but also the necessity to occupy their minds and energies, as well as to develop in them a desire to improve their condition. With the same object he introduced new trades, encouraged and facilitated their ancient industries of hunting, fishing, and gathering berries, and arranged for the exportation of their various products, such as salt and smoked fish, fish-oil, dried fruits, and furs.

Owing to the want of capital, civilization tended to impoverishment of the Indians, by calling for an increased outlay in their expenses, without augmenting their income. Notwithstanding, an earnest desire for progress and enlightenment; the native mind was not fertile in conceiving fresh and permanent modes of industry; therefore, it became necessary for their leader to think out for them, new sources of revenue.

All did not run smoothly in Mr. Duncan's aggressive movements to wrest the heathen from the thraldom of their abominations; at every step in the beginning, he encountered insidious resistance.

Slavery with attendant horrors almost indescribable, was common throughout the entire North Pacific country, on Mr. Duncan's arrival.

From the time of the earliest voyagers to this region, explorers and travellers have recorded the most revolting cruelties practised upon the slaves. Mears in his "*Voyages to the Northwest Coast of America*" writes :—

"The number of Maquilla's slaves were very considerable, not only at Nootka, but in other parts of his territories. And when the fatal day arrived which was to be celebrated by the feast of a human victim, a certain number of these slaves, were assembled in the house of the sovereign chief, who selected the object to be eaten by him and his guests, in the following curious manner :—the inferior chiefs were invited to partake of the ceremonies which were appointed to precede it :—these consisted of singing the war song, dancing round the fire, and fomenting the flames by throwing oil into them. A bandage is then tied over the eyes of Maquilla, who in this blindfold state is to seize a slave. His activity in the pursuit, with the dread and exertions of these unhappy wretches in avoiding it, form another part of this inhuman business. But it is seldom a work of delay,—some one of these slaves is soon caught; death instantly follows, —the devoted carcass is immediately cut in pieces, and its reeking portions distributed to the guests: when an universal shout of those who have escaped declares the joy of their deliverance."

It has been the custom of many tribes up to our day, to sacrifice, the life of a slave to wipe out

an insult, or on the grave of his master that he
should go to the other world attended, as became
his dignity.

Chiefs and other important men often celebrated
the erection of their houses, by planting the four
posts, on the bleeding bodies of slaves slaughtered
for the occasion. Slaves were marked by having
their hair cropped short. They were subjected to
all manner of abuse, sold and hired out for prostitution, and at death their bodies were cast into the
sea, or were feasted upon by cannibals.

Even within close proximity to the white settlements the vile traffic in human beings was open, and
common. Touching this topic Whymper writes, of
Victoria, B. C. :—

" These Indian slaves squatting in considerable
numbers in the bush, for what purpose it is not
difficult to imagine, and the extent to which the
nefarious practices referred to are encouraged by the
crews of her Majesty's ships, is a disgrace to the
service they represent, and a scandal to the country.
Hundreds of dissipated white men, moreover, live
in open concubinage with these wretched creatures.
So unblushingly is this traffic carried on, that I have
seen the husband and wife of a native family, can-
vassing from one miner's shanty to another with
a view of making assignations for the *clootchman*
(squaws) in their possession. On one occasion I
saw an Indian woman offering to dispose of her
own child, the offspring of the guilty alliance with

a white man, for $31, at the door of a respectable white dwelling."—"*Travels in Alaska.*" London, 1868.

D. G. F. McDonald, C.E., writes :— "These wretched slaves are horribly abused. They are made to do all the filthy work under the torture of the lash, which their fellow-savage lays on unmercifully. Should such enormities be perpetrated, or their continuance be allowed, in a British colony? Surely slavery is a curse so intolerable and degraded that it ought not to be suffered to exist, even for a single hour."

Upon the matter of slavery the Bishop of Columbia writes :—" Slavery has increased. Female slaves are in demand. Distant tribes make war upon each other, and bring their female slaves to the market. You will hardly credit it, but it is strictly true, women are purchased as slaves to let them out for immoral purposes. A female slave has been known recently to be purchased for $200 (£40)."—"*British Columbia.*" London, 1862.

While at Fort Simpson, Mr. Duncan, found it impossible to do more, than urge upon the people the iniquity and injustice, of holding their fellow-men in servile bondage. But, as soon as he was firmly established at Metlakahtla, he devoted himself arduously to freeing all slaves who came within his range of power, and also, harbored fugitives, until they could be restored to the native tribes from which they, or their ancestors had been seized.

As may be expected this called down upon him the retaliatory fury of many powerful chiefs, among whom was the treacherous Sebassah who ultimately was convicted for the murder of two white men. He and his confederates confessed the crime, he was condemned to death, but on the recommendation of Mr. Duncan, this sentence was commuted to five years' surveillance at Metlakahtla.

For his determined rescue of slaves Mr. Duncan's life was many times endangered, but he was heartily supported by the Metlakahtlans, and he continued his humane work in defiance of all threats. Finally Metlakahtla became known as an asylum of emancipation, and slaves from all parts of British Columbia and Alaska, sought a refuge within its sheltering precincts. As the result of the bold onslaught upon slavery begun by Mr. Duncan, to-day the practice has greatly diminished, and is now I believe only common among the inland tribes of British Columbia and Alaska.

One of the most serious difficulties to be dealt with was the sale of intoxicating liquors. White men trading along the coast in small sailing vessels made liquor selling their principal business. Some Indians also engaged in this traffic by means of their canoes. Their visits to Indian camps were invariably followed by brutal outrages, usually with murder and not unfrequently intertribal wars. By strictly prohibiting indulgence or traffic in intoxicating liquors, within his own precincts, Mr. Duncan, at once brought himself into collision with these traders, and earned their eternal hatred. Being vested by the government with the powers of a magistrate, he found it necessary to exercise his functions, by fining and imprisoning several of the liquor traders; and finally, as an example, seized the vessel of one who defied his authority and burned it on the beach. The owner, on returning to Victoria, in fitting out a new liquor-selling vessel, out of spite named it " The Duncan."

One of the white traders imprisoned at Metla-kahtla was singularly enough converted during his term of imprisonment, by the Indian guard, whose exemplary Christian life so impressed him, that he abandoned the nefarious traffic and became a Christian. However, some of these traders even went so far as to threaten Mr. Duncan's life, and did kill one of his constables and wound several others while attempting to make arrests. On one occasion a party of Kitahmaht Indians landed a quantity of liquor: Mr. Duncan, at once caused it to be seized. The Kitahmahts, out of revenge for this, stole a little boy belonging to Metlakahtla, while he was on a fishing expedition with his parents. He was worried to death, and literally torn to pieces and devoured by these cannibals!

To this was added the hostility of the Hudson's Bay Company's agents, who regarded Mr. Duncan's introduction of the trades and industries of civilization as undermining their close monopoly. They would no longer bring his supplies in their vessels. From this time forth the Hudson's Bay Company's agent and the coast traders lost no opportunity to revile him, charging that his mission was simply a private money-making scheme ; therefore, he had as his sworn enemies not only the slave-traders and the Shamans and chiefs, who saw him destroying their power and influence ; but also the white traders of the coast, who were plotting for his overthrow and that of his mission.

Just at this time there fell upon the coast a fearful plague of small-pox, destroying thousands of lives, and spreading universal destitution and terror. Five hundred Tsimsheans alone succumbed to its ravages. Thanks to the wise sanitary precautions taken by Mr. Duncan, who vaccinated all who came to him, only five deaths occurred among his original settlers who came with him from Fort Simpson, and several of these contracted the fatal malady while caring for outside sufferers.

But the ravages of this scourge along the coast caused frightful misery and suffering. Seeing so many fellow-creatures stricken down on all sides about them, the Indians were so demoralized with terror that they could hardly be induced, during its depressing reign, to continue their avocations ; and trading between the tribes was almost wholly suspended. Mr. Duncan, humanely sent succor far and near, and numbers flocked to him for assistance ; he ministered to them as far as possible, always

GOLD AND SILVER BRACELETS.

guarding the welfare and safety of his own people as his prime duty. His heroic conduct and indefatigable devotion during this trying ordeal, was not lost upon the Indians.

These were certainly grave difficulties to be met single-handed by a lone white man, with an infant community of but half-enlightened savages. But the brave man who had not feared to face death, in the performance of the work to which he had so nobly dedicated himself, did not falter.

He determined to purchase a vessel, and thereby secure independent transportation. For this purpose he obtained subscriptions from his Indians in sums of five dollars to ten dollars, paid in their products; in total amounting to an equivalent of four hundred dollars; then, appealing to the government, he secured a contribution of five hundred dollars (this latter sum being afterward apportionately refunded), and added the deficit of six hundred dollars from his own private funds, and purchased a schooner costing fifteen hundred dollars.

During the first voyage this schooner made down the coast to Victoria Mr. Duncan, was obliged to navigate the vessel himself. It proved a highly remunerative investment, carrying their own products down the coast, and bringing up various goods to supply their own wants, and for traffic with the neighboring tribes.

At the end of a few months a handsome dividend was declared on each share. This part of the proceedings somewhat puzzled the Indians, who, when the money was paid to them, imagined that they must necessarily be parting with their interest in the vessel. As soon, however, as the matter was made clear to them, they evinced their appreciation by calling it "Kahah," or "Slave," signifying that *it* did all the work, and that *they* reaped all the profit. His own share of the profits Mr. Duncan, devoted entirely to the objects of his mission.

An important step in these commercial developments, was, the establishment of a village store on the plan of a co-operative stock company, in which each villager held at least one share. This institution also served as a savings-bank. Blankets, furs, etc., were received, and the value credited as a deposit, upon which a yearly interest of ten per cent. was allowed. On the payment of the first year's interest some of the Indians were surprised, for they imagined that they ought instead, to pay for the safe-keeping of their treasures. It was, indeed, a revelation when they found that their ten blankets had "swollen" (to use their quaint expression) to eleven! It was their first idea of usury. Formerly, in storing up their furs and blankets in their own huts, they became injured and depreciated by mildew and insects.

After a time, prosperity began to smile upon this novel Arcadian community. The untiring zeal and energy of their leader, enabled them to override the many obstacles which had threatened their progress.

The minds of the people exhibited signs of development, and their benefactor was alive to the requirements of their advancing intellects; he delivered simple lectures, illustrated by maps and a stereopticon; on history, geography, astronomy, natural history, and morals. He was at one and the same time pastor, missionary, secretary, treasurer, magistrate, school-master, physician, carpenter, builder, chief-trader, friend and adviser.

The growing exigencies, demanded modifications in the form and organization of the village government, also new and modified laws. The native council was increased in numbers and was made an elective body, without compensation; they were allowed to wear a badge of office on special occasions. The constabulary force was also increased, and free uniforms were supplied; the constables received a small remuneration when on duty. The entire male population was divided into ten companies, each having an equal number of councilmen and constables, who acted as monitors; and, in order to enlist the younger men in the public weal, a fire brigade was organized of six companies, ten men in each company.

At one of these elections a little incident occurred that would amuse some politicians. The ballot in favor of a candidate for the council must be unanimous, in order to secure election. On one occasion a black ball was cast, and as the nominee enjoyed an excellent reputation, Mr. Duncan, gave out that

he would like to see the dissenter privately. Early
the next morning the individual called, and explained that on a certain day, the candidate had
been given one dollar too much change at a store,
and had asked him if he ought to keep it—

" He ought to have known himself that he ought
to be honest without asking me! That, is why I
thought he ought not to be a councillor."

These people, just wrested from dark superstitions and vicious habits, and liable to the natural
weaknesses of mankind, required the most anxious
watch-care. And, as was to be expected, some
transgressions of the rules occurred. Those guilty
of offences of a grave character such as threatening
or attempting bloodshed, after being adjudged by
Mr. Duncan, and the council, and condemned, were
publicly whipped by Mr. Duncan. This was the
severest form of punishment inflicted, which occurred only four or five times and one much dreaded;
for the inherent pride and vanity of the people
caused them to regard it as a stinging disgrace
Banishment, was also resorted to, in the cases of
some incorrigible malefactors. A very novel mode
of dealing with a certain class of offences was the
hoisting of a black flag over the prison ; whenever
this flag was raised the people inquired of each
other, "Who is the offender ? " and soon public
opinion made it so warm for him, that he was obliged to make ample amends or quit the village.

To keep pace with the general moral and mental

progress, and furnish them with the comforts and conveniences of modern civilization, it was necessary to improve the dwellings, and, it was decided to pull down all the old houses and erect new ones. The new town was laid out in lots of 60 by 120 feet, on each to be erected a double house. As the new dwellings were to be substantial and commodious, and somewhat beyond their means, Mr. Duncan, pledged himself to assist them in lumber to the amount of $60 for each double house. A new church, seating 1,200 people, a town-hall, dispensary, reading-room, market-house, blacksmith, carpenter, cooper, and tin shops; work-sheds, and a soap-factory were built. And not the least important undertaking, was the building of a massive sea-wall to protect the village. In order to carry out the proposed improvements, it was necessary to erect a water-power saw-mill. One old Indian who heard that Mr. Duncan intended to make water saw wood, said :—

"If it is true that Mr. Duncan, can make water saw wood, I will see it and then die!"

And thus prosperity continued. The public improvements were largely the result of the profits accruing from the schooner, the store, and the trading expeditions of the villagers, but were assisted by the contributions of friends of the mission and Mr. Duncan's private funds. As time passed on, one practical trade and industry after another was added—the people were kept busy and happy. Mr.

Duncan, paid a flying visit to England in 1870, during which he procured machinery and learned various trades, such as weaving, rope-making, twine-spinning, brush-making, etc. During his stay he learned the gamut of several instruments, and on his return to Metlakahtla; gratified the musical tastes of the people, by organizing a brass band of twenty-one instruments, which has long since gained great renown on the coast. And an organ was placed in the church.

Had Mr. Duncan, at any time doubted the Indians' appreciation of his labors, every vestige of this must have been dispelled; when on his return from England, the population of his ideal mission paid him all the honors that they could have accorded to a king. His brief absence had seemed to them an age. The touching incidents of this greeting are best recounted in his own modest words :—

" The news of my arrival travelled to Metlakahtla, and on the following morning a large canoe arrived from there to fetch me home. The happy crew, whose hearts seemed brimful of joy at seeing me back, gave me a very warm welcome. I at once decided to leave the steamer and proceed at once to Metlakahtla with my Indian friends, who assured me that the village was in a great state of excitement at the prospect of my return. We were favored with a strong, fair wind, and with two sails up, we dashed along merrily through a boiling sea. I now felt I was indeed homeward bound. My

SEA VOYAGE IN NATIVE CANOE.

happy friends, having nothing to do but to watch the sails and sit still, could give free vent to their long-pent-up feelings, and so they poured out one piece of news after another in rapid succession, and without any regard to order, or the changes their reports produced upon my feelings; thus we had good and bad, solemn and frivolous news, all mixed indiscriminately.

"On sighting the village, in accordance with a preconcerted arrangement, a flag was hoisted over our canoe, as a signal to the villagers that I was on board. Very soon we could discern quite a number of flags flying over the village, and Indians hurrying toward the place of landing. Before we reached the beach large crowds had assembled to greet me. On my stepping out of the canoe, bang went a cannon, and when fairly on my feet bang went another. Then some of the principal people stepped away from the groups and came forward, hats off, and saluted me warmly. On my advancing, the corps of constables discharged their muskets, then all hats were doffed, and a general rush to seize my hand ensued. I was now hemmed in with the crowds of solemn faces, many exhibiting intense emotion, and eyes glistening with tears of joy. In struggling my way to the mission-house, I had nearly overlooked the school children. The dear little ones had been posted in order on one side, and were standing in mute expectation of a recognition. I patted a few on the head, and then with my feel-

ings almost overcome, I pressed my way to my
house. How sweet it was to find myself again in
my own little room; and sweeter still to thank God
for all His preserving care over me. As numbers
of the people were pressing into and crowding my
house, I ordered the church bell to be rung. At
once they hurried to the church, and when I entered it was filled. Such a sight! After a minute's
silence we joined in thanksgiving to God, after
which I addressed the assembly for about twenty
minutes. This concluded, I set off, accompanied by
several leading Christian men, to visit the sick and
very aged, whom I was told were anxiously begging
to see me. The scenes that followed were very affecting. Many assured me that they had constantly
prayed to God to be spared to see me once again,
and God had answered their prayers and revived
their hearts after much weeping. On finishing my
visit I made up doses of medicine for several of the
sick, and then sat down for a little refreshment.
Again my house becoming crowded, I sat down with
about fifty for a general talk. I gave them the
special messages from Christian friends which I had
down in my note-book, told them how much we
were prayed for by many Christians in England,
and scanned over the principal events of my voyage
and doings in England. We sat till midnight, but
even then the village was lighted up, and the people
all waiting to hear from the favored fifty, what I
had communicated. Many did not go to bed at

all, but sat up all night talking over what they had heard.

"Such is a brief account of my reception at Metlakahtla. I could but reflect how different this to the reception I had among the same people in 1857. Then they were all superstitiously afraid of me, and regarded with dread suspicion my every act. It was with feelings of fear or contempt they approached me to hear God's word, and when I prayed among them I prayed alone; none understood, none responded. Now how things have changed! Love has taken the place of fear, and light the place of darkness, and hundreds are intelligently able and devoutly willing to join me in prayer and praise to Almighty God. To God be all the praise and glory."

It was not long after the founding of Metlakahtla; that, the example of its inhabitants began to produce a marked impression, upon the surrounding tribes, and even far in the interior, and up and down the coast.

Among the converts had been numbered the chiefs Legaic, Neachshlakah-Noosh, Leequneesh, and Quthray, the leader of the cannibal feast witnessed by Mr. Duncan, on his first arrival.

It was only after a hard struggle that the fierce barbarian Legaic yielded, and sacrificed his proud and powerful position as chief of all the chiefs of the Tsimsheans. This brutal murderer, who boasted of the number of lives he had taken—was at length humbled and led like a lamb. He had once, as I had previously shown, attempted to assassinate Mr. Duncan, and had never ceased to persecute and harass him and his followers, until now, like Saul when stricken, he was transformed into a faithful disciple of him whom he had bitterly reviled, and had mercilessly pursued. Likewise, as Saul, when baptized he chose the name Paul. He became a simple citizen of Metlakahtla, an industrious carpenter and cabinet-maker, a truly exemplary Christian. While he was away on an expedition to some tribes in the Nass River Country, he was taken with a fatal illness, and feeling that he was approaching death, he sent pleading letters to Mr. Duncan to come to his bedside; but to his great sorrow, circumstances rendered this impossible, and Mr. Duncan, could only send comforting messages.

Legaic's last words to Mr. Duncan, written down by his own daughter, were as follows :

" I want to see you. I always remember you in my mind. I shall be very sorry if I shall not see you before I go away, because you showed me the ladder that reaches to heaven, and I am on the top of that ladder now. I have nothing to trouble me; I only want to see you." Then he passed peacefully away.

Thus died the once haughty chieftain Legaic.

Mr. Duncan, had visited many outside tribes, but most of his time was occupied with his work at Metlakahtla.

LEGAIC AS A SIMPLE CITIZEN AND CARPENTER OF METLAKAHTLA.

Remembering how the white Christian, who with so much self-sacrifice had come among them, to bring them out of darkness; the Indians of Metlakahtla felt it to be incumbent upon themselves, as soon as they had sufficient light, that they should carry the knowledge to their less privileged brethren. Native missionaries went out at their own expense. These men gave their message in a simple, figurative language, yet with an earnestness and directness of purpose that carried conviction. The following is an example which will serve to illustrate their method of thought:

"Brothers, sisters, you know the way of the eagle? The eagle flies high, and the eagle rests high! He rests on the highest branch of the highest tree, then, he is free from fear of all beneath him!—Brothers, sisters, Jesus, to us is the highest branch of the highest tree! Let us rest on Him, then, we too need not fear, all our enemies are beneath us."

Nor were the regular native missionaries the only workers; the hunters and fishermen in mingling with the people of other villages, told them of the changes wrought by the new life; and the trading parties who journeyed far inland, or voyaged along the coast in their canoes bartering for furs, each did his mission work. Nor was it in their words alone that they gave evidence. These men, who had formerly been a terror to the whole coast and only received with suspicion, were, to the contrary, now mild and peaceful. What had wrought this change?

After a visitation of the Metlakahtla voyagers, a chief and several of the head men of the Chilkats, a fierce tribe living some five or six hundred miles north on the Alaskan coast, ventured to pay a visit to Metlakahtla, of which they had heard such wonderful stories. Just before landing they, as usual on visiting a settlement, arrayed themselves in all their magnificence of barbaric finery, intending to impress the people with their greatness and importance. As they approached in solemn state, Mr. Duncan, was notified of their coming and urged to attire himself in his Sunday best, because the savages were in gorgeous trappings and would despise him if he was poorly dressed. He had on his common work clothes, and was in the midst of some important work, which he could not drop at the moment.

As the Chilkats' superb canoes kissed the beach they leaped out and were cordially received by the Metlakahtlans. They were struck with utter amazement at the sight of the buildings, the manner in which the people were clothed, and the general appearance of thrift and civilization on every hand. They were impatient to see the great master, who had wrought all these wonders.

Mr. Duncan, had not dressed up,—at all times he sought to discourage the assumption of pomp and foolish display, which he found so wefted in these naturally vainglorious people. When the Chilkats were escorted to him, and he was pointed out as the benefactor, they looked over and beyond him, saying that they could not see him, but when this modest, plainly clad little man greeted them, and his personality was made clear, they preserved their countenances in stolid rigor to maintain their own great dignity, never uttering a word, save, the ceremonies of a formal greeting.

Despite their efforts to conceal their thoughts, they betrayed great astonishment; it was evident that they suspected some deception was being practised upon them. Mr. Duncan, evincing great cordiality conducted them to his house, and gave them the customary seats of honor for distinguished guests. They continued to look at him in utter silence for some time, when finally they could restrain themselves no longer they broke out, saying:

"Surely *you* cannot be the man! Why, we expected to see a great and powerful giant, gifted in magic, with enormous eyes that could look right through us and read our thoughts! No, it is impossible! How could *you*, tame the wild and ferocious Tsimsheans, who were always waging war, and were feared throughout the whole coast? It is only a few years ago that all this country was a streak of blood, now we see nothing but white eagle's-down (their emblem of peace and amity)! We can hardly believe our own eyes, when we see these fine houses and find the Tsimsheans have become wise like white men! They tell us that you have God's Book, and that you have taught them to read it; we wish to see it."

On the Bible being placed before them, and on being told that it was by following the teachings of this Book, that the Metlakahtlans had become enlightened, each one touched it reverently with the tip of his finger and said, " Ahm, ahm "—It is good, it is good.

Gifts were exchanged, and bartering went on, and the visitors tarried for several days, during which time, they marvelled at every new wonder of civilization which they beheld.   Mr. Duncan, seized every opportunity to impress upon them, the fundamental truths, which had brought about this change. He showed them, that the prosperity, and material benefits, which they witnessed, were but the reward of the adoption of the new life.   This lesson was not lost upon them ; they returned to their homes resolved to adopt the Christian white man's ways. And thus, came many from afar to view the wonders of civilization, all to return, and proclaim to their people, that, the Christian white man's ways were good.

CHAPTER III.

HALCYON DAYS.

AN era of prosperity now shone upon Mr. Duncan's civilized Indian community, however, in the acquirement of those things essential to human comfort and refinement ; the material, was never allowed to crowd the spiritual ; the material was only the means to a spiritual end. With these people it was, as it has ever been, in dealing with the infant-mind of the savage, necessary to hold up the benefits of civilization as the guerdon of a better life.

No better evidence, of the depth, and integrity, of the conversion of these recently groping savages, could·be required, than the attestation of those distinguished dignitaries of the Church who visited them, and observed the practices of their daily life, and after thoroughly testing the candidates, administered the rites of baptism.

This chapter I shall devote to several such citations for a twofold purpose, which will discover itself in the progress of this volume.

The Bishop of Columbia's first visit to Metlakahtla, was during the oolichan fishing season, 1863. He came with the special purpose of baptizing those

whose probation indicated their worthiness to receive that rite.   His own narrative vividly pictures
the incidents of his arrival :

" The Christian Indian settlement of Metlakahtla
lies retired upon a recess of a bay, and is marked by
a row of substantial wooden houses.   An octagon
building is the school, and a flagstaff stands near,
upon which ascended the national flag when we
hove in sight, and fired the gun to announce our
approach.   We could soon distinguish a canoe putting off to us, and presently it approached, flying a
flag.   It was a large canoe, which had a warlike
appearance, manned by ten Indians, and in it was
seated Mr. Duncan, the missionary of Metlakahtla.
There was placed, too, by his side, a murderer, who
had last year committed a cold-blooded murder
upon an Englishman, and who had given himself up
against the coming of the man-of-war."

According to the Bishop of Columbia's account,
the man-of-war " *Devastation* " had in vain directed
her guns against the village of this man's tribe,
threatening it with annihilation if they did not give
him up.   The Indians defied the man-of-war, but
after its departure the murderer, knowing Mr. Duncan's renown for justice and clemency, surrendered
himself at Metlakahtla, saying to Mr. Duncan,
" Whatever you tell me to do I will do.   If you say
I am to go on board the gun-ship when she comes
again, I will go."

The Bishop continues.   " For six months he had

been there at large, and when our gun sounded he might have escaped; but he said, 'What am I to do?' and the answer was 'You must come with me a prisoner.' He was accordingly handed over to us a prisoner, to be taken to New Westminster to be tried for his life. The scene was touching when his wife and children came to bid him farewell, and she earnestly besought Mr. Duncan, the captain, and myself to say some one word which might give her a ray of hope. Thus we see that what the ship of war with its guns and threats could not do for civilization, for protection of life, for justice, the simple character and influence of one missionary could accomplish for all those importuous objects. . . .

" Among the crew in Mr. Duncan's canoe was one man who had been a noted drunkard and a violent chief, a slaughterer of many human victims in his day—indeed, the head man of the Tsimshean tribes —who had given up all evil ways, and was now as a little child, a candidate for baptism. . . .

" We were met," he writes, " by the whole village, who stood on the bank in a long line, as fine a set of men, well-dressed, as could anywhere be seen where men live by their daily toil; certainly, no country village in England would turn out so well-clad an assemblage. . . .

" I addressed the assembly, and was interpreted by Mr. Duncan, who made himself, also, an earnest and telling discourse. *This change is the result of four and a half years of his faithful and earnest work as a catechist. Beyond the expectation of all persons acquainted with Indians, success and blessing have attended his labors."* . . .

The Metlakahtlans are very dependent upon the catch of fish during the season, but many of them made great sacrifice of their time to receive the ordinance of baptism. The Bishop of Columbia, dwells very particularly upon their strict observance of the Sabbath while so strongly tempted to seek a store of food.

"But what did the Christian Indians do when Sunday came? The first Sunday of their first fishing-season, as Christians, although the fish had come up in greater abundance than ever, and the season was so short, the Christians said, 'We cannot go and fish.' The heathen were full of excitement, gathering in the spoil; but the Christians said, 'No, we are God's people; God will provide for us, and we will spend His day as He tells us to do.' *And they kept holy each Lord's Day in the midst of the fishing-season."* An example which a later Bishop would have done well to copy.

"Got to the mission-house at eight to breakfast. Afterward engaged the whole day seeing catechumens till one o'clock next morning. One after another the poor Indians pressed on to be examined. They had been under training for periods, varying from eight months, to three years. They had been long looking for a minister to admit them to baptism. It was a strange yet intensely interesting sight in that log cabin, by the dim glimmer of a small lamp, to see just the countenance of the Indian, sometimes with uplifted eyes, as he spoke of the blessedness of prayer; at other times, with downcast melancholy, as he smote upon his breast in the recital of his penitence. The tawny face, the high cheek-bone, the glossy jet-black flowing hair, the dark, glassy eye, the manly brow, were a picture worthy the pencil of the artist. The night was cold —I had occasionally to rise and walk about for warmth—yet there were more. The Indian usually retires as he rises, with the sun, but now he would turn night into day, if he might only be allowed to ' have the sign,' and be fixed in the good ways of God. . . .

"Converts from heathenism can fully realize renunciation of the world, the flesh, and the devil. *Among these Indians pomp of display, the lying craft of malicious magic, as well as all sins of the flesh, are particularly glaring, and closely connected with heathenism. So are the truths of the Creed in strongest contrast* to the dark and miserable fables of their forefathers, and heartily can they pledge themselves to keep the holy will of God, all the days of their life, seeing Him a loving and true Father, of whom now so lately, but so gladly, they have learnt to know."

The Bishop of Columbia continues: "I first drew forth their views of the necessity of repentance, its details, and their own personal acquaintance with it. I then questioned them as to the Three Persons of the Trinity, and the special work of each, with allusion to the Judgment, and the state of the soul hereafter, inquiring into their private devotion, to learn their personal application of repentance and faith. I questioned their anxiety for baptism, and demanded proof of their resolution to keep the will of God for their guide, to speak of God, and to labor for God's way, all their life long. I sought to find out the circumstances under which they first became seriously inclined, and to trace their steps of trial and grace. Admitting them to the promise of baptism, I exhorted them to prayer and devotion, as a special preparation until the time came."

The following extracts from the Bishop of Columbia's report convey a most convincing testimony to the honesty, and depth, of conversion of these recently reclaimed savages.

The simplicity, and apparent sincerity of the answers, will bear a thoughtful comparison, with those rendered in our home churches. I beg my readers will bear this examination in mind while reading the reference I shall make to the report of the Society's Deputation in Chapter VII. of this volume.

MALES.

CLAH, aged 35 —*Answers :*—I have made up my mind to live a Christian Must try to put away all our sins I believe in Jesus Christ, the Son of God, who died for our sins. God is good to us, and made us. God gives us His

Spirit to make us clean and happy. I pray to God to clean my heart, and wipe out my sin from God's book. It will be worse for us if we fall away after we have begun. I repent I was not baptized a year and a half ago.

LEGAIC (principal chief), aged 40.—*Answers :*—We must put away all our evil ways. I want to take hold of God. I believe in God the Father, who made all things, and in Jesus Christ. I constantly cry for my sins when I remember them. I believe the good will sit near to God after death. Am anxious to walk in God's ways all my life. If I turn back it will be more bitter for me than before. I pray God to wipe out my sins ; strengthen me to do right ; pity me My prayers are from my heart. I think sometimes God does not hear me, because I do not give up all my sins. My sins are too heavy. I think we have not strength of ourselves.

Remarks.—Under instruction about nine months. On two occasions before attended for a short time, but fell away. Mr. Duncan says this man has made greater sacrifices than any other in the village. Is the principal chief, and has left his tribe and all greatness. Has been a most savage and desperate man ; committed all crimes. Had the offer of forty blankets to return to his tribe. He now bears the ridicule of his former friends. Yet his temper, formerly ferocious, bears it patiently, and he returns kindness, so that some have melted and are ready to come with him.

LEE-QU-NEESH (a chief), aged 39.—*Answers :* When young was brought up in sin. No one ever told me the good news. Cannot tell how great a sinner I am. I believe in God, and cannot turn back to any of my old ways. The great Father Almighty, Maker of the earth. Jesus Christ, the only Son of God, died for our sins that God might pity us on that account. God is a Spirit, full of love and goodness ; but we must pray for God's Holy Spirit. We must all stand before God. God will know who are good and bad. By-and-by I shall know if God hears me. My heart is dark; I cannot clearly tell now. A long time I felt it was contrary to God, and when I heard the good news I gave up evil ways.

NEEASH-LAKAH-NOOSH (called "the Lame Chief;" he is blind also of an eye; fine old man); aged 70.—*Answers :*—When asked if he wished to become a Christian, said—For that object I came here with my people. I have put away all lying ways, which I had long followed. I have trusted in God. We want the Spirit of God. Jesus came to save us. He compensated for our sins. Our Father made us, and loved us because we are His work. He wishes to see us with Him because He loves us. When asked about the judgment, said, The blood of Jesus will free those who believe from condemnation.

Remarks.—Under regular instruction for a year, and before that for some time by his daughter. Is most consistent, trying to do simply what is right. Recently he was benighted on a Saturday, on his way to spend the Sunday at Metlakatillo, seven miles off. Would not come on, nor let his people gather herring-spawn, close under their feet; he rested the Lord's Day according to the commandment.

YILMAUKSH, aged 22.—*Answers :*—I believe in Jesus as my Saviour, who died to compensate for my sins to God.

Remarks.—Appears very earnest; speaks devoutly and freely. Long time under serious impressions. Brought out from heathenism three of his relations. Eight months under special instruction.

LEHT, aged 25.—*Answers :*—I feel my unworthiness, but trust to God's pity. We must pray constantly to God. I have not two hearts; have given myself to God.

Remarks.—Was in the "Cariboo" steamship when blown up: turned to God then. Three years under instruction. Son of a chief. Much tempted to go to heathen feasts, but has steadily refused.

KANGISL, aged 22.—*Answers :*—I am striving against my sins, determined to follow God's way. God's way good and right, without doubt. Our way full of mistakes. Christ searched out (exposed) man's way and showed God's way, and then was punished to make satisfaction for our sins. I pray for a good heart and for pardon from my sins.

Remarks.—Four or five years ago under instruction ; fell away. A year preparing for magic ; a year and a half earnest.

SHKAH-CLAH, aged 35.—*Answers :*—I have not long come forward for baptism, but have long been wishing to be fixed in God's way, and have been struggling against my sins. God punishes the wicked who persevere in their sins. I must pray for God's Spirit. God teaches us humility, and to love one another. I pray for God to pardon my sins, and to dress me in His righteousness.

Remarks.—Confesses he has been very wicked. Lately his child died. As it lay dying, with tears he touched it, and said, "This is for my sins." Was moved strongly to turn to God by the death of his child. Belongs to a leading family. His brother, a heathen chief, tells him he will be nobody if he becomes a Christian.

LAPPIGH KUMLEE, aged 30.—*Answers :*—I have given up the lucrative position of sorcerer. Been offered bribes to practise my art secretly. I have left all my mistaken ways. My eyes have been bored (enlightened). I cry every night when I remember my sins. The great Father Almighty sees everything. If I go up to the mountains He sees me. Jesus died for our sins upon the cross to carry our sins away.

Remarks.—Dates his change from seeing a convert reading a book, and he felt ashamed that he knew nothing, and he determined to learn, and soon he found his own system false. One case, when his spirit said there would be recovery, death came ; and another, when he foretold death, life remained.

COW-AL-LAH, aged 30.—*Answers:*—A Christian must put away sin, lies, drunkenness. I had wished to come forward at the last baptism, but was held back by those around. I have now broken away, and am ready to give myself to God. God is the maker of heaven and earth. God pitied our sins, and sent Jesus to save us. The Spirit helps our weakness. If we follow God here we shall find God after death. All must stand before God and receive according to their works. Was struck at the dark death of many of his relations. He and they knew nothing about the future. So when Mr. Duncan came and spoke about those things, he gladly heard, and determined to follow him.

QUIL-AH-SHKAHKS, aged 25.—*Answers:*—I have put away my sins. I have long sinned against God. I am afraid of my sins. God sees me. Jesus has opened the door of heaven to us. God sends His good Spirit to help us. God will measure our ways when we die. So long as I live I will try to give the news of God to others. The word of God has taught us to hope. In the summer saw the people die from small-pox. Saw the hand of God, and trembled and resolved to turn to God. We are not strong to resist the hand of God

NEEASH-AH-POOTK, aged 35.—*Answers:*—I have long followed sins which made God angry. I have put away sin, but if I am ever so ignorant in my endeavors I will persevere. Used to be a great drunkard. Have given up magic and display of property. Felt God last summer. We have turned back to our great Father. He sees all; His Spirit is with us. The blood of Jesus cleanseth us from all sin. How happy the angels will be to see us good, and how they will cry if we are sinful! At the last God will divide us. Lost ten relatives by the small-pox last year, and it opened my eyes to my sins. God's hand was strong to cut down sinners.

KSHIN-KEE-AIKS, aged 36.—*Answers:*—I will fight against my sins, and continually cry to find God. I will endeavor not to retaliate when ridiculed. I believe in the Lord in heaven, who made the earth and heaven, and us, and the food we eat. Jesus the only Son of God died to save us from our sins. God gives us the Holy Spirit to help us to contend against the evil spirits who come against us. If we are sinful when we die, God's face will be against us. Wherever I go my mind is fixed to serve God. At the last God will divide the good from the bad. Used to hear God's Word, and always went back to my sin. But at last came away with the others, and was fixed then.

KOW-KAYTH, aged 18.—*Answers:*—We must leave all sinful ways, and take hold of God's ways. I have long carried sin, but must not carry sin to God. God is a great Spirit. Made earth and heaven. Jesus died in our stead. The Spirit of God ever with us ; the hand of God ever near. If we carry our sin till we die, God will punish us. We must all meet God when we die. God will show us our ways. My father was cut down in his sins. I purpose to do differently.

KAHLP, aged 35.—*Answers:*—I shall fight against my sins. My heart truly says I will turn from sin to God. God is perfectly right in His ways. Sees all, good and evil. God made all things—heaven and earth and us. The Son of God our Saviour, Jesus. The blood of Jesus Christ cleanseth us from sin. God does not withhold His Spirit when we cry for it. Whosoever believes in God, the Spirit of God lives in his heart. Those who die in their sin go to darkness and to fire. I will fear God as long as I live. I pray for God's Spirit and light to lead my own spirit along the path to Himself when I die. Was a slave ; was poor in spirit, and was drawn to cry to God to take my heart.

Remarks.—Answers freely. He was taken slave by the Hydahs ; brought back and sold to his old chief, and was some years a slave. The chief's son sold him to his own friends, who set him free.

SKULLOH, aged 30.—*Answers :*—From my birth I have been a sinner. I cannot understand the size of my sinfulness. Cannot of myself give up my sins, but God will help me. Jesus our Saviour came from heaven ; that is the reason why we can be saved. I feel God sees and understands all we do, and think, and speak. Am not afraid of the judgment, for God is full of love and mercy, and the Son of God has made our peace   I pray God to prepare my heart to see Him.

Remarks.—Was in a canoe with a child, who fired a gun by carelessness. A portion of the boat turned the shot from going into his back. He was led to think why a little piece of wood should thus save his life ; he became thoughtful ; heard Mr. Duncan was to come to speak about God, and at once joined.

OOSHI-NEEYAM-NAY, aged 24.—*Answers ·*—I will try to take hold of God's ways, and leave sin   When I remember my sin my heart cries. I believe in God, who made heaven and earth, and who is almighty. Our sins were the death of Jesus. The blood of Jesus cleanseth us from sin. We must pray to put our hearts to Him. Jesus will dress us in His goodness. God sends His Spirit to make us good. I am not afraid of the judgment, for I hope my heart will be right to see God before I die. If our hearts are not right to see God, He will cast us into darkness.

KISHEESO, aged 16.—*Answers :*—A duty to give up the ways of the Tsishseans. Was very wicked when quite young. Will try to put away my sin   I cannot eat again what I have vomited. God is almighty. Jesus the Son of God, our Saviour. God will hear me if I cry to Him. We must seek God first before any other thing. My father and mother still in heathenism, but I cannot go back to them. I rather cry when I think of them. I pray night and morning for God to pity and to pardon me.

Remarks.—Came by himself in a tiny canoe, across the sea, away from home, to join the Christian people.

THRAK-SHA-KAWN (sorcerer), aged 50.—*Answers* ·—I wish to give up all wicked ways. Have been a medicine-man, and know the lies of heathenism. I believe in the great Father who made us, in Jesus who died on the cross that God would pity us. I want the Spirit of God to touch my heart. We must all stand before God. God will measure our ways. No one to be his master but God. I will not keep my eyes on the ground any more, but will look up to heaven all my life.

Remarks.—He has had to bear much scorn, and to go through much struggle.

QU-TL-NOH, aged 19.—*Answers :*—I wish to put away all sin, lies, drunkenness. Have erred in following man. Must now try to follow God. I believe in Jesus Christ, who died for our sin. God's Spirit prepares us for baptism. We shall rise from the dead and see God's face, if we are God's children. I am wishful to serve God as long as I live.

FEMALES.

WAHTHL (wife of Legaic), aged 40.—*Answers :*—I wish to put away evil and have a clean heart. Feel the pain of the remembrance of sin so bad I would sometimes like to die. I want to seek God's face, but feel little hope ; still I determine to persevere, though miserable. Loss of relatives, and finding no peace and rest, and feeling in darkness, led me to look to God. I know that God sent His Son Jesus to die for our sins

Remarks.—About nine months under regular instruction. She is evidently anxious for her soul ; knows the truth, but her sins are a burden that she has not found peace. She has been anxious her husband should go forwards in good.

LOOSL (widow of the cannibal chief who died penitent),

aged 25.—*Answers :*—I know how blind I have been. Was first turned to God by the news of the Saviour. Was struck that He came down amongst us. God is a Spirit full of love. Christ came to carry away our sins. We must pray for the Spirit to help us. I confess my sins to God and cry for pity. I pray for my friends. After death the judgment We must stand before God. Jesus will answer for those who trust in Him.

Remarks.—Upheld her husband in his wickedness. Was turned by his turning at his death.

SHOODAHSL (wife of Clah), aged 30.—*Answers :*—We must give up all sin. God sees and knows us all through. Jesus died in our stead because we were bad By the Spirit of Jesus we must learn to walk in the good way I feel struggle in my mind, but persevere. I pray for pardon. Will do all I can to keep God's way. God's own Word promises that He will heal.

NISHAH-KIGH (chieftainess of the Nishkahs), aged 45.— *Answers :*—I must leave all evil ways. I feel myself a sinner in God's sight. I believe in God the Father Almighty, and in Jesus Christ, who died for our sins. God sends down His Spirit to make us good. Jesus is in heaven, and is writing our names in God's book. We must stand before God and be judged by Him. I feel God's Word is truth. Have been for some time accustomed regularly to pray.

Remarks.—Two years ago she was found giving Christian instruction to a sick and dying person. Her husband tells me she passed much time in devotion. When she first heard the Word of God her sorrow was great, and her penitence more than she could bear. Some five years she has been earnestly seeking God.

NAYAHK, aged 30.—*Answers :*— I have been a great sinner, but God has opened my heart to see good, and I am resolved by His help to put away all evil and live to God. I pray for pardon and God's Holy Spirit. I feel unhappiness now amongst my heathen friends, and have pleasure only with God's people.

Remarks.—Her husband has been sent away. She remained, although at the cost of much privation to herself; but she would not go back to heathenism. Replied well as to the special work of each Person of the Trinity.

NAYAHK (wife of Lapplighcumlee, a sorcerer), aged 25. —*Answers:*—Answers well and clearly upon the separate work of each Person of the Trinity. Prays for pardon—for the Holy Spirit.

Remarks.—Suffered much from the mockery of her husband. At her earnest demand he gave up devilry. Under eighteen months' regular instruction. Been consistent in the midst of opposition; adhered to the Mission when many were against. Has been a blessing to her family, all of whom have renounced heathenism. Her husband, the sorcerer, laments his past life, and would be the first to put his foot upon the evil system.

AD-DAH-KIPPI (wife of a Christian Indian), aged 25.— *Answers:*—I must put away sin. I know I have been making God angry, but must put away all my old ways, lies, and the evil of my fathers. God gave us commandments. God would not hear us till we put away our sins, Jesus would make peace for us and add His spirit. Am resolved to endeavour to live to God all my life. Was much moved last fishing at my sinfulness, and then repented strongly, and resolved to walk with God. I pray morning, noon, and night for pardon and God's Spirit.

Remarks.—Had opposed her husband, who is a Christian.

WAH-TEE-BOO, aged 16.—*Answers:*—Have been sorely tempted. Jesus came down from Heaven to save sinners, and to make our peace with God. Jesus shed His blood for our sins. Jesus will be as a ladder for us to heaven when we die. We must stand before God. We must cry to God before we die, and not put off. I pray for a clean heart to God.

Remarks.—Made a touching confession of her sins, when applying for baptism.

PAIEK (wife of Slulloh), aged 25.—*Answers :*—Want to find God   I repent of my sins.   First led to think by the shock of my father being shot in the house by another Indian.   Sought peace and came to Metla-katla.   God is almighty, full of goodness, and truth, and love.   Jesus, the Son of God, died for our sins.   Asked what we should ask God for.   She said, light.   The good will dwell with God for ever, the bad be cast away.

LAHSL, aged 22.—*Answers ·*—I wish to be a Christian   Must put away all sin.   I believe in our Lord Jesus Christ, who takes away my sin.   The Spirit is almighty ; strengthens my breath.   We must all stand before God.   We must try to be good.   Knowing this, I pray to God morning and evening.   Death in the family first led me to think.   I have been made bad by my people, but have now turned to God.

Remarks :—Eighteen months under instruction.   Been afflicted, and shown great constancy.

AHK-YAIK, aged 22.—*Answers :*—My sins I must leave. I pray to God for pardon.   Believe in God who made us, and heaven and earth.   Jesus Christ the son of God, our Lord.   He came down from heaven to our world to save sinners.   God is a great spirit.   God will measure our ways. I have struggled against my friends who wish to get me away from here.

Remarks :—About ten months under instruction.

SHYIT-LEBBEN (wife of Kow-al-ah), aged 23.—*Answers :* —I have a miserable heart when I think of my sins.   Jesus had compassion, and died on the cross for our sins, that we might live after His death   God sends down His Spirit to make us good.   After death God will show us our sins and divide us.   I pray when I wake in the night.   If only my tongue speaks, my prayers do not go to God ; but if my heart speaks, God hears my prayers.

TAH-TIKS, aged 24.—*Answers :*—I must give up all my old ways. I believe Jesus Christ died for my sins. We shall be happy with the angels if we are good here. The people of heaven and earth will be brethren. God will be to us a brother. Long time ago I knew good, but it died in my heart, and I followed sin , but I had an illness, and determined to do differently, and when the move here was made, I followed. Did follow evil, but am changed.

OO-AH (wife of Thrak-sha-kaun), aged 38.—*Answers :*—I wish to be a Christian. Was long time in sin, but now hope to give up every sin. Jesus died for our sins. Our Father made us and all things. The spirit helps us. We shall find God when we die, having lost our sins. Those who remain in their sins will be carried away. I prayed to God for salvation.

Who can read these simple childlike professions of faith, without being impressed with the mighty change, from the vicious, defiant, bravado which many of the self-same men and women, had exhibited when Mr. Duncan, began to show them " the way."

On the day appointed, fifty-six, accepted candidates for baptism, assembled in the church, and, ranged themselves in a large circle, in the midst of which the ceremony was to be performed.

The Bishop of Columbia thus describes the scene :—

" The impressiveness of the occasion was manifest in the devout and reverent manner of all present. There were no external aids—sometimes thought necessary for the savage mind—to produce

or increase the solemnity of the scene. The building is a bare and unfinished octagon of logs and
spars—a mere barn—sixty feet by sixty, capable of
containing seven hundred persons. The roof was
partly open at the top ; and, though the weather
was still cold, there was no fire. A simple table,
covered with a white cloth, upon which stood three
hand-basins of water, served for the font, and I officiated in a surplice. Thus there was nothing to impress the senses, no colour, or ornament, or church
decoration, or music. The solemnity of the scene
was produced by the earnest sincerity and serious
purpose with which these children of the Far West
were prepared to offer themselves to God, and to
renounce forever the hateful sins and cruel deeds
of their heathenism ; and the solemn stillness was
broken only by the breath of prayer. The responses
were made with earnestness and decision. Not an
individual was there, whose lips did not utter in
their own expressive tongue, their hearty readiness
to believe, and to serve, God." .   .   .

On the following day, the Bishop was called upon
to unite in marriage three native couples.

" Nothing could be more pleasing, than the manner in which the young people conducted themselves. The service evidently impressed both them
and their friends who came to witness the ceremony.
The custom of the wedding-ring was quite novel to
them, in connection with marriage. Rings they have
in abundance generally. I have counted thirty on a

A NATIVE BELLE.

single pair of hands. All rings were, however, absent on this occasion, except the third finger had on a gold ring. There was no confusion; all evidently were properly impressed. Two of the young ladies had white dresses. I presented each of the couples with a fifty-pound bag of flour and five pounds of sugar.

" It is customary amongst Indians for the newly married pair to give presents to their friends, sometimes to their own impoverishment. We desire to establish rather the more healthful practice of encouraging the new home by substantial help."

On the same day fourteen children were also baptized.

" It was pleasing to see the strong desire of the Christians for the admission of their children to the same privilege of union with Christ's Church as themselves. They all took places—parents, sponsors, and children—in the same ring as the adults of yesterday, and came up, leading the little ones between two, and, on returning, reverently knelt down, remaining in private devotion for a while, as was the case with the adults. Several questions were necessary to be decided which are not incidental to old-established countries. Parents, still unbaptized, sought baptism for their children; prudence prevented this. Children, of one parent Christian, the other heathen, were admitted. Two parents, still unbaptised, came to say they had given their child to a sister who was a Christian, and who had adopted it for her own, that it might be baptised and trained as a Christian. This I allowed. Children over seven I did not admit, considering they might be imbued with heathen ideas, and should undergo training in Christianity as a preparation for baptism, though to be baptised as infants. It was interesting to see, afterwards, children brought by their parents, and coming of their own accord to have their names set down for preparation."

Before his departure, the Bishop gave a feast of rice and molasses to all the village.

"They assembled in the octagon. Cloths were laid; all brought their own dishes and spoons. There were three tables, at each of which one of the chiefs presided. Their custom is to eat little at the time, but take away the principal part of the allotted portion : all rise before and after the meal, for grace. Singing was then introduced, and excellent, certainly, were the strains of harmony poured forth in the English tongue. Several well-known rounds were capitally sung. First, a boat song; then—

'When a weary task you find it,
   Persevere, and never mind it.'

'Come tell me now, sweet little bird,
   Who decked thy wings with gold?'

'See our oars, with feather'd spray;'

and last, 'God save the Queen.' In this they were as quick and lively as any children in the world the men joining, too, in good time, voices soft and sweet. Mr. Duncan afterwards addressed them in an earnest speech."

The Bishop of Columbia, reporting upon *another* visit to Metlakahtla, about three years later, writes :

" Groups of well-dressed Indians were waiting to receive us. With many of them I shook hands, having baptised most of them. The great octagon was well filled. It was a thankful sight to behold the clean, neat, and orderly flock gathered with a devotional object to the Christian house of prayer. In a front row were ten young girls, all with English Bibles in their hands, as modest and devout as could be seen in any village church of Old England. I was glad to see so many children, and never have I seen better behaved ones anywhere. The first hymn was in English, ' How sweet the name of Jesus sounds !' I then said some prayers, and Mr. Duncan said the Litany in Tsimshean, after which a hymn in that language was sung; I then gave an address. It was pleasing to hear the fervent Amens, both in English and Tsimshean prayers, and also the responses to the Litany universally made."

The Bishop visited the attractive island-gardens of the mission lying in the bay opposite the village; he was particularly struck by the intelligent methods of agriculture, and the industry of men, women, and children.

The Queen's birthday occurred during the Bishop's sojourn, and the officers and men of H. M. S.

"*Sparrow-hawk*," anchored off the village, participated in the celebration. This holiday was the one always most observed, for they had been taught to worship God, and honor their Queen. The following account of this day's festivities, I quote from Dr. Halcombe's report :

"At an early hour a party from the ship landed, to help decorate the mission-house, and bastion, with a festoon of flags of various nations. The day was delightful; the sun shone bright, and all the beautiful scenery of the islands, placid sea, and distant mountains contributed to the charm.

"The proceedings of the day commenced in the house of God, where seventeen children were baptized. 'It was pleasing,' writes the Bishop of Columbia, who officiated, 'to witness the devout manner of the sponsors, and to hear their audible responses. None anywhere could behave better, or show more appreciation of this sacrament of the Gospel.'

"A distribution of gifts then took place. First came 140 children, as orderly, and nicely dressed, as the children of the best village school in England. After singing 'God Save the Queen' in English, they were each presented with a biscuit. Next came 120 elderly men and women, to whom a few leaves of tobacco were an acceptable token of friendly feeling; the sick, too, were remembered; and last, not least, the councilmen and constables.

"Precisely at twelve o'clock, a royal salute of

twenty-one guns boomed forth from the ship, to the great satisfaction and some astonishment of the groups of Indians, who, in their Sunday-best, had gathered to the village square, to join in the festivities, which now commenced in earnest. Children playing at ball, and taking turns at a merry-go-round ; young men competing at gymnastic bars ; the eighteen policemen of the village in regimentals, ready for review ; and the elders walking about comparing the old time and the new, made up a scene which for interest, and enjoyment, could not well be surpassed.

" But the most exciting part of the programme for the day was the regatta. The course was about two miles, round the island. In the first race, five canoes, manned by forty-one young men in their prime, were engaged. The canoes flew through the waves, throwing the white foam on every side ; and right gallantly were the efforts sustained until the goal was reached. Three canoes, rowed by women, also contended for a prize.

" Next, came foot-races, running in sacks, blindman's buff, and such like amusements. It so happened that on this day a large body of Quoquolt Indians came to Metlakahtla. As they landed from their fleet of Bella Bella canoes, the contrast which they presented to the well-dressed and respectable Metlakahtlans, was very striking. They were clothed in tattered blankets which scarcely covered their nakedness. Their faces were painted black and red, and their hair was matted and dishevelled. Not a little astonished at all they saw around them, they eventually retired, as though wishing to hide themselves from observation. Their chief, a stately personage, alone remained as the guest of Legaic. The evening was devoted to a public meeting, and a magic-lantern entertainment.

"At the meeting several of the officers from the '*Sparrow-hawk*' addressed the Indians. Some of the chief men replied; Mr. Duncan, acting as interpreter for both sides. The time being short, the speakers were limited to a few minutes each. Two or three quotations will serve to give some idea of the general line of the addresses, and the highly figurative language peculiar to Indian oratory:"

ABRAHAM KEMSKAH.—"Chiefs, I will say a little. How were we to hear, when we were young, what we now hear? And being old, and long fixed in sin, how are we to obey? We are like the canoe going against the tide which is too strong for it; we struggle, but, in spite of our efforts, we are carried out to sea. Again, we are like a youth watching a skilled artisan at work: he strives to imitate his work, but fails; so we: we try to follow God's way, but how far we fall short! Still we are encouraged to persevere. We feel we are nearing the shore; we are coming nearer the hand of God, near peace. We must look neither to the right nor left, but look straight on and persevere."

PETER SIMPSON (*Thrak-shah-kawn—once a sorcerer*).—" Chiefs, I will speak. As my brothers before have entreated, so do ye. Why have you left your country and come to us ? One thing has brought you here : one thing was the cause. To teach us the way of God, and help us to walk in it. Our forefathers were wicked and dark ; they taught us evil, they taught us *ahlicd* (sorcery). My eyes have swollen. Three nights I have not slept ; I have crept to the corner of my house to cry, reflecting on God's pity to us in sending you at this time. You are not acting from your own hearts : God has sent you. I am happy to see so many of my brothers and sisters newly born to God. God has spoken to us : ' let us hear.' "

RICHARD WILSON.—" Chiefs, as we have now heard, so do ye. Indeed, father " (addressing Mr. Duncan), " we are sinners before you ; we often make your voice bad in calling us ; we must persevere, we must try, though we are bad ; we are like the wedge used in splitting the trees ; we are making the way for our children : they will be better than we are. The sun does not come out in full strength in early morn ; the gray light at first spreads itself over the earth ; as it rises the light increases, and, by-and-by, is the mid-day sun. We shall die before we have reached much, but we shall die expecting our children to pass on beyond us, and reach the wished-for-goal."

DANIEL BAXTER (*Neeash-ah-pootk*).—" Chiefs, I

am foolish, I am bad, bad in your sight. What can our hearts say? What shall we do? We can only pray and persevere. We will not listen to voices on this side or that, but follow on till we reach our Father in heaven."

CHEEVOST (*Jacob*).—"Chiefs, we have heard you. Why should we try to mistake the way you teach us? rather we must try to follow on; though our feet often slip, we must still try; we have rocks all round us; our sins are like the rocks, but the rudder of our canoe is being held. She will not drift away. We are all assisting to hold the rudder and keep her in her course. What would she be without the rudder?—Soon a wreck upon the rocks. So we must cry to God for help to follow on. We must beg God's Holy Spirit to strengthen us and to guide us. Chiefs, do you but speak, and we will obey."

WOODEEMEESH (*Simeon*).—"I will speak to my brethren. What has God done to us? What does He see in us that He should be working for us? We are like the fallen tree buried in the undergrowth. What do these chiefs gain by coming to us? Did we call them? Do we know from whence they are, or did we see the way they had come? Yet they have arrived to us. They have torn away the undergrowth; they have found us; and they have lifted up our hands and our eyes to God, and showed us the way to heaven."

To those men who now in attempting to destroy

the Native Christian Church in Metlakahtla declare
—that Mr. Duncan's work is superficial—"he is too
much of a trader"—"he is a misleader"—"incites
them to lawlessness"—"he influences them for evil"
etc., I commend the following expressions of the
Bishop of Columbia ; and, the Bishop spoke with a
knowledge, and with a personal experience ; and
after watching the development of this little
oasis :—

" *All former work, varied, and interesting, and im-*
pressive as ministerial life is, seems insignificant,
before this manifest power of the Spirit of God,
touching the heart and enlightening the understand-
ing of so many recently buried in the darkness and
misery of ignorant and cruel superstition.

" *To a worthy, zealous, and gifted lay brother, is*
this reward of his loving and patient labors. Few
would believe what Mr. Duncan has gone through
during the past four years and a half, laboring
alone among the heathen. Truly is the result an
encouragement to us all."

Speaking of Legaic's reformation, the, Bishop
says :—

" He is industrious, and gains a good livelihood, and lives in a comfortable house of his own
building, with good glass windows and a veranda.
Chairs were set for visitors, and we had much talk
about the Mission, and the work, and the tribe.
His only, child Sarah is one of the most promising
girls of the Mission-house."

Rev. R. Dundas also writing at about the same time alludes, to Legaic's family :—

"He and his wife have one child only, a young girl of fourteen. She was a modest-looking, pleasing child, very intelligent; one of the first class in the school. She did not look like one who had been 'possessed with a devil'; and yet this is the child whom three years ago her teacher saw naked in the midst of a howling band, tearing and devouring a bleeding dog. How changed! She who 'had the unclean spirit sits now at the feet of Jesus, clothed and in her right mind.'"

The Bishop of Columbia, was very much impressed by the methods, and results, of Mr. Duncan's instruction, of the youth, and says,—

"I had observed on Sunday a row of well-behaved and devout young girls with Bibles in their hands. As I gave out my text they found the passage. *On Sunday evening I heard them read the Bible, and they sang chants and hymns, some in English, and some in Tsimshean. To-day I examined several of them in reading, and was much pleased by the accurate, and devout manner, in which they read the Word of God.**

"These were to be the future mothers of a new generation. Already has he seen one set go forth from the Institution, well, and respectably married

---

* Compare this with Deputations Statement Chapter VII. this volume.

to young men, who had proved worthy of the
Christian profession.

"Those now in the Institution are the second set,
several of whom are about to be married, and there
are others, waiting to come and supply their place.
So great is Mr. Duncan's influence, that none are
married without his consent, and he is entirely
trusted by the parents. Constantly is he applied to
by the many young men who desire this, or, that
one, for a partner; and not a little interesting, if not
amusing, are the accounts he can relate, of the care
and watchfulness with which he guards the tender
plants from too early or ill-advised exposure to the
blasts and storms of the voyage of life."

In his charges to newly-wedded couples, Mr.
Duncan impressed upon both bride and groom, the
necessity of unity of heart, unity of thought, and
unity of purpose. On one occasion, to illustrate
the folly of antagonism, he aptly related the incident of a man and wife, who, when seeking advice
as how to combat each, the other's obstinacy, were
bidden to throw a rope over the roof of their house,
and each to pull an end on opposite sides, with
their might, and see which should pull it over;
they did so and pulled in vain; then, they were
told to both take hold of one end and pull together;
then it was drawn over without resistance, or assistance. They saw the point, and profited.

The Rev. R. Dundas visited Metlakahtla about
a year after the Bishop of Columbia's first visit.

During his stay arrangements, were made for the baptism of a considerable number of converts who had shown themselves worthy of that sacrament.

The Rev. Mr. Dundas depicts the mission, and the incidents of his visit :—

" It was a pretty sight to see the whole population, old and young, at the sound of the bell, thronging to worship God. No need to lock doors, for there is no one to enter the empty houses. Every soul is assembled in the one place, and for one purpose. As they entered, the men took the right and the women the left hand of the great circular hall. I was surprised to learn from Mr. Duncan afterward that he had never bidden them to do this; they seemed to have adopted the arrangement instinctively. Service began with a hymn in Tsimshean. He led with his concertina. The air was very plaintive and beautiful—sung by some 200 voices, men, women, and children—it thrilled through me. Then followed prayers in Tsimshean, at the close of which all joined in the Lord's Prayer in English. Then followed a chant; one of the Psalms he had translated and taught them, to a fine old Gregorian. His address, or sermon, of nearly an hour, was upon the story of Martha and Mary. His manner and gesticulation were animated and striking, very much after their own style. Their attention never seemed to flag throughout. He asked me to address them, which I did, shortly, upon their present light as compared with their past darkness, and the difficulties they must expect in their new cause of Christian discipleship. Mr. Duncan interpreted for me. Before separating they sang again in Tsimshean a sort of sacred air, which seemed familiar to me, and was exquisitely beautiful. I found afterward it was the anthem, ' I will arise, and go to my Father,' somewhat altered, and made more Indian in its character. It suited their voices admirably. I closed with a short prayer in English, and pronounced the Benediction.

" The service was most striking. *It was hard to realize that three years ago these had all been sunk in the deepest heathenism, with all its horrible practices. What hours, what whole nights of wrestling in prayer, have been spent by this single-minded faithful servant of God, in humble supplication that he might ' see of the travail of his soul,' and how has he been answered!* There is nothing too hard for the Lord.

.   .   .   .

" I went on shore in the afternoon, to take up my quarters with Mr. Duncan. About four o'clock the bell was rung, and the whole village assembled at the school-house, when Mr. Duncan told them that on the following Sunday, those who desired it, and also on examination approved themselves, would be admitted to Holy Baptism. Candidates were to assemble that evening at seven, to give in their names. In his address to them he was very pointed and stringent—fencing in, as he afterward told me, the door of admission. *He told them the strict, un-compromising requirements in those who thus sought to join themselves to Christ and His service. Better that they should postpone so solemn and awful a step than come to it unprepared.* At the hour appointed the candidates were assembled. Fifty-five gave in their names. Several were absent who would have come forward had they been there; but, as my coming was not anticipated, at least 150 to 200 were away for their last hunting and fishing excursions before the winter, and would not be back for some weeks. . . .

"*I was strongly impressed with the real earnest-ness and devotion of those who came forward, and with their acquaintance with the simple, saving truths of the Gospel message.*

"A few answers may interest."

"COMKAHGWUM, aged about twenty-five, a fine young man—to the inquiry, what led him first to think of Christ—said, 'It was the winter before last. The new school was built at Fort Simpson. Mr. Duncan asked all the Indians one Sunday to come to church. I had never been. I went then. He told us of our evil ways, and of God who loved us. It was good to my heart; I was *deep in the ground* then; but now, when I heard this, I wanted to be free, and to love God: that was the first time I thought of him.'

"In answer to the inquiry about God's view of sin, and His feeling toward sinners, he said, 'God's heart is against sin, He is angry with it But He pitied us. It was all for Jesus' sake.' (What did Jesus Christ do for us?) 'Jesus came down from His Father to die for our sins on the Cross.

(Is He dead still?) 'Oh, no! He rose up from death. He is in heaven now. He is working for us there. He is sprinkling us with His blood to make us clean.' (What must we *leave* and *do* to be Christians?) 'We must leave our sinful ways; we must have new hearts; our old hearts are bad. We must believe in our Lord.' (Who will help you?) 'Jesus sends down His Holy Spirit to strengthen our hearts: we must keep praying for His good Spirit.' (Do you pray for it?) 'I am always working in prayer for God to pity me.' (If you are tempted, what will you do?) 'I will fight my sins. God will help me to fight.' This poor man has been a murderer in his heathen state. Three years ago he was provoked by another of the tribe, and wronged in the same way. He watched him out of the village at Fort Simpson, and then shot him dead. It weighs much upon his mind now.

"Here are some answers of an elderly woman : 'I want to take hold of the hand of God. He is willing to pity me; our sins killed Jesus; but His blood saves us. I must leave all my sins, for Jesus suffered for them. We shall stand before God; we must see God's righteousness. He will give His hand to the good, but He will put the wicked away from Him' This woman, who cannot be less than fifty, has had no instruction, save what she has heard in church. It has come chiefly from her own daughter of fifteen, who is one of the Mission-house inmates, and has been with Mr. Duncan for four years, his best and most promising young convert. She has been baptized by the Bishop, and has now been the instructress of her parents, both of whom will be baptized by me to-morrow.

"From two, or three elderly men, I got of course answers less full. It is hard for them to *remember* truths so as to give definite answers in *words*. They feel, and know, more than they can explain.   In a few cases Mr. Duncan said, if I would allow him, he would not put any questions to them formally, but would leave them to tell in their own way why they sought for baptism.   And very touching it was even to listen to them, though I could not understand them.   One, with tears streaming down, said he was very old, and must soon die; but he wanted to be at peace with God.   He knew his ways had been bad all his life; but he had had no light; and now he wanted to belong to Jesus, for he knew Jesus loved him and died for him.

"All Saints' Day.   To-day I was privileged to perform the most interesting scene I have ever taken part in since I left England.   Fifty-two souls have been baptized with water and the Spirit, and added to the Church of Christ, most of whom were walking a few years ago in the darkness that might be felt of degraded heathenism.

"After service on board, Lieutenant Verney accompanied me on shore.   The Baptismal Service was arranged to take place at two, for adults, of whom there were thirty-nine.   A second service was fixed for the infants of some of the Christians, thirteen in number, at five o'clock.   A large number of the sailors from the gun-boat were present, and seemed greatly interested in the solemn rite.   A small table was arranged on a low platform at one side of the great circular Mission-house.   On it were placed four silver dishes containing water, which Lieutenant Verney lent for the occasion; they were the best substitute we could obtain for a font.

"The service of course had to be gone through twice: after each prayer and exhortation, in the adult form, had been offered or spoken by me in English, Mr. Duncan repeated it in Tsimshean. The candidates were arranged in rows—the men behind, the women in front. On either side of them, all round the hall, were the rest of the congregation, Indians and sailors. At the proper point in the service, one by one, the candidates stepped forward in front of the assembled congregation. Mr. Duncan called up each by his heathen name. In answer to my request, 'Name this person,' he gave the new Christian name, and by it I baptized the candidate.

"As I held the hand of each, while receiving him or her into the Church of Christ, and signing him with the sign of the Cross, I could often feel that they trembled with deep emotion. On returning one by one to their places, each knelt down in silent prayer. The Baptism being ended, I offered up the two concluding prayers, all joining in the Lord's Prayer in English. I then addressed the newly baptized.

"In describing his departure he said, 'Up anchor, and started at seven. Mr. Duncan came off in his canoe to say good-by. The Indians ran the British ensign up as we passed the flag-staff, which Lieutenant Verney acknowledged by hoisting all his colors —red, white, and blue—at main, fore, and mizzen.

And so I bid good-by to this most interesting place. *It takes its position now as one of the civilized towns or villages of British Columbia. But it is more than that: it is the enduring witness of the faith and patience and love of one unaided Christian teacher, whose sole reward (the only one he has ever coveted) is the souls he has been the honored instrument of bringing from darkness to light. 'I have seen Missions in various parts of the world before now' (said Lieutenant Verney to me), 'but nowhere one that has so impressed me with the reality of what has been accomplished.'"*

Bishop Cridge, then, (Dean of Victoria), gives the following picturesque account of his inspection of Mr. Duncan's school,* and of an evening gathering.

" Examined the writing exercises of the first class of girls. The words 'whale,' 'shark,' 'salmon,' 'seal,' were written on the black-board, and, each girl wrote a short theme in connection with each word. Some of the exercises were as good as in an English school in respect to composition, spelling, and penmanship.

" In the evening, the girls sang some of their native nursery rhymes. Some were very pretty, some ludicrous, some pathetic. Among the latter is that of the little slave-child, who is told by her captors

---

* It is worthy of mention that Mr. Duncan from the first, in his indefatigable devotion to the progress of his people, realizing the necessity of their daily toil, held night-school for the adults.

that her mother is gone getting clams; and the little thing lisps,

'Raven, have you seen my mother?
Sea-gull, have you seen my mother?'

After this, one of the party commenced the legend of 'The Chief's Proud Daughter;' but the night advancing, we were obliged to defer the conclusion.

"On Tuesday Mr. Duncan gave the girls a merry evening with the galvanic battery, introducing the bucket of water and the silver coin, which none succeeded in getting. Mr. Duncan has great art in keeping them cheerful, telling them humorous stories, the point of which they always remember; *c.g.*, 'A man with a wry neck fell and hurt himself; a friendly by-stander picked him up, and began to set him generally to rights, and among the rest to straighten his neck. The man, terrified, cried out, 'Hold hard there! Born so, born so!'" One evening some one made a remark on their Indian gait, which Mr. Duncan interpreted to the girls, to their great amusement; and one of them exclaimed, in English, 'Born so!' which was immediately taken up by the rest, some of them jumping up and caricaturing their own peculiarities; upon which Mr. Duncan, explained to us the allusion.

"This evening Mr. Duncan, showed me a letter, just received from one of the girls whom he had occasion to reprove in the morning. · In broken

English she bewailed her ingratitude and hard heart, asked his forgiveness, and entreated his prayers that she might be a better girl."

A letter written by one of Mr. Duncan's first set of scholars, illustrates, how efficaciously he had cultivated in them, the affectionate ties of brothers and sisters. It was a part of his plan, to create in them a love of home, and a love of each other, and purity of relationship.

This letter was sent to a sister who was leading an evil life in Victoria. Eliza had already succeeded in rescuing one of her sisters from a life of shame. Many are the Magdalens whom Mr. Duncan has fully reclaimed from degradation.

" METLAKAHTLA.

"MY DEAR SISTER: I send this little news to you. I very much wish to see you, my sister. I tell you sometimes I very much cry because I remember your way not right. I want you to hear what I speak to you. Come now, my sister, I hope you will return and live in your own place. Do not persevere to follow bad ways. You must try to forsake your way; repent from your heart. You hear our Saviour Jesus Christ. Cast all your bad ways on Jesus. He know to save us when we die. I very happy because I see my brother and sister come again. I thank God because He hear always cry about you.

" I am your crying sister,

" ELIZA PALEY."

If letter-writing be any gauge of progress, it may be worthy of note that in 1866 the Metlakahtlans posted about 200 letters, each voyage of their schooner.

Bishop Cridge in writing of the store and schooner says :—

"No step of a temporal nature was, perhaps, so loudly demanded, or has conferred such important benefits on the people of Metlakahtla, in conducing to their comfort, and contentment in their new home. Instead of having to go seventeen miles for supplies to a heathen camp, they can procure them at their own doors at a cheaper rate. Persons who come hither to trade, carry away some word or impression to affect their countrymen at home. During my sojourn at Metlakahtla, there has not been a single Sunday, in which there have not been hearers of this description, attendant on the word of life. This is one of those branches of the work taken up by Mr. Duncan, simply because it was pressed upon him by the force of circumstances, as necessary to his entire success.

"A striking benefit of the trade is the disposition of the profits, for with a view to transferring it, when possible, to other parties, he has always conducted it on business principles, in order that the parties so assuming it might be able to live by it. Hitherto the profits realized on this principle, absorbed by no personal benefits, have been expended on objects conducive to the public benefit, in the erection of public buildings, in subsidies to the people, in aid of improving the roads, and wharves for canoes, in charity to the poor, and even in the redemption of slaves. The sum of £600, has already been expended on such objects, and £400, are in hand ready to be applied to similar uses. *In fact, the only person who suffers is Mr. Duncan himself*, who has sacrificed his comfort, his repose, and almost his health, for the sole benefit of the people but has been more than compensated by the rich reward of feeling that God has owned and blessed the sacrifice. Besides this, the trade affords industrial occupation for the people, and thus aids them in a more steady advancement in the comforts of civilized life. It is quite a lively scene to witness the various parties of laborers engaged, some in bringing the rough timber in rafts from the forest, others in sawing it into planks, others planing, others cutting the shingles, others with nail and hammer erecting the building—all devoting themselves to their daily task, rather with the constancy of the English laborer, than, with the fitful disposition of the savage."

In reference to the emancipation of slaves, mentioned by Bishop Cridge, the following passage from a letter of Mr. Duncan's dated March, 1876, has interest as a touching illustration, of the reputation of Metlakahtla, as a refuge, for the suffering, and oppressed:

" A poor slave woman, still young in years, who had been stolen away when a child, and carried to distant tribes in Alaska Territory, where she had suffered many cruelties, fled from her oppressors last summer, and though ill at the time, took to the sea in a canoe all alone, and determined to reach Metlakahtla or perish in the attempt. On her way (and she had upwards of one hundred and fifty miles to travel, she was seen and taken by a party of Fort Simpson Indians, who would no doubt have been glad to hand her back to her pursuers for gain, but on hearing of her case, I demanded her freedom, and finally she was received into a Christian family here, and tenderly cared for. Both the man and his wife who received her into this home had themselves been slaves years ago. They understood her language, sympathized deeply with her, and laboured hard to impart to her the knowledge of the Saviour of sinners. After three months her cruel master with his party came here to recapture her, but they had to return home unsuccessful. In three months more her strength succumbed to the disease which had been brought on by cruelty and hardship. She was a great sufferer during the last few weeks of her life, but she died expressing her faith in the Saviour, and rejoicing that she had been led here to end her days."

Archdeacon Woods—rector of the Holy Trinity Church, New Westminster, British Columbia—

visited Metlakahtla in 1871 for the purpose of baptizing converts. He recounts his approach to the
village as follows :—

" I left Will-a-claw (at the mouth of the Skeena
River) about 9 A.M. by canoe, being paddled by an
Indian and his wife. . . .

" As we drew near to Metlakahtla the sound of
the church-bell over the still waters of the bay
could be heard for a considerable time before we
reached the village. The man called my attention to it, and said it meant ' *school ;* ' the woman,
however, promptly corrected him, saying it meant
' *death :* ' of course my own ear had told me that this
was its meaning, and now we could see the funeral
procession passing in canoes from the villages to a
small island, which has been set apart as a grave-
yard ; so that when I actually reached the landing-
place, I learned, as I expected, that Mr. Duncan
was away at the funeral."

The Metlakahtlans now inter their dead after the
manner of Christian burial. When the old heathenish customs were in vogue they disposed of their
dead by earth, water, aerial and canoe burials,
and by burning. All of these customs prevailed
along the coast ; none were peculiar to any one
tribe, and some individual tribes practised all.
The ceremonies of burning were the most hideous, being made the occasion for frightful religious
orgies ; in some cases the widow or slaves, were
burned on the pyre. The most picturesque was the

BURNING THE DEAD.

canoe burial.   Julia McNair Wright thus describes
one :—

"The canoe—often a very handsome one—covered with pictures and thirty feet long, is suspended
between poles.   The dead lies in this canoe, and
over the body a smaller canoe is turned, affording
protection from birds or from the weather.

"These canoe burial-places—in the solemn stillness and darkness of the spruce and cedar woods, and
usually on the bank of some wide stream—are picturesque and touching.   The bowls, the cups, the
weapons of the dead one, suggest the occupations
of his life, and also the blackness that brooded over
his future when he drifted into another world, utterly unknown, that all his life had bounded his
horizon with a wall of darkness."

Chieftains and Shamans were laid out in state
mid great ceremony—and were arrayed in all the
splendors their people could command.

Archdeacon Woods, visited the Niskah Mission
Station on the Naas River some seventy miles distant, before performing the rites of baptism at Metlakahtla.   He records an incident, of the journey,
which very forcibly illustrates, how consistently the
Metlakahtlans lived their religion.

"Having paddled from daylight till dark with a
brief rest of about an hour, we reached the only
available camping-ground on the coast, where we
rested for the night under such shelter as the canoe
sail stretched across the mast could afford ; and hav-

ing lighted a fire, prepared supper. Mr. Duncan, having provided me with food already cooked, my supper was soon made, and I laid down to rest, wearied with sitting all day in the canoe. The Indians cooked their venison and salmon Indian fashion, and then, all reverently taking off their caps, one said grace with every appearance of devotion. After supper I was amused at the evident fun that was going on amongst them, for though I could not understand their language, a laugh is understood all over the world; and certainly, if laughter be an evidence of jokes and fun, they were rich in merriment, notwithstanding the discomfort of camping out on wet ground and under heavy rain. By-and-by, as I was dropping asleep, I was roused by their sudden stillness. My first impression was that they were getting wearied; but it was not so, they were only calming down before retiring to rest, and soon I observed them all, with heads uncovered and reverently bowed, kneel round the camp fire while one said prayers for all. And as the Lord's Prayer (for I could recognize it in the strange language in which it was clothed) ascended from beneath the shades of the forest from lips which only lately had acquired the right to say 'Our Father,' and as I doubt not from hearts which truly felt the mighty privilege which holy baptism had conferred, I could not fail to realize how grandly catholic is that prayer which He Himself gave to those to whom alone He gives the right to use it.

" The miners and traders reach Skeena mouth by steamer for Victoria, but thence to the mines the transit is made for a considerable distance up river in a canoe. Consequently in the spring and autumn (the seasons for going to and returning from the mines), there is considerable traffic up and down the river, and those Indians who choose to put their canoes on the river command good wages and constant employment. The Metlakahtla Indians freely avail themselves of this means of earning money, and in connection with this valuable testimony of the sincerity of their profession came under my notice from the miners who took passage down to Victoria on the return trip of the ' *Otter.*' All agreed in witnessing to the honesty, the self-denial, and the determination to resist temptation of the Metlakahtla Indians. ' *They won't work on Sunday, they won't drink, they won't lend themselves in any way, to any, kind of immorality.*' The truth of the first part of this statement I observed for myself during the time of my stay at Metlakahtla. I noticed how the Indians flocked home on Saturday nights, some of them from long distances, many of them from Skeena mouth, to enjoy the Sunday peace and quiet of their own village, and to avail themselves of those ' means of grace ' which the Sunday Church services and Sunday-schools afforded."

Returning to Metlakahtla the Archdeacon examined the candidates for baptism. The ceremonies that ensued are best expressed in his own words :—

"Sunday, the 12th of November, is a day to be remembered by me. *I have had in the course of a ministry of over twenty years many solemn experiences, and witnessed many touching scenes, but never since the day of my own ordination as a priest in the Church of Christ, have I felt anything like the solemnity of that day,* when I saw before me a crowded congregation of Christians—of heathen seeking after Christ, and of the little band of fifty-nine about to be received through holy baptism into the ark of Christ's Church.

"Holy Baptism, at all times a most solemn rite, seemed to me specially so at this time, when I was called upon to administer that Holy Sacrament to men and women who, of their choice, yet influenced, as I fully believed, by the power of the Holy Ghost, came forward to renounce heathenism —to give up in more than one instance all that was dear to them in this world, and to enlist in the army of Christ. Oh, may the merciful God grant that they may have power and strength to have victory and to triumph against the devil, the world, and the flesh !

"In the evening, accompanied by Mr. Duncan, I visited several houses in the village and baptized five adults, who, through sickness or the infirmities of age, were prevented attending the service in church, making a total of eighty-four persons baptized at Metlakahtla, which, with the twenty-two baptized at Kincoulith, gives a grand total of 106 persons added to the Church on this occasion."

In alluding to the industries at Metlakahtla Archdeacon Woods says :—

"A marked and important feature of the Metlakahtla Mission is the aspect imparted to it by the fostering and utilizing of native industry ; at present there are carried on a lumber-mill, the manufacture of soap, the dressing of skins, and blacksmithing, while preparations are being actively urged forward for weaving, rope-making, and shoe-making, the materials for weaving and rope-making being found in abundance in the immediate neighbourhood. *These, in combination with the trading store in the village, have a very practicable bearing on the well-being of the Mission, quite apart from the mere money gain,* though this too is a matter of considerable importance to the success and prosperity of the Mission.

"The trade store in the village brings to the Indians all the necessaries of life beyond what their own labour can provide, and takes from them in exchange the skins and oil which are the chief results of their hunting and fishing, so that they have within the limits of their own village the means of exchanging the produce of their labour for necessaries and luxuries beyond their own ability to procure, and this without bringing them in contact with the temptations which must necessarily beset them if compelled to carry their skins,

oil, etc., to the trading-posts outside their own reserve."

In the winter of 1877 and 1878, the Bishop of
Athabasca, visited Metlakahtla. It was, at a very
critical moment, in the history of the Mission, as
Mr. Duncan had resigned, and had left the settlement but a short time previously, to make way for
an ordained Church of England clergyman ; who,
through various indiscretions soon threw the mission into confusion, and necessitated Mr. Duncan's
return. He had barely succeeded in restoring
order in the village, when the Bishop of Athabasca
arrived. I give his account of the Christmas festivities in his own words.

" The festivities of the season commenced here
on Christmas Eve, when a party of about twenty-
five of the elder school girls were invited to meet
us at tea. After tea we were all entertained by
Mr. Duncan, with the exhibition of a galvanic battery and other amusements. This party having
dispersed to their homes in good time, at a later
hour came together the singers who were appointed
to sing Christmas carols during the night along the
village street, led by the schoolmaster. After their
singing they returned to supper at the Mission before retiring to rest.

" On Christmas morning the first sight which
greeted us was that of the constables ; lengthening
to its full height the flag-staff on the watch house,
to hoist the flag for Christmas, and all the village

street was soon gaily dressed with flags. The constables then marched about the village to different houses to shake hands and make Christmas,—peace with all whom they had been called to interfere with in the course of the year. At eleven o'clock the church bell rang, and the large church was thronged with a well-dressed and attentive congregation.

" After service all the villagers, to the number of about six hundred, had to come and pass through the Mission-house to shake hands with all the inmates. In doing this they so crowded the verandah that the boards actually gave way beneath them, but the ground being only about two feet below no injury resulted. After all the shaking of hands was over, the villagers returned home to their own private entertainments, and most of us at the Mission enjoyed a quiet Christmas evening together; but Mr. Duncan entertained at tea a party of the chiefs and principal persons of the village, whom we did not join, from inability to converse in the Tsimshean tongue.

" The day after Christmas was a gay one. The constables, twenty-five in number, paraded and exercised on the green with banners and music, and about fifty volunteers, in neat white uniforms, with drums and fifes and banners flying, went through creditable evolutions and exercises. All the strangers who had come from neighbouring villages to spend Christmas at Metlakahtla were collected by

Mr. Duncan, in the Mission Hall, and, after a suitable address, all of them received presents of soap, apples, sugar, tobacco, etc. In the evening the usual week-day service was held in the school-room, always crowded.

"The following day all the children were assembled by Mr. Duncan at his house, first the girls and then the boys, about two hundred in all; and, after being amused by him, were treated to sugar-plums and apples, and each one received some article of clothing (cap or cape, etc.), so as to be sent away to their homes rejoicing.

"Next day all the men in the village, about 300, were assembled in the market-house to be addressed by Mr. Duncan. After he had given them the best advice he could their Christmas presents were distributed to them in the presence of all the Mission party. These consisted of one-half pound sugar, and six apples to each one, with copy-book and pencil, or tobacco for the older men.

"The day after this, Mr. and Mrs. Schult kindly entertained the widows of the village, about sixty in number, to a substantial dinner. It was a pleasure to see even the old and decrepit able to sit at table and enjoy their meal, and it made us enter fully into the idea of the renovating influence of Christmas blessings, to think in what dark and murderous heathenism, these aged widows, had been reared when young. After dinner Mr. Duncan brought them to his Hall to listen to an address, so that they might not return home without words of Gospel truth, and comfort, to cheer for struggling days.

"The morrow, being Sunday, was marked by the usual services. These consist, first, of morning Sunday-school at half-past nine, at which about 200 are present, both children and adults, males and females being in separate buildings. All the elder scholars learn and repeat a text both in English, and Tsimshean, and have it explained to them, and *they are able to use intelligently their English Bibles* for this purpose. At eleven is morning service in church, attended at Christmas time by 700 to 800. Hymns are sung both in English and Tsimshean, and heartily joined in by the congregation. This being the last Sunday in the year, the service was made a specially devotional one to seek mercy for the offences of the past twelvemonth.

"After morning service the adults met again in Sunday-school to learn in English and Tsimshean the text of the sermon, and have it again explained to them by the native Sunday-school teachers, who are prepared for this duty at a meeting with Mr. Duncan on Saturday evening. It is very interesting to see about 300 adults gathered together in the three schools at midday, entirely in the hands of native-teachers, and with English Bibles in their hands poring intelligently over the text, and following out again the subject of the morning discourse.

I cannot but think it would be a great gain if this scheme of Mr. Duncan's could be largely followed in other missions.

"Afternoon service is held in the church at three o'clock, with a Litany, and after this, when the daylight lasts long enough, there is a second Sunday-school. The church is as full in the afternoon as in the morning, and the punctuality of the attendance is surprising. In the evening at seven o'clock service is again held in the school-room, which is crowded, and occasional meetings are held by the elder converts for the benefit of any aged people unable to come to church.

"To return to the Christmas doings : on the Monday, all the women of the village, about three hundred, assembled in the market-house, and, after suitable addresses, valuable presents were made to each, viz.: one pound soap, one pound rice, and several apples, etc., so, that they returned home laden and rejoicing. Altogether about £50 ($250) must have been spent upon the Christmas presents.

"On Monday evening, being the last night of the old year, a suitable service was held in church, the subject being Psalm xc. : 'So teach us to number our days,' etc. On New-Year's day, the festivities were renewed. Bugle-notes and drums and fifes, and the exercises of the volunteers, enlivened the scene. The youth of the village played foot-ball on the sands. All the men of the village were assembled in the market-house, and were permanently enrolled in ten companies, the members of each company receiving rosettes of a distinguishing colour. Each company has in it, besides ordinary members, one chief, two constables, one elder, and three councillors, who are all expected to unite in preserving the peace and order of the village. The ten chiefs all spoke in the market-house on New-Year's day, and in sensible language promised to follow the teaching they had received, and to unite in promoting what is good. After the meeting all adjourned to the green in front of the church, and joined in singing 'God save the Queen,' in English, before dispersing to their homes. The rest of the day was spent in New-Year's greetings.

"Wednesday evening was occupied by the usual week-day service, and Thursday and Friday evenings were devoted to the exhibition in the school-room, first to the women and then to the men, of a large magic-lantern, with oxygen light, and also a microscope showing living insects and sea-water animalcules, as well as various slides.

"The above is but an imperfect sketch of the efforts made by Mr. Duncan for the increase and happiness of his village."

We read these testimonies, according one with another, to a perfect corroboration and repeat to ourselves,—"what hath God wrought"—through his faithful servant—but wait, and we shall see, how, when this devout flock, becomes the object of persecution, and relentless tyranny, men wearing "*the cloth*" presume with temerity to declare that white is black.

CHAPTER IV.

EARL DUFFERIN AND OTHERS TESTIFY.

STATESMEN, explorers, naval officers, travellers, merchants, and missionaries, on returning to England and the United States, after visiting the North Pacific, gave impressive accounts of Mr. Duncan's remarkable work. These accounts are, unfortunately, for the most part buried in huge reports, or interspersed through books which are of a more or less technical or special character, having interest but to the few.

However, I shall quote some extracts which I have gleaned from the writings of a few of those who have visited Mr. Duncan's mission, or studied his methods and work.

An event of no little importance in the history of Metlakahtla, during the year 1876, was the visit of Lord Dufferin, when Governor-General of Canada— accompanied by Lady Dufferin. Their reception was extremely cordial.

The following address was presented by the natives.

"To His Excellency the Earl of Dufferin,
    Governor-General of the Dominion of
    Canada:

"*May it Please Your Excellency,*—We, the inhabitants of Metlakahtla, of the Tsimshean nation
of Indians, desire to express our joy in welcoming
your Excellency and Lady Dufferin to our village.
Under the teaching of the Gospel we have learned
the Divine command, 'Fear God, honor the King,'
and thus as loyal subjects of her Majesty Queen
Victoria we rejoice in seeing you visit our shores.

"We have learned to respect and obey the laws
of the Queen, and we will continue to uphold and
defend the same in our community and nation.

"We are still a weak and poor people, only lately
emancipated from the thraldom of heathenism and
savage customs; but we are struggling to rise and
advance to a Christian life and civilization.

"Trusting that we may enjoy a share of your
Excellency's kind and fostering care, and under your
administration continue to advance in peace and
prosperity,

"We have the honor to subscribe, ourselves, your
Excellency's humble and obedient servant,

"For the Indians of Metlakahtla,

"DAVID LEASK,

"*Secretary to the Native Council.*"

The Governor-General replied as follows:—

" I have come a long distance in order to assure you, in the name of your Great Mother, the Queen of England, with what pleasure she has learned of your well-being, and of the progress you have made in the arts of peace and the knowledge of the Christian religion, under the auspices of your kind friend, Mr. Duncan.   You must understand that I have not come for my own pleasure, but that the journey has been long and laborious, and that I am here from a sense of duty, in order to make you feel, by my actual presence, with what solicitude the Queen, and Her Majesty's Government in Canada, watch over your welfare, and how anxious they are that you should persevere in that virtuous and industrious mode of life in which I find you engaged. I have viewed with astonishment the church which you have built entirely by your own industry and intelligence.   That church is in itself a monument of the way in which you have profited by the teachings you have received.   It does you the greatest credit, and we have every right to hope that, while in its outward aspect it bears testimony to your conformity to the laws of the Gospel, beneath its sacred roof your sincere and faithful prayers will be rewarded, by those blessings which are promised to all those who approach the throne of God, in humility and faith. *I hope you will understand that your White Mother and the Government of Canada are fully prepared to protect you in the exercise of your religion, and to extend to you those laws which know no difference of race or of color, but under which justice is impartially administered between the humblest and the greatest in the land.*

"The Government of Canada is proud to think that there are upward of thirty thousand Indians in the territory of British Columbia alone. She recognizes them as the ancient inhabitants of the country. The white men have not come among you as conquerors, but as friends. We regard you as our fellow-subjects, and as equal to us in the eye of the law as you are in the eye of God, and equally entitled with the rest of the community to the benefits of good government, and the opportunity of earning an honest livelihood.

"I have had very great pleasure in inspecting your school, and I am quite certain that there are many, among the younger portion of those I am now addressing, who have already begun to feel how much they are indebted to that institution, for the expansion of their mental faculties, for the knowledge of what is passing in the outer world, as well as for the insight it affords them into the laws of nature, and into the arts of civilized life; and we have the further satisfaction of remembering that, as year after year flows by and your population increases, all those beneficial influences will acquire additional strength and momentum.

"I hope you are duly grateful to him to whom, under Providence, you are indebted for all these

benefits, and that when you constrast your own
condition, the peace in which you live, the comforts that surround you, the decency of your habitation—when you see your wives, your sisters, and
your daughters contributing so materially by the
brightness of their appearance, the softness of their
manners, their housewifely qualities, to the pleas-
antness and cheerfulness of your domestic lives,
contrasting as all these do so strikingly with your
former surroundings, *you will remember that it is to
Mr. Duncan you owe this blessed initiation into your
new life.*

"By a faithful adherence to his principles and his
example you will become useful citizens and faithful subjects, an honor to those under whose auspices
you will thus have shown to what the Indian race
can attain, at the same time that you will leave to
your children an ever-widening prospect of increasing happiness and progressive improvement.

"*Before I conclude I cannot help expressing to Mr.
Duncan and those associated with him in his good
work, not only in my own name, not only in the name
of the Government of Canada, but also in the name of
Her Majesty the Queen, and in the name of the people
of England, who take so deep an interest in the well-
being of all the native races throughout the Queen's
dominions, our deep gratitude to him for thus having
devoted the flower of his life, in spite of innumerable
difficulties, dangers, and discouragements, of which
we, who only see the result of his labors, can form only*

a very inadequate idea, to a work which has resulted in the beautiful scene we have witnessed this morning. I only wish to add that I am very much obliged to you for the satisfactory and loyal address with which you have greeted me. The very fact of you being in a position to express yourselves with so much propriety is in itself extremely creditable to you, and although it has been my good fortune to receive many addresses during my stay in Canada from various communities of your fellow-subjects, not one of them will be surrounded by so many hopeful and pleasant reminiscences as those which I shall carry away with me from this spot."

Subsequently, Lord Dufferin, in a speech delivered in Government House, Victoria, before about two hundred leading citizens, including the members of the Provincial Government, said:

"I have traversed the entire coast of British Columbia, from its southern extremity to Alaska. I have penetrated to the head of Bute Inlet; I have examined the Seymour Narrows, and the other channels which intervene between the head of Bute Inlet and Vancouver Island. I have looked into the mouth of Dean's Canal, and passed across the entrance to Gardener's Channel. I have visited Mr. Duncan's wonderful settlement at Metlakahtla, and the interesting Methodist Mission at Fort Simpson, and have thus been enabled to realize what scenes of primitive peace, and innocence, of idyllic beauty, and material comfort, can be presented by the stal-

wart men, and comely maidens of an Indian community under the wise administration of a judicious,
and devoted Christian missionary. I have seen the
Indians in all phases of their existence, from the
half-naked savage, perched, like a bird of prey, in a
red blanket upon a rock, trying to catch his miserable dinner of fish, to the neat maiden in Mr. Duncan's school at Metlakahtla, as modest and as well
dressed as any clergyman's daughter in an English
parish. . . . What you want are not resources,
but human beings to develop them and consume
them. *Raise your thirty thousand Indians to the level
Mr. Duncan has taught us they can be brought, and
consider what an enormous amount of vital power
you will have added to your present strength.*"

A further quotation will be given later on in
reference to the land question, from this speech
of Lord Dufferin.

Lord, and Lady Dufferin, were greatly impressed
by the evidences they beheld on every hand, at
Metlakahtla, of the *substantial creation* of a civilized
community, from a people rescued in a single generation, from the lowest degradation, and savagery.

Lady Dufferin, especially noted a remarkable refinement of taste and the choice of quiet colors, and
modest dresses of the women.

Mr. St. John who accompanied Lord Dufferin
and reported the above address, writing of Mr.
Duncan's plan of dealing with his people, among
other things says :—

"It struck me that he threw, and successfully threw, cold water on the Governor-General's bestowing any special mark of recognition on the chiefs. He has to conduct his operations in a peculiar way, and it can be easily shown, he understood that much of his advice and direction, would be thrown away, were there a recognized authority over the Indians other than himself. *He strives to make industry and merit the standards by which the men of the village are measured* and in presenting an address to the Governor-General, which was done immediately after the singing was concluded there was no apparent priority or distinction among them."—"*Sea of Mountains.*" London, 1877.

The Church of England Missionary Society of London, was so proud of Mr. Duncan's work, that it published, and widely circulated, a book entitled "*Metlakahtla,*" in which it extols Mr. Duncan's work, giving him unstinted praise, for the marvellous things he had accomplished, among the ferocious, wild savages, of the great Northwest. This book was the means of bringing many thousand pounds in contributions to the Society's coffers "for the purpose of converting the heathen of foreign lands." The Church Missionary Society's publications continually chronicled the progress of his work, and held him up as an example for missionaries throughout the world.

The Society for the Promotion of Christian Knowledge, London, published a book, edited by the Rev. J. J. Halcombe, M.A., titled "*Stranger than Fiction.*" This book, devoted entirely to Mr. Duncan's mission work, has passed through many editions, and I have been informed; something like twenty thousand copies have been sold. The author begins by saying that Mr. Duncan's work "presents a series of incidents without parallel in the missionary annals of the Church," and from beginning, to end, lauds his methods.

In reference to the founding of Metlakahtla he says :—

"Gradually assuming shape and consistency, until it finally issued in the establishment of the native settlement, the singular and successful development of which has already constituted it *one of the marvels of the day,* . . .

"Thus we have seen the foundation laid, and the superstructure begin to rise upon it. What the nature of the foundation has been we have sufficiently indicated. 'Other foundation can no man lay than that is laid, even Jesus Christ,' seems to have been pre-eminently the principle upon which, as a true missionary—'a wise master builder'—Mr. Duncan from the first proceeded in his work. 'Jesus Christ and Him crucified,' all the historical facts of our Lord's life and death, the causes which led to, and the results which followed from, the 'one all-sufficient sacrifice, oblation, and satisfaction for the sins of the whole world,' offered by Christ upon the cross; these had been, so to speak, the materials ceaselessly thrown in amongst the quicksands of ignorance, and superstition, which would otherwise have baffled all hope of erecting any solid superstructure upon them.

"It is difficult, in a narrative like the present, to convey any sufficiently adequate idea of the untiring perseverance with which Mr. Duncan seems thus to have made his preaching, and teaching *rest upon and centre round the great facts of the history of man's redemption.* Line upon line, precept upon precept, in season, and, as some would have thought, out of season the same theme was evidently regarded as the only motive-power, which could be brought to bear with any reasonable hope of a successful result attending it. . . .

"*But of all tests of progress in such a settlement as Metlakahtla the development of a missionary spirit is the most trustworthy. Nor was this sign wanting. Amongst all classes of the community there seems to have been a constant desire leading to continued and earnest efforts to bring home the truths of the Gospel to their heathen brethren.*" . . .

In narrating the remarkable career of Legaic, Dr. Halcombe writes ·—

"The case of Paul Legaic was, be it remembered, no exceptional one, though rendered somewhat more remarkable by his former rank. His history is only one out of a very large number of a similar kind which the experience of this Mission would furnish. . . .

"That, humanly speaking, a great part of Mr. Duncan's success, especially at first, was due to the persistency with which he went to those who would not come to him, and to his resolute determination to declare to all 'whether they would hear or whether they would forbear,' the counsel and will of God regarding them, there can be no doubt.

"How far the moral and social elevation of the whole Indian race may be affected by what is being done in Metlakahtla, and what may be the result of the formation of a sort of native capital and model settlement, it is impossible to predict. That with God's blessing it may result in the saving of a goodly remnant of a whole race we would fain hope.

"What Mr. Duncan's own plans are, and how far he will hereafter devote himself to the extension of the great work which he has so successfully inaugurated, we have no means of judging. Being himself a layman, he naturally wishes to see a clergyman permanently established in charge of the settlement, *and speaks continually of the time of his own retirement from the work as being near at hand.*

"That a man possessed of such singular administrative ability, such great earnestness, and such unusual power of influencing others, and who has gained so thorough a mastery in the language as 'to think and dream' in it, should entirely withdraw himself from the work to which he has hitherto devoted himself would be a cause of general and deep regret, and we may well express the hope that

the day for his doing so may yet be far distant.
Great as has been the work which has been already
done, a greater still remains to be accomplished.
*If Metlakahtla is really to become the centre of any
widely extended efforts to evangelize the native tribes
of North-West America, it must be under the guid-
ing and controlling influence of such a mind as that
of Mr. Duncan.* Most sincerely do we trust that
he will meet with such encouragement and assistance
as will enable him to complete that which he begun
so well, and that the Christian Community which
we have seen so successfully organized may only be
the first of many other settlements modelled on the
*same plan and showing the same signs of material
prosperity, combined with a thorough appreciation
and practical application of the saving truths of Christianity.*

*"Yielding to ' no consideration of comfort, taste,
interest, reputation, or safety (in all which respects
he has been severely tried),' did Mr. Duncan labor on
year after year resolutely, sacrificing himself, and his
own interests to the work which he had undertaken,
and refusing to decline or abandon any undertaking
which he believed to be, under the providence of God,
essential to its success. Who that reads the story of
what the strong will and entire self-devotion of one
man has effected will deny that it is indeed ' stranger
than fiction' ? "*

We shall have occasion in succeeding chapters,
to ponder over some of these strong terms of praise,

and wonder which is the strangest feature of Mr. Duncan's experience; his anxious struggle to wrest these people from heathendom, or, his resistance of ecclesiastics, who seek to destroy his life's work.

The Encyclopædia Britannica, in its treatise on missions says:

"At Columbia, on the coast of the Pacific, a practical missionary genius, named William Duncan, has succeeded in civilizing a body of Indians, degraded by cannibalism, and, at his Metlakahtla mission, stands at the head of a community of some thousand persons, which has a larger church than is to be found between there and San Francisco. Testimony to the value of the results was borne in 1876 by Lord Dufferin, then Governor-General of Canada, who declared that he could hardly find words to express his astonishment at what he witnessed."

Admiral R. C. Mayne, R.N., F.R.G.S., devoting nearly five years to exploration, and study, of the natives of the North Pacific, in his highly instructive report writes:

"There is no doubt that men of Mr. Duncan's stamp, who will in a frank, manly spirit go among them (the Indians), diffusing the blessings of religion and education, will meet a cordial reception and an abundant reward. But without any desire to disparage or dishearten others, I must say that Mr. Duncan impressed us as a man out of ten thousand, possessing with abundant energy and zeal that talent for acquiring the confidence and love of his fellow-creature which all who come in his way, were they whites or Indians, could not fail to acknowledge and feel subject to.

"The labors of men of his class among the distant heathen are undervalued by the world, which refuses to credit the fact that savages such as these coast Indians undoubtedly are, can receive and retain impressions so utterly at variance with their nature or habits." Then Admiral Mayne quotes Captain Richards, R.N., commanding H. M. S. Plumper, who, having been ordered by the government to quell an outbreak at Fort Rupert, reported:

"I have had some trouble with the Indians, and at a large meeting they asked me why Mr. Duncan was not sent to teach them, and then insisted on the injustice of his being sent over their heads to the Tsimshean Indians. The business I have just had with the Indians convinces me that it is not our ships of war that are wanted up the coast, but missionaries. The Indian's ignorance of our power and strong confidence in his own, in addition to his natural savage temper, render him unfit to be dealt with at present by stern and unyielding men of war, unless his destruction be contemplated, which of course is not. Why do not more men come out, since Mr. Duncan's mission has been so successful; or, if the missionary societies cannot afford them, why does not government send out fifty, and place them up the coast at once? Surely, it would not be difficult to find fifty good men in England willing to engage in such work! And their expenses would be almost nothing compared with the cost which the country must sustain to subdue the Indians by force of arms."

To this the Admiral adds : " Such are the earnest sentiments of one of Her Majesty's naval captains while among the Indians. And such, I may add, are the sentiments of myself—in common, I believe, with all my brother officers—after nearly five years' constant and close intercourse with the natives of Vancouver's Island and the coast of British Columbia."

Matthew Macfie, F.R.G.S. (" *Vancouver's Island*"), London, 1865, commenting upon the utter degradation in which he found the British Columbian Indians, writes :

" From these facts, some idea may be formed of the vexations borne by Mr. Duncan at the beginning of his career. But a noble ambition to elevate the social and religious condition of the Indian lightened the burden of his toils. Such an enterprise was sufficiently onerous to one cheered by the presence of Christian sympathy ; but his isolated situation, struggling without a pious companion of either sex to share his anxieties and labors, was fitted to deepen the interest felt by the religious public at home. A work has been accomplished there whose success has rarely, if ever, been equalled in the history of missions to the heathen.

" These indispensable auxiliaries of civilization did not, I know, formerly receive from foreign missionaries in the Sandwich Islands the attention they merited, and consequently, the results of their zealous and severe exertions were, in most instances, sadly out of proportion to the time, strength, and money expended in connection with their work. I trust I do not detract from the dignity of the missionary calling, or from the power of the Christian religion, in suggesting that the arts and institutions of civilized life ought to be fostered side by side with the communication of religious instruction. These arts and institutions create new and elevating social relations, and open up the most worthy spheres to be found in this world for the exercise of Christian virtues, the strengthening of heavenly principles, and the development of the divine life. To those missionaries, therefore, who have been exclusively ecclesiastical in their plan of action, I commend the enlightened example of Mr. Duncan.'

Whymper, the distinguished English traveller, made an extended journey of exploration through the North Pacific country. In his book, " *Travels in Alaska,*" London, 1868, after giving his own ideas regarding the civilization of the aborigines, says, referring to Metlakahtla :

" The success of this station is, doubtless, due in part to its isolation from any large white settlement, but Mr. Duncan must have labored earnestly and incessantly in his noble work.

" I think it is fair to allude to one objection I have heard used, both in and out of the colony, to Mr. Duncan's work. It is this, that for a missionary he is 'too much of a trader.' I cannot say to what extent, or in what sense, this may be true; I do not myself believe it in any offensive sense. If, however, Mr. Duncan, from a little pecuniary advantage accruing to him, should be induced to prolong his stay among the Indians, and follow out the work of civilization he is engaged in, no one can rightly complain. The majority of missionaries do not stop long enough in any one locality to acquire a thorough knowledge of the native dialects, and this of itself must be a fatal hindrance to their efforts.

" If this gentleman, by giving up a large part of his life for the benefit of these savages, can at the same time make a fortune, may success attend him."

This report of the accusation against Mr. Duncan, is given in order to show how industriously the liquor traders, and the Hudson's Bay Company's agents, circulated their slanders against him, (see Chap. II. of this volume) simply because he endeavored to prevent the sale of intoxicating drink to the Indians, and, because he introduced industries that enabled the natives to cheaply manufacture articles, that, the Hudson's Bay Company had previously supplied at exorbitant prices. Mr. Duncan desired peaceful relations, and on founding Metla-kahtla endeavored to induce the Hudson's Bay

Company to open a store there, and thus avoid the necessity of his engaging in the venture. But in their bitterness, they obdurately refused.

The liquor traders of Alaska maligned him, because he would not allow them to poison his people; they even accused him of complicity in smuggling,* and based their charges on the fact, that the Tsimsheans bartered their goods, up and down the coast; as they had ever done from the earliest time. It is needless to add that the accusation was false. Had Mr. Duncan been greedy of gain he would hardly have abandoned a lucrative position, with bright future prospects, in England to encounter the dangers, and hardships, of missionary life among the North Pacific savages.

The Nanaimo *Tribune* (British Columbia) published, the following account of a visit paid to Metlakahtla, in 1866 by a Roman Catholic gentleman, he writes :—

"Though *not* of the same denomination as Mr. Duncan, and *having no interest to subserve*, by my advocacy of his great claims to the respect and

---

* Bancroft, in his History of Alaska, in error, attributes a report of this accusation to Dr. Sheldon Jackson , but, Dr. Jackson positively denies that he has ever published or made such a statement, and credits, its circulation solely to Alaskan liquor traders, or, early officials, who were mixed up with them, or, were anxious to stamp out mission work, and education. The early history of Alaska is very unsavory in this respect.

gratitude of all true Christians, for his meritorious
services in the good cause, it is with feelings of the
utmost pleasure, that, I bear testimony to the great
good effected by this worthy man, during his period
of self-exile at Metlakahtla. Some time ago reports were industriously circulated that his influence
over the aborigines was rapidly on the wane, and
that he used every means to prevent his people
from trading with the vessels calling at the Mission.
With regard to the first assertion, it is simply ridiculous. *The confidence reposed in Mr. Duncan by
his dusky flock has never for a moment been shaken,
in fact is daily on the increase,* as the many additions
to the population from outside sources will attest,
as well as the alacrity with which he is obeyed in
every command, having for its object, the good of
the community. A notable instance of the latter I
witnessed in the ready manner in which they turned
out to do their quota of statute labor on the
streets, or paid its equivalent in blankets, &c.: no
coercion, all was voluntary, for they see the benefit
in front of their own doors. Their hearts seem to
be centred in their little town, and you can inflict
no greater punishment on them, than to exile them,
from it and its founder.

" In regard to the allegation about the prohibition
to trading, I have only to remark that it is as groundless as the other. I myself was on a trading voyage,
and stopped ten days at Metlakahtla, and had every
facility afforded me by Mr. Duncan in trafficking

with the natives. The reason is obvious enough: our trade was not in whiskey. That branch of trade is certainly discouraged at the Mission, hence the outcry about 'interfering with commerce.' . . .

"A word or two now about Metlakahtla and its beautiful environs, all blooming with the blossoms of that useful esculent the potato, some twenty acres of which were under cultivation and looking splendid. The town is triangular in shape; the Mission-buildings being located on a bold promontory forming the apex. The view from the southern entrance of the harbor, looking townward, is extremely pretty. The church, of octagonal form,* having a handsome portico and belfry, and surmounted with the emblem of Christianity and peace, occupies a prominent position in the foreground, adjacent to this are the parsonage, store, and saw-pits, the latter supplying lumber of good quality, the product of native labor, at the rate of fifteen dollars per 1,000. The houses, numbering about fifty, are nearly all of a uniform size—16 by 24 feet— good frame, weather-boarded and shingled, glazed windows, and having neat little gardens in front; the whole forming two handsome esplanades, one fronting the outer and the other the inner harbor.

"The interior of the houses did not belie the promise held out by the exterior. Everything was neat and scrupulously clean. The inmates were as

---

* The old church.

well supplied with the requisites to make life comfortable as any of our laboring class here. Cooking-stoves and clocks were common to every dwelling, and, in a few instances, pictures adorn the walls of the more luxuriously inclined.

"The sight at church on Sabbath morning was pleasant to behold. The congregation numbered about 300, the females preponderating, the major portion of the males being at that time away at the fishing-station. They were all well clad—the women in their cloth mantles and merino dresses; the men in substantial tweeds and broadcloth suits, and having the impress of good health and contentment on their intelligent features. Their conduct during divine service was strictly exemplary, and would have done credit to many a more pretentious edifice than that at Metlakahtla.

"As a whole, Mr. Duncan's people are industrious and sober; they are courteous and hospitable to strangers, and, if properly protected by the Government against the poison-venders of this land, will in time become a numerous wealthy people."

One of the British Columbian journals, publishes the following concerning the visit of Mr. McKenzie, a Scotch gentleman, to Metlakahtla during a prospecting tour on the North Pacific Coast :—

"On reaching the Metlakahtlan settlement, the party were astonished to witness all the external, and internal evidences of civilization. The interior of each dwelling is divided into separate apartments, and what little furniture they contain is kept in good order, and clean.

"The people, both male and female, are all comfortably clad, the result of their own industry and provident habits.

"The village contains a church, part of which is used as a school during the week. Mr. McKenzie attended divine service on Sunday, and was amazed at the sight of the large congregation of native converts assembled. Their deportment and solemnity during the service, he declares, could not be excelled by any Christian congregation which he had ever previously united with in worship. Mr. Duncan read the Church Service, and afterward preached in the Indian language. It was evident to Mr. McKenzie and his companions that the natives took a deep, and intelligent interest, in the services from beginning to end. The apathy, and listlessness, which is observable in the countenance of an untutored Indian has entirely departed from the Metlakah-tlans. Most of their faces are remarkable for an animated appearance and intelligent expression.

"Mr. Duncan teaches school during the week, and instructs the natives how to use the appliances of modern civilization in cultivating their gardens, building their houses, and sawing timber, as well as many other useful arts. He also superintends the village store, acts as magistrate, settles all disputes that may arise, and, in fact, has his hands full in performing the arduous labors which devolve upon him, and which have resulted in such complete success as scarcely to be believed, unless, as Mr. McKenzie states, it has been witnessed.

"The contrast between the Fort Simpson Indians, among whom Mr. McKenzie resided last winter, and the inhabitants of Metlakahtla, is like that between darkness and light: at Fort Simpson all is gross ignorance, barbarism, degradation, filth, and evil: whilst at Metlakahtla civilization, progress, enlightenment, cleanliness, and Christianity are everywhere observable.

"Mr. McKenzie bears willing testimony to the amazing amount of substantial good done by Mr. Duncan. The beneficial influence which he exerts over the natives is not confined to those under his charge alone. The improvement, which he has been the zealous instrument of bringing about, has become extensively known among the wandering Arabs who inhabit the British possessions of the Pacific, and the tribes are now desirous of being instructed by Missionaries. Mr. McKenzie, in his travels up Naas and Skeena rivers, has heard the Indians express the most fervent wishes to have 'good men' laboring among them. Mr. McKenzie in his narrative has only spoken of what he witnessed himself, and he is not a bad witness to facts coming under his own observation. He is an intelligent Scotchman, who has travelled a good deal, and, like most of his countrymen, is not easily deceived, being of 'an inquiring turn of mind.'"

William F. Bainbridge, in his book, " *Tour of Christian Missions around the World*," New York, 1882, speaking of the Church of England Missions, writes:

" Their most interesting station is at Metlakahtla, near Fort Simpson, upon the Pacific coast of British Columbia. When, in 1857, Mr. Duncan was located among the Tsimsheans, his task seemed as hopeless as when the explorer Hudson was cast adrift by the mutineers. He found twenty-three thousand of the most blood-thirsty savages. Physically a superior tribe, they yet seemed to have sunken lower than all others in wretchedness and crime. Soon after, the " fire-water " was introduced by the Victoria miners, and a reign of terror began. But the missionary felt that Christianity was equal to even such a situation of unparalleled horrors, and he kept to work. By 1862 he had influenced some fifty to a better life, and with them formed a new settlement a few miles distant. Now over a thousand are gathered there about him, in well-built cottages, with the largest church edifice north of San Francisco, the Sabbath kept, all the children at school, every citizen in health attending divine worship. No intoxicating drink is allowed in the community. This prosperous, well-ordered, Christian settlement shows what evangelization can do under the worst possible embarrassments."

Rev. Sheldon Jackson, U. S. General Agent for Education in Alaska, has several times visited Metlakahtla, and has repeatedly borne emphatic testimony, to the great influence of Mr. Duncan's Christianizing, and civilizing work upon the Alaskan Natives. Dr. Jackson's extensive experience in mission and educational work among the Indians, lends peculiar force to his opinions; he says of Mr. Duncan's mission :—

"The new settlement has now grown to one thousand people, forming the healthiest and strongest settlement on the coast." . . .

"These Indians are a happy, industrious, prosperous community of former savages and cannibals, saved by the grace of God. This is the oldest and most successful Indian Mission on that coast, and illustrates what one consecrated man by Divine help can accomplish." . . .

"Some three or four years ago the head chief of the Indians upon the northern end of Vancouver Island, at Fort Rupert, visited Metlakahtla, and asked for a teacher, saying that 'a rope had been thrown out from Metlakahtla which was encircling and drawing together all the Indian tribes into one common brotherhood.'"—*Alaska and the Missions of the North Pacific Coast. New York,* 1880.

I shall make further quotations, from Dr. Jackson, in the last chapter of this volume, together with a quotation from the Governor of Alaska.

The Hon. James G. Swan, was appointed a Special Commissioner of the Department of the

Interior, in 1875, to visit Alaska. In his official report we find the following :—

" From Fort Simpson we proceed to Fort Tongass, in Alaska, some 15 miles distant from Simpson. This is an abandoned military post, belonging to the United States, and now occupied by a band of 700 Tongass, under a chief named Ya-soot. He came on board and expressed a great desire to have a missionary teacher. He said he felt ashamed when he went to Fort Simpson to see all the children learning to read and write, and all the Indians going to church, while the Tongass Indians had neither a missionary nor teacher and he thought that ' Washington ' does not take as good care of the Alaska Indians as King George (the name they give the English) does of the Indians at Fort Simpson. He wished me to ask ' Washington ' to send them a missionary, and he would make his people build him a house, and he, would compel all the Indians to send their children to school. Now this apparent eagerness for a missionary is simply owing to a feeling of jealousy of the Tsimheans, who are given to boasting to the Alaska Indians that the English Government take better care of them, than the American Government does of the Alaskans. Still, a beneficial influence is exerted by the feeling ; for in all my experience of over twenty years among the coast tribes, the great difficulty has been to get them to allow a missionary to reside among them. This same feeling was exhibited in every village we visited during our cruise. It was the old cry, 'Come over from Macedonia and help us.' I sincerely believe if this matter was placed in the hands of various missionary societies, and they could send men like Mr. Duncan and Mr. Crosby, free and untrammelled by any of the restrictions that now necessarily surround the Indian agents, under our present plan, that far more good would be effected among the natives, and at far less cost than by our present system."

Referring to a Sunday spent in Fort Simpson he says :—

"I was so impressed with what I had seen that day that I could not help the thought that the people whom we dare to call savages can teach the so-called Christians lessons of humility. I left Fort Simpson with a feeling of respect for those Indians that I have never before felt for any tribe I have lived with on the Northwest Coast, and I feel confident if missionaries, and teachers, are sent them by the various missionary societies, of all denominations of Christians in the same untrammelled manner accorded to Messrs. Duncan and Crosby, that the Alaska tribes will not only stay at home and trade with our own people, but they will be morally, physically, and pecuniarily, better off than they will be should our present miserable policy of Indian agencies be thrust upon them."

Colonel Vincent Colyer reporting as a Special Commissioner to the U. S. Government after a tour of inspection through Alaska laid great stress upon our nation's neglect of the natives there and made forcible comparison with Mr. Duncan's achievements in British Columbia :—

" ' You ought to see Duncan's Mission before you leave the Pacific Coast,' said many people to me on my journey. . . .

" ' It is really astonishing what he has done for the Indians in a short time,' said they. . . .

" We arrived at the mission at three o'clock having started at eight. Mr. Duncan, was away on a visit to another mission which he looks after up in Nass Bay. We landed at a well-constructed stone wharf, built for canoes, and passing up this about one hundred feet ascended a flight of steps and entered the market-house.

" This market-house is a neat, well-built house, of about forty by eighty feet, dry, clean, and comfortable. A number of Indians were in it, sitting beside their heaps of oolichan, boxes, piles of bear and deer-skins, fish, &c., and seemed as contented, cheerful, and enterprising as many white people I have seen in like places. Ascending from the market-place a flight of about twenty steps, which are lengthened out on either side along a terrace two hundred feet, you come to the plateau on which the mission village is located.

" The two streets on which the houses are built form two sides of a triangle, at the apex of which

the church, mission-house, trading store, market and
and 'lock-up' are erected.

"The store was well furnished with substantial
articles of daily necessity, and at fair prices. Up-
stairs there was a good stock of marten, mink, fox,
bear, and beaver-skins, which Mr. Duncan had
received in exchange for the goods. The missionary's own residence is simple and commodious.

"But the chief interest is in the construction and
condition of the dwellings of the Indians. In these
Mr. Duncan has shown much practical good sense.
Taking the common form of habitation peculiar to
all Koloshan tribes along this coast, he has improved
upon it by introducing chimneys, windows, and
doors of commodious size, and floors elevated above
the ground. For furniture he has introducd chairs,
and tables, bedsteads, looking-glasses, pictures, and
window curtains. In front he has fenced off neat
court-yards, and introduced the cultivation of flow-
ers, while in the rear of their dwellings are vegetable
gardens. Altogether the village presents many instructive and encouraging features.

"Mr. Duncan is invested with the powers of
a civil magistrate under the Colonial laws of Great
Britain, and is thus enabled to settle disputes and
nip all petty misdemeanors in the bud. He has
organized a police of Indians and they are said to
be well disciplined and effective. There is a small
'lock-up' or caboose built of logs in a picturesque

form, in which the disorderly are temporarily confined.

"It will be noticed that Mr. Duncan is thus invested with the powers of an Indian agent, teacher, missionary, trader, and justice of the peace, and as he is considered an honest man, and his books of record are open to inspection, among a primitive people, as Indians are, he can be a most efficient officer."

Chas. Hallock on his return from Alaska, wrote:—

"I am pleased to be able to give fair sketches of the remarkable Indian settlement of Metlakahtla, above referred to, not only, as an instance of the advanced state of civilization to which some of the Pacific Coast Indians have already been brought, but because it is an earnest of the enviable results which must surely crown our own endeavors, if properly applied, and therefore, an encouragement to persevere.

"*Metlakahtla is truly the full realization of the missionaries' dream of aboriginal restoration.* The population is 1,200. . . . Its residents, have a rifle company of forty-two men, a brass band, a two-gun battery and a large co-operative store, where almost anything obtainable in Victoria can be bought. We visited this port on our return trip from Sitka, and were received with displays of bunting from various points, and a five-gun salute from the battery, with *Yankee Doodle* and *Dixie* from the band. The Union Jack was flying. The church

THE METLAKAHTLA CHURCH : BUILT ENTIRELY BY THE NATIVES.

is architecturally pretentious and can seat 1,200 persons. It has a belfry and spire, vestibule, gallery across the front end, groined arches and pulpit carved by hand, organ and choir, Brussels carpet in the aisles, stained glass windows, and all the appointments and embellishments of a first class sanctuary; and it is wholly native handiwork! This well ordered community; occupy two story shingled and clap-boarded dwelling houses of uniform size, 25 × 50 feet, with three windows and gable ends, and door in front; and enclosed flower gardens, and macadamized sidewalks ten feet wide along the entire line of the street."

"These people have also a large town hall or assembly room of the same capacity as the church, capable of accommodating the whole population. It is used for councils, meetings, and for a drill room. It is warmed by three great fires placed in the centre of the building, and lighted by side lamps. The people dress very tastefully in modern garb, and I am not sure but they have the latest fashions. The women weave cloth for garments, and there are gardens which afford vegetables and fruit in abundance. It is as cleanly as the most punctilious Shaker settlement.

"The best testimony that can be offered to demonstrate the disposition of the Indians to receive the lights, rights, and benefits of Christian civilization is contained in the simple appeal made by Chief Toy-a-att, at Wrangell, as long ago as 1878,

to an assemblage of several hundred whites and
Indians; and that appeal has not yet been regarded!
Is philanthropy a sop to Indian credulity? Read
what follows :—

(TRANSLATION).

" My Brothers and Friends : I come before you
to-day to talk a little, and I hope that you will
listen to what I say, and not laugh at me because I
am an Indian. I am getting old and have not many
summers yet to, live on this earth. I want to speak
a little of the past history of us Sitka Indians and
of our present wants. In ages past, before white
men came among us, the Indians of Alaska were
barbarous, with brutish instincts. Tribal wars were
continual, bloodshed and murder of daily occurrence, and superstition controlled our whole movements and our hearts. The white man's God we
knew not of. Nature showed to us that there was
a first great cause; beyond that all was blank. Our
god was created by us; that is, we selected animals
and birds, which we revered as gods.

" In the course of time a change came over the
spirit of our dreams. We became aware of the fact
that we were not the only beings in the shape of
man that inhabited this earth. White men appeared
before us on the surface of the great waters in large
ships which we called canoes. Where they came
from we knew not, but supposed that they dropped
from the clouds. The ship's sails we took for wings,

and concluded that, like the birds of the air, they could fly as well as swim. As time advanced, the white men who visited our country introduced among us everything that is produced by nature and the arts of man. They also told us of a God, a superior being, who created all things, even us the Indians. They told us that this God was in the heavens above, and that all mankind were His children. These things were told to us, but we could not understand them.

"At the present time we are not the same people that we were a hundred years ago. Association with the white man has created a change in our habits and customs. We have seen and heard of the wonderful works of the white man. His ingenuity and skill have produced steamships, railroads, telegraphs, and thousands of other things. His mind is far-reaching; whatever he desires he produces.

"Each day the white man becomes more perfect while the Indian is at a stand-still. Why is this? Is it because the God you have told us of is a white God, and that you, being of His color, have been favored by Him?

"Why brothers, look at our skin; we are dark, we are not of your color, hence you call us Indians. Is this the reason that we are ignorant; is this the cause of our not knowing our Creator?

"My brothers, a change is coming. We have seen and heard of the wonderful things of this

world, and we desire to understand what we see
and what we hear. We desire light. We want
our eyes to become open. We have been in the
dark too long, and we appeal to you, my brothers,
to help us.

"But how can this be done? Listen to me.
Although I have been a bad Indian, I can see a
right road and I desire to follow it. I have changed
for the better. I have done away with all Indian
superstitious habits. I am in my old age becoming
civilized. I have learned to know Jesus and I desire to know more of Him. I desire education, in
order that I may be able to read the Holy Bible.

"Look at Fort Simpson and at Metlakahtla,
British Columbia. See the Indians there. In years
gone by they were the worst Indians on this coast,
the most brutal, barbarous, and blood-thirsty. They
were our sworn enemies and were continually at
war with us. How are they now? Instead of our
enemies, they are our friends. They have become
partially educated and civilized. They can understand what they see and what they hear; they can
read and write and are learning to become Christians. These Indians, my brothers, at the places
just spoken of, are British Indians, and it must
have been the wish of the British Queen that her
Indians should be educated. We have been told
that the British Government is a powerful one, and
we have also been told that the American Government is a more powerful one. We have been told

that the President of the United States has control over all the people, both whites and Indians. We have been told how he came to be our great chief. He purchased this country from Russia, and in purchasing it he purchased us. We had no choice or say in change of masters. The change has been made and we are content. All we ask is justice.

"We ask of our father at Washington that we be recognized as a people, inasmuch as he recognizes all other Indians in other portions of the United States.

"We ask that we be civilized, Christianized and educated. Give us a chance, and we will show to the world that we can become peaceable citizens and good Christians. An effort has already been made to better our condition, and may God bless them in their work. A school has been established here which, notwithstanding strong opposition by bad white men and by Indians, has done a good work among us.

"This is not sufficient. We want our chief at Washington to help us. We want him to use his influence toward having us a church built and in having a good man sent to us who will teach us to read the Bible and learn all about Jesus. And now, my brothers, to you I appeal. Help us in our efforts to do right. If you don't want to come to our church don't laugh and make fun of us because we sing and pray.

"Many of you have Indian women living with

you. I ask you to send them to school and church, where they will learn to become good women. Don't my brothers, let them go to the dance-houses, for there they will learn to be bad and learn to drink whiskey.

" Now that I see you are getting tired of listening to me, I will finish by asking you again to help us in trying to do right. If one of us should be led astray from the right path, point out to us our error and assist us in trying to reform. If you will assist us in doing good and quit selling whiskey, we will soon make Fort Wrangell a quiet place, and the Stickeen Indians will become a happy people. I now thank you for all your kind attention. Goodby."—*Our New Alaska*. New York, 1886.

Mr. N. H. Chittenden in his book, " *Travels through British Columbia*," Victoria, B. C., 1882, writes :—

" Metlakahtla.—The field of the remarkably successful work of Mr. Duncan, in civilizing and christianizing the Tsimshean Indians. He first established a mission at Fort Simpson, a post of the Hudson's Bay Company, but for the purpose of greater isolation in 1862 removed to Metlakahtla, where he has gathered about 1,000 of that tribe, and through a firm government and faithful secular and religious training raised them from barbarism to the condition of civilized people. They live in comfortable houses, dress like the whites, school their children, and worship in one of the largest churches in the Province, erected at a cost of $10,000."

Julia McNair Wright, in her book devoted to the study of the natives of Alaska, writes :—

"William Duncan of the Church of England, is another of these bright names. Forgetting ambition, despising ease, forsaking his own country and his father's house, counting even life not dear if he might win those simple Indian souls for the Son of God, he has created a civilization in Metlakahtla and brought many souls to glory." . . .

"The longest established, and most successful work among any Alaskan Indians, is that maintained by Mr. Duncan. . . .

"The Chilcats had occasionally visited Fort Simpson, and Metlakahtla, where one of the most remarkable of all missionary enterprises is located, and also Sitka and Fort Wrangell, and they had carried to their friends wonderful tales of Indians 'become white,' who could 'talk on paper' and 'hear paper talk' and who wore white folks' clothes, and lived in houses with windows, and forsook the Shaman, and ate no more dog-flesh, and no longer killed one another." . . .

Alluding to the wretchedness, of the Alaskan Indians in their native villages, she adds :—

"The houses of the Indians are not fitted for any decency of home-life, nor for maintaining health. The houses are often without partitions, and are inhabited by many Indians together, of all ages and

both sexes. There is no possibility of securing
modesty of demeanor, purity of thought or cleanliness of living under these circumstances. Polygamy of the most shameless type exists, and child-marriages are common. There is no need to
expatiate on the moral degeneration resulting from
twenty, thirty or more persons living in one room :
the results would be evident to any idiot."—"*Among
the Alaskans.*" Philadelphia, 1883.

The Church at Home and Abroad. New York,
February 1, 1887. In a leader on Mr. Duncan's
work headed "*A Notable Stranger among Us,*"
says :

"He has built a self-supporting civilized Christian community of about one thousand souls, in a
neat, well-ordered town called Metlakahtla, well
known to all the late tourists that have visited
Alaska, and seen by great numbers of them.

"Metlakahtla is one of the most successful undertakings in the elevation of the Indians, and, as a
model, is a fit and inspiring study for all the Indian
workers on the continent.

"It has been often said that there is no trouble
between the Canadian authorities and the Indians
The Riel affair of last year was a sufficient answer
to this statement. But these Metlakahtla Indians,
as it is understood, find that they have far less hold
on the land of their fathers, than have the Indians
of the United States, and no such guarantee for
permanent possession. They are liable to have the

land on which Metlakahtla stands sold from under their feet."

"*The influence of these Christian Indians for good has been very great on our Alaska tribes.* Some of them were first employed as laborers while we had troops at Fort Wrangell. They were sober and Sabbath-keeping Indians : and through their influence a considerable number of the Stickeens at that place were led to Christ before Mrs. McFarland, our first missionary teacher, reached Alaska. They became members of the first church organized there under the successful labors of Rev. Mr. Young. Philip the first teacher and native preacher, and Mrs. Dickinson, the interpreter, were both educated at Metlakahtla.

"One Sabbath morning, soon after the church was organized, as the people were gathering for public worship, five stalwart-looking Indians, clad in army blue and each with a waterproof on his arm, walked into the chapel and reverently worshipped God there, though it appeared afterward that they could not understand the dialect used in the services. They proved to be Metlakahtla Indians, who had been carrying goods up the Stickeen River to the Cassiar mines ; on their return, Saturday night overtook them at Fort Wrangell, and, true to their principles, they fastened their boats to the shore and kept the Sabbath. Monday morning they went on their way homeward. But such an object-lesson could not fail of its influence on the ruder and less

Christianized race. So have they influenced for good all the tribes among which our missions are located."

I might add to these, many other direct, and indirect tributes, that have been paid to Mr. Duncan, and his work, but it will suffice for my purpose to close this chapter, with extracts from Admiral Prevost's narrative of his late visit to Metlakahtla. It will be remembered, that it was through his graphic portrayal, of the barbarous, degradation of the Tsimshean savages, that Mr. Duncan, was inspired to dedicate himself to the enlightenment, of these people; we shall now observe with what wonderment, he beheld the transformation. He says :

"Three A.M., Tuesday, 18th June, 1878. Arrived at Fort Simpson in the U. S. Mail Steamer '*California*,' from Sitka. Was met by William Duncan, with sixteen Indians, nearly all Elders. Our greeting was most hearty, and the meeting with Duncan a cause of real thankfulness to God, in sight, too, of the very spot (nay, on it) where God had put into my heart the first desire of sending the Gospel to the poor heathens around me. Twenty-five years previously H. M. S. '*Virago*' had been repaired on that very beach. What a change had been effected during those passing years. Of the crew before me nine of the sixteen were, to my knowledge, formerly medicine men, or cannibals. In humble faith, we could only exclaim, 'What hath God wrought!' It is all His doing, and it is marvellous in our eyes.

"After twenty-five years' absence, God had brought me back again, amidst all the sundry and manifold changes of the world, face to face with those tribes amongst whom I have witnessed only bloodshed, cannibalism, and heathen devilry in its grossest form. Now they were sitting at the feet of Jesus, clothed, and in their right mind. The very church-warden, dear old Peter Simpson, who opened the church door for me, was the chief of one of the cannibal tribes. . . .

"Words cannot describe the happy month I spent in this happy Christian circle. I can only copy from my rough notes, written on the spot, some of the events which occurred to me.

"Peter Simpson (Thrakshakann). 'I remember when you put your ship on shore at Fort Simpson. I remember how nearly we were fighting, and the guns were prepared. You had a rope put out to keep us off, and we heard it said that you would fire at us from your ship when you got afloat. We knew not what you had rather planned to do. You planned to bring us the Gospel and that has opened our eyes to heavenly things, and oh! how beautiful, very beautiful indeed! Metlakahtla is like a ship just launched. You are here to give us advice, where to put the most in, and how to steer. I address you thus, though you are great and I am poor. But Jesus despises not the poor. The Tsimsheans

were very low, yet Jesus raised us, and we are
now anxious for all our brethren, the tribes around
us, to be made alive. We see them now willing
to hear, and we are trying to help them. We
know God put it into your heart to come here,
and brought you here; God bless you for coming.'

"Sunday, 23rd.—To me, all days at Metlakahtla
are solemnly sacred, but Sunday, of all others especially so. Canoes are all drawn up on the beach
above high-water mark. Not a sound heard. The
children are assembled before morning service to
receive special instruction from Mr. Duncan. The
church bell rings, and the whole population pour
out from their houses—men, women, and children—
to worship God in His own house, built by their
own hands. As it has been remarked, ' No need
to lock doors, for no one is there to enter the empty
houses.' Two policemen are on duty in uniform,
to keep order during service time. The service begins with a chant in Tsimshean, ' I will arise and
go to my Father,' &c., Mr. Schult leading with the
harmonium ; the Litany Prayers in Tsimshean follow, closing with the Lord's Prayer. The address
lasts nearly an hour. Such is the deep attention of
many present, that having once known their former lives, I know that the love of God shed abroad
in their hearts by the Holy Ghost can alone have
produced so marvellous a change.

"First, there was a very old woman, staff in hand,

stepping with such solemn earnestness; after her
came one who had been a very notorious gambler;
though now almost crippled with disease, yet he
seemed to be forgetting infirmity, and literally to
be leaping along. Next followed a dissipated youth,
now reclaimed; and after him a chief, who had
dared a few years ago proudly to lift up his hand
to stop the work of God, now with humble mien,
wending his way to worship. Then came a once
still more haughty man of rank; and after him a
mother carrying her infant child, and a father leading his infant son, a grandmother, with more than
a mother's care, watching the steps of her little
grandson. Then followed a widow, then a young
woman, who had been snatched from the jaws of
infamy; then; a once notorious chief; and the last
I reflected upon was a man walking with solemn
gait, yet hope fixed in his look. When a heathen
he was a murderer: he had murdered his own wife
and burnt her to ashes. What are all these now, I
thought, and the crowds that accompany them!
Whither are they going? And what to do?
Blessed sight for angels! Oh, the preciousness of
a Saviour's blood! If there is a joy in heaven over
one sinner that repenteth, with what delight, must
angels gaze on such a sight as this! I felt such a
glow of gratitude to God come over me, my heart
was stirred within me, for who could have joined
such a congregation as this in worship and have
been cold, and who could have preached the Gospel

to such a people and not have felt he was standing
where God was working?

"After morning service, a class of female adults
remain in the church and receive further instruction
from the native teachers. At the same time the
male adults meet Mr. Duncan in his own room. At
three, the church bell again assembles all the village to worship; and again at seven, when they
generally meet in the school-room, the address being given by one of the native teachers." . . .

"July 16th. Before my departure from Metlakahtla, I assembled the few who were left at the
village, to tell them I was anxious to leave behind
some token both of my visit to them after so long
an absence, and also that I still bore them on my
heart. What should it be? After hours of consultation they decided they would leave the choice to
me, and when I told them (what I had beforehand
determined upon) that my present would be a set
of street lamps to light up their village at night,
their joy was unbounded. Their first thought had
a spiritual meaning. By day, God's house was a
memorable object, visible both by vessels passing
and repassing, and by all canoes as strange Indians
travelled about; but by night all was darkness—
now no longer so—as the bright light of the glorious
Gospel, had through God's mercy and love shined
in their dark hearts, so would all be reminded, by
night as well as by day, of the marvellous light
shining in the hearts of many at Metlakahtla, even

the Indians who came with him were in such fear from the neighboring tribes, that they begged him not to have a fire burning at night or show a light in his house. The system of murder was then so general, that whenever an enemy saw a light he sneaked up to it, and the death of the unsuspecting Indian was generally the result. Thus my selection was a happy one, and I thanked God for it."

In the testimony of these independent, and intelligent observers, who have investigated with scrutiny, the development, of this ideal community, we have evidence beyond question that Mr. Duncan's work is an unqualified success; totally free, from any underlying motives of personal emoluments, or actuated by ambition for self-aggrandizement.

CHAPTER V.

THE SAVAGE.

WE have now followed Mr. Duncan in the noble
work, which he has fearlessly pursued through grave
perils and sore trials; we have always found him
faithfully at his post, sacrificing everything for his
cause ; we have followed him in his joyful delight
at the successes, which had crowned the struggles
he had sustained with such manly fortitude, yet,
with modesty and Christian simplicity. We have
received the impressive testimony of those whose
privilege it has been to visit his modern Arcadia,
and to see with their own eyes, how he has brought
order out of chaos—how he has builded on a rock.
Now, it remains for us to scan his methods, and
then to follow him through a course of cruel events,
unlooked for, uncalled for, and almost without
precedent in the modern history of sectarian persecution.

We have observed how Mr. Duncan began his
work, by first mastering the tongue and then studying, in their own homes, the minds and inner life,
the habits and customs of these painted, half-naked
savages, as at night, clustering around their hearth-

stone, the blazing fire cast a weird glow over their swarthy faces. He learned from them their ideas of the creation, of the mystery of death, their religious superstitions, their history as told in legends; in short, he studied them, and their capacities, as a scientist studies, the relative equivalents of the elements in chemistry.

As a samaritan to their sick, as a peacemaker when fierce passions stirred strife, as a comforter in their hours of trouble and woe, he not only won their affection and confidence; but, he also implanted in their hearts, the germs of good-will and forbearance toward each other. He exemplified and upheld by his own pure, every-day, Christian life, those true principles of morality that stood the crucial test, of the ever suspicious scrutiny of the savage.

Dr. Livingston tells us, how essential it is that missionaries, should teach by their lives, as well as by their words.

"No one ever gains much influence in Africa without purity and uprightness. The acts of a stranger are keenly scrutinized, by both old and young. I have heard women speaking in admiration of a white man because he was pure, and never guilty of secret immorality. Had he been, they would have known it, and, untutored heathen though they be, would have despised him everywhere."

The moment a white man indulges in the common vices among savages he reduces himself, in their estimation to their own level.

The unbounded, all-absorbing devotion of heathen peoples in their worship, and their subservience to their own deities and avowed cults, and that they often make voluntary sacrifice of their own lives, or the lives of their kin, to glorify their god or propitiate his wrath is well known. The late Dean Stanley dwelt much upon their honest, unreserved devotion, and declared that however revolting their beliefs they lived consistently to their teachings, this he held up in vivid contrast to the canting hypocrisy invading so large a portion of the Christian Church.

It is recorded that some Brahmins, conversing with the Danish Missionary Schwartz, replied to his arguments in behalf of Christianity:

"We do not see your Christian people live according to that Holy Word. They curse, they swear, they get drunk; they steal, they cheat, they deal fraudulently with one another; they blaspheme and rail upon matters of religion, or often make a mock of those who profess to be religious; they behave themselves as badly, if not worse, than we heathen. Of what advantage is all your profession of Christ's religion, if it does not influence the lives of your own countrymen? Should you not first endeavor to convert your own countrymen before you attempt to proselyte Pagans? But turning to him they said, 'Of a truth you are a holy man, and if all Christians thought and spoke and lived as you do, we would without delay undergo the change and become Christians also.'"

Based on his study of the infant minds, and the needs of these people, Mr. Duncan began by teaching them the simple truths of the Christian religion. He dispensed with everything in the way of form or ceremony that would distract their minds; he represented to them as the central idea the One Omnipotent God,—Creator of all,—Ruler of human destinies,—Controller of the elements, of the earth, and of the heavens.

He told them of the fall of man, and how God had sent His own Son into the world to suffer and to be sacrificed, for the redemption of all sinners. He told them of the reward for the righteous, and the punishment of the wicked. He did not tell them, that his God was better than theirs; he taught them, that there was but one God, and it was the Supreme Ruler Who had blessed the earth with light, and warmth, and verdure; stocked the sea and rivers with fish, and the forests with game.

He was dealing with simple, primitive minds, whose only idea of creation, and, the origin of surrounding wonders of nature, had been conveyed through tribal legends.

Notwithstanding, the many plausible speculations and theories advanced by learned investigators, primitive autochthonic life, not only in America but throughout the entire world, is enshrouded in mystery. Neither science, nor theology, has conclusively solved the problem of the manner in which the world was peopled. However, we may consistently

conjecture that man primordially was without a
knowledge of the true God, knew absolutely nothing.
His development was like the babe from birth, and
his gradual unfoldment was the result of necessity,
and, the impulsion of the inevitable.   His cravings
to appease hunger caused him to seek wherewith
to satisfy his need; the fruits and the weaker creatures about him served as his food ; in his struggles
with nature he devised means to ensnare and kill
animals, whose skins should protect him from cold.
His very strife in self-defence against ferocious animals quickened his intellect. He sought shelter from
the inclemency of the elements in caves.   Communal life was adopted for security, and the strongest
naturally assumed the chieftainship.   Consequent
upon being thus thrown together, attrition of one
mind with another, enlarged their mental horizon.

The savage beheld with awe the phenomena of
nature.   Light, darkness, the storms, the tides, the
seasons, his own origin, all signified some hidden
power, which, unable to solve, he attributed to the
workings of some good or evil spirit, visible or invisible. Many of their beliefs hung upon the figments of
their dreams, which were to them realities.   " So
strong was the [aboriginal] North American faith
in dreams, that on one occasion when an Indian
dreamt he was taken captive, he induced his friends
to make a mock attack on him, to bind him, and
treat him as a captive, actually submitting to a con-

THE DEVIL DANCE.

siderable amount of torture, in the hope thus to fulfil his dreams. The Greenlanders, also, believe in the reality of dreams, and think that at night they go hunting, visiting, courting, and so on " (Sir John Lubbock).

These children in intellect ever struggled with the mysterious problems of nature. M. Ambrousset was told by Sekesa a Kaffir: " Your tidings are what I want; and I was seeking before I knew you as you shall hear and judge for yourselves. Twelve years ago I went to feed my flock. The weather was hazy, I sat down on a rock and asked myself sorrowful questions; yes sorrowful because I was unable to answer them. 'Who has touched the stars with his hands? On what pillars do they rest ?' I asked myself. 'The waters are never weary; they know no other law than to flow, without ceasing, from morning till night, and from night till morning; but where do they stop? And who makes them flow thus? The clouds also come and go, and burst in water over the earth. Whence come they? Who sends them? The divines certainly do not give us rain, for how could they do it? And why do I not see them with my own eyes, go up to heaven to fetch it? I cannot see the wind but what is it? Who brings it, makes it blow, and roar and terrify us? Do I not know that the corn sprouts? Yesterday there was not a blade in my field; today I returned to the field and found some. Who can have given to the earth the wisdom and power to produce it?' Then I buried my face in both my hands."

Awe, wonderment and reverence were commanded by the mundane environments of the savage. "Thick black clouds, portentous of evil, hung threateningly over the savage during his entire life. Genii murmur in the flowing river, in the rustling branches are felt the breathings of the gods; goblins dance in vapory twilight, and demons howl in the darkness" (Bancroft).

Even the personality of dead heroes, whose valiant deeds, oft recounted, became, in the passage of time, merged with their deities.

Heathen peoples in their worship have invariably exhibited a gradual development and advancement from, polytheism towards monotheism : first, paying homage to objects of nature, finally conceiving that there is One Supreme Power, which controls the universe.

This supreme being ever remains to them a mystery, as for the matter of that, does their own duality of soul and body, which is suggested to them by shadows and dreams, and the realization that when breath leaves the body, the light goes out.

Idolatry comes from an attempt to materialize and render tangible their deities. Recognizing mankind as the highest type, naturally they often essayed to model their gods after man's image—600 B. C. Xenophanes wrote, " Men seem to have created their gods, and to have given to them their own mind, voices and figure. The Ethiopians made their gods black and flat-nosed ; the Thracians theirs, red-haired and blue-eyed."

As the inexorable domination of the strongest in brute force prevailed, so alike in mental force the strongest, with most creative imagination, asserted and assumed knowledge of all supernatural things, and finally claimed to be vested with the power of controlling the forces of nature. The natural desire for an intermediary between themselves, and their vague deities, and the desire to propitiate such, made this supremacy not difficult for the crafty to attain.

"There are several ways in which the worshipper can hold personal intercourse with his deities. These, being souls or spirits, are of course to be seen at times in dreams and visions, especially by their own priests or seers, who thus get (or pretend to get) divine answers or oracles from them. Being a soul, the god can also enter the body, and act and speak through it, and thus hysterical and epileptic symptoms, which we have seen to be ascribed to an evil demon possessing the patient, are looked on more favourably when the spirit is considered to be a deity, come to inspire his minister, and talk by his voice. The convulsions, the unearthly voice in which the priest answers in the name of the deity within, and his falling into a stupor when his god departs, all fit together, and in all quarters of the world the oracle-priests, and diviners, by familiar

spirits seem really diseased in body and mind, and
deluded by their own feelings, as well as skilled in
cheating their natives with sham symptoms and
cunning answers " (E. B. Tylor).

Thus began priestcraft or Shamanism; and as
the valiant chieftain led and commanded them in
warfare, so the Shaman, manifested and exercised
his power when sickness or calamity fell upon them:
aye, from chief, to slave, all bowed in submission to
his mandate.

The power of the priest was thus recognized and
yielded to; he became an important factor, and must
needs be consulted in all personal or State affairs;
sometimes, supernatural and temporal power were
merged in one and the same person.

Church and State, superstition and despotism,
were thus united in the darkest ages of mankind.

Variety and similarity characterized the cults of
primitive man in every part of the globe. Whatever the form of worship it is a noticeable fact,
there has been a gradual progressive awakening in
the formation of society, with the recognition of
the rights of others.

At the very dawn of civilization in the old world,
as we may still see in any museum, "the scene of
the weighing the soul of the deceased, and his trial
by Oseris the Judge of the dead, and the forty-two
assessors, while Thoth, the writing-god stands by to
enter the dread record on his tablets. In the columns of hieroglyphics, are set down the crimes, of

which the soul must clear itself, a curious mingling of what we should call ceremonial, and moral sins, among them the following; 'I have not privily done evil against mankind. I have not told falsehoods in the tribunal of Truth, I have not done any wicked thing. I have not made the labouring man do more than his tasks daily. I have not calumniated the slave to his master. I have not murdered. I have not done fraud to men. I have not changed the measures of the country. I have not injured the images of gods. I have not taken scraps of the bandages of the dead. I have not committed adultery. I have not milked milk from the mouths of sucklings. I have not hunted wild animals in the pasturage. I have not netted sacred birds. I am pure, I am pure, I am pure!'" (E. B. Tylor).

Despite the recognition of moral responsibilities, many anomalies occur in the ethics of the savage.

As the savage fought with beasts of prey to secure subsistence, so battled he with his fellowman for spoils. Warfare caused a uniting of communities for defence and offence; conquest enriched and increased the power of the triumphant few. Avarice, greed, pride, ambition, all contributed their quota as an incentive to gain dominion and precedence. Human conflicts then, as to-day, wrought good as well as evil; they were attended with mental activity that largely tended to the unfolding of the intellectuality. With the gain of wealth, came the desire for pomp and splendor.

They built pretentious huts or wigwams. The patrons of art in those days, as now, found ready hands, deft in fashioning their frippery.

Development was but the sequence of the ever reaching after the unattainable, hence the unfolding continued. When individual desires had been gratified — communal and national desires, arose and grew apace. In some lands advancement was rapid, in others, resisted, retarded, and ofttimes defeated.

We who enjoy the benefit of an advanced state of civilization, often forget, that it is but a few generations since our own forefathers, grovelled, in the darkest superstitions.

" The nations now most civilized were once barbarians. Our ancestors were savages, who, with tangled hair, and glaring eyes, and blood-besmeared hands, devoured man and beast alike.

" The difference between the cultured and primitive man lies chiefly in the fact that one has a few centuries the start of the other in the race of progress " (Bancroft).

The American aborigine is among the least favored of mankind in the progress of enlightenment. We find him still, the associate of wild beasts, and still, groping in darkness, but, seeking for light. One of the most touching and romantic incidents in history, is that of the pilgrimage of four Nez Percés Indians from the Columbia River, Oregon, to St. Louis, Mo., in 1832, when that town was but a military outpost and fur-trading station. The

AN ABORIGINAL STOCKADE.

Nez Percés had learned from an American trapper much about the white men's arts and wisdom; he told them that the pale-faces owed their greatness to the teachings of the supreme God; that they possessed God's book of wisdom, which they could read; this book revealed the secrets of life and of the hereafter; taught them to be good and wise.

The Nez Percés talked much among themselves about this wonderful book, held anxious councils over their camp-fires. The desire to learn more about the white man's God grew upon them, and became their uppermost thought. Finally two trusted old braves, and two stalwart young braves, were chosen for the mission. On foot they journeyed the trail of many moons toward the rising sun, enduring unspeakable hardships, encountering many perils, crossing the great rivers on improvised rafts, scaling the mountain ranges, stealing silently by night, through the land of the fierce Black Feet and other hostile tribes, covering their tracks, subsisting solely on the game of the forest and plains. Thus for more than two thousand miles they wended their way to the white man's camp. They arrived and though they marvelled at the many strange sights, the great lodges, and the huge fire-canoes as large as islands, paddled without hands; yet their sacred errand was uppermost in their thoughts. They were feasted cordially and abundantly; decked with finery, and clad in showy blankets; in truth, for kindliness and entertainment they lacked naught; but to them their mission was a failure, they sought in vain for " The Book." St. Louis was exclusively a Roman Catholic town, and, as is well known, it is not the custom or policy of that church, to give the Bible to the people.

The two old braves died in St. Louis, and one of the young men contracted a disease, from which he died on his homeward journey. On taking their departure, their hearts burdened with disappointment, one of them delivered the following speech to General Clark,* then commanding the station, in the presence of a small group of officers and traders :

" I came to you over the trail of many moons from the setting sun. You were the friend of my fathers, who have all gone the long way. I came, with one eye partly opened, for more light for my people, who sit in darkness. I go back with both eyes closed. How can I go back blind, to my blind people ? I made my way to you with strong arms, through many enemies and with strong hands, that I might carry back much to them.

" I go back with both arms broken and empty. The two fathers who came with us, the braves of many winters—we leave asleep here by your great water and wigwam. They were tired in many moons, and their moccasins wore out. . My peo-

---

* It was this general who had with Lewis made the famous overland journey to Oregon and the Pacific.

ple sent me to get the white man's Book of Heaven. You took me where you allow your women to dance, as we do ours, and the Book was not there.

"You showed me the images of good spirits, and pictures of the good land beyond, but the Book was not among them to tell us the way. . I am going back the long, sad trail to my people of the dark land. . You make my feet heavy with burdens of gifts, and my moccasins will grow old in carrying them, but the Book is not among them.

"When I tell my poor blind people, after one more snow, in the big council, that I did not bring the Book, no word will be spoken by our old men, or, by our young braves. One by one, they will rise up and go out in silence. . My people will lie in darkness, and they will go on the long way to the other hunting-grounds. No white man will go with them, and no white man's Book to make the way plain. . I have no words."

Then sadly and silently they took their homeward trail.*

But the Nez Percés mission was not a failure, for after many months the story of their pilgrimage reached the ears of Mr. Spaulding, and that noble martyr Dr. Whitman, who planted Christianity, accompanied by seed-wheat and wagon-wheels. It was the indirect effect of the Nez Percés' journey,

---

* Portraits 207 and 208 in Catlin's collection represent these two handsome young Nez Percés braves.

which brought about the fruitful mission work and
Dr. Whitman's heroic midwinter, horseback ride of
four thousand miles, in four months from the Columbia to the Potomac, that resulted in England's concession of Oregon to the United States—this, too,
at the time when the air was afume with "*fifty-four
forty, or fight.*"

"There have been eminent express rides, full of
import to families and states; these have carried
messages of war and for peace, for trade and tower-
ing ambition. It would be difficult, however, to find
one that for distance, time, heroic daring, peril, suffering, and magnificent consequences, could equal
Whitman's ride" (Barrow).

Nor was this the only benefit. In time the Hudson's Bay Company, which had previously discouraged missionaries and settlers, found the American
missionaries making such invasions within their territory, that they opened their gates hospitably to
English missionaries; and, it was after this change of
their policy that Mr. Duncan, was allowed to begin
his work at Fort Simpson.

I have thus digressed to show that the savage is a
seeker after light, but a seeker when that light brings
a benefit, which he can see, and feel, and measure.
The Nez Percés hoped by means of the white
man's book to acquire his arts, his wisdom, to learn
therefrom an easy trail to the "Happy Hunting
Ground."

We have every evidence that it is mankind's incarnate selfishness, more or less, blended with cowardice and fear, that has in all eras, in all parts of the world, prompted the outreaching for or acceptance of deities and creeds, having always in view self-preservation, and betterment of condition. Sometimes this selfishness has taken the form of self-aggrandizement; sometimes has found vent in the gratification of a grand passion.

How quaintly comes to us now, Nestor's story [as given by Dean Stanley] of the conversion of that ferocious Russian Prince Vladimir, when he and his people were still pagans and in the depths of barbarism. He, who was as much distinguished for his zeal for the rude idolatry of his own countrymen, as for his savage crimes.

Vladimir having gained great renown through the known world, there came to him in about the year 986 envoys of the various religions.—" First the Bulgarian mussulmans from the Volga, saying: 'Wise and prudent prince as thou art, thou knowest neither law nor religion. Believe in ours, and honor Mahomet.'—'In what does your religion consist?' asked Vladimir. 'We believe in God,' they replied, 'but we believe also in what the Prophet teaches. Be circumcised, abstain from pork, drink no wine; and after death choose out of seventy beautiful wives the most beautiful.' Vladimir listened to them for the last reason. But that which he did not like was circumcision, the abstinence from pork, and above all the prohibition of drinking. 'Drinking is the great delight of Russians,' he said; 'we cannot live without it.'

"Next came the representatives of Western Christendom. 'The Pope,' they said, 'begs us to tell you, your country is like ours, but not your religion. Ours is light. We fear God, who made the heaven and earth, the stars and the moon, and every living creature, whilst thy Gods are of wood.' 'What does your law command ?' asked Vladimir.—'We fast,' they said, 'to the best of our power; and when one eats or drinks, he does it in honor of God, as we have been told by our master S. Paul.'—'Go home,' said Vladimir.—'Our fathers did not believe in your religion, nor receive it from the Pope.'

"Next, came some Jews (who lived among the Khozars). 'We have heard say that the Mahometans, and the Christians, have tried to persuade thee to adopt their belief. The Christians believe in Him whom we have crucified. We believe in one God, the God of Abraham, Isaac and Jacob.'—'In what does your law consist ?' asked Vladimir.—'Our law requires circumcision, prohibits pork and hare, and enjoins the observance of Saturday.'—'Where then is your country ?'—'At Jerusalem.'—'What is Jerusalem ?'—'God was wroth with our forefathers; he dispersed us for our sins throughout the world, and our country has fallen into the hands of Christians.' —'What,' said Vladimir, 'you wish to teach others —you whom God has rejected and dispersed? If God had loved you, and your law, He would never have scattered you abroad; do you wish, perhaps, that we should suffer the same?'

"In each of these answers we detect the characteristic temper of the Russian; his love of drinking, his tenacity of ancestral customs, his belief in the Divine right of success.

"Another agency now appears on the scene. It is not a nameless barbarian, as before. It is, so the chronicler tells us, 'a philosopher from Greece.' The glory of Grecian culture still hung about its ancient seats, and the fittest harbinger of Christian truth, even in dealing with the savage Vladimir, was thought to be a Greek; not a priest or a missionary, but a philosopher.

"'We have heard,' said he, 'that the Mahometans have sent to lead you to adopt their belief. Their religion, and their practices are abominations in the face of heaven and earth, and judgment will fall upon them, as of old on Sodom and Gomorrah. This is what they do who call Mahomet a prophet.'

"This calls forth the first moral spark that we have seen in Vladimir's mind. He spat upon the ground and said, 'This is shameful.'

"'We have also heard,' said the philosopher, 'that messengers have come from Rome to teach you. Their belief differs somewhat from ours. They celebrate mass with unleaven bread, therefore, they have not the true religion.' Such was the point on which the two greatest Churches of the world had been torn asunder, and into which Vladimir did not further inquire. He then took up the word himself and said : ' I have also had Jews here who said that the Germans and Greeks believe on Him Whom we crucified.'" The philosopher assented. 'Why was He crucified ?' asked Vladimir.—' If you will listen,' replied the philosopher, ' I will tell you all from the beginning.' ' With pleasure,' replied Vladimir. And the philosopher then proceeded to relate all the Divine acts, and deeds, from the beginning of the world; the whole course, we may say, of ecclesiastical history, coming to a characteristic close in the Seventh General Council. He then defined the true faith, and spoke of the future reward of the just, and the punishment of the impious, and at the same time showed to Vladimir, a tablet on which was painted the scene of the last judgment. Then, showing him on the right the just, who, filled with joy, were entering Paradise, he made him remark on the left the sinners who were going to hell. Vladimir, as he looked at the picture, heaved a sigh and said,—' Happy are those on the right ; woe to the sinners on the left.'—' If you wish,' said the philosopher to enter with the just, who are on the right, consent to be baptized.'—Vladimir reflected profoundly, and said, ' I will wait yet a little while.' For he wished first to be instructed about each religion. But he loaded the philosopher with presents and sent him away.

" Vladimir in the next year sent for the nobles and elders, and told them of the different interviews. 'You know, O Prince,' they said, 'that no one talks evil of his religion, but that all, on the contrary, praise their own. If you wish to know the exact truth, you have wise men; send them to examine each faith of each, and the manner of their worship.'

"We need not follow them throughout their journey. They reported that the Mussulmans prayed with their heads covered, and that their stench was insupportable; and that the German and Roman churches had no ornaments nor beauty, though better than the Mussulman mosques.

"But the nobles insisted, that the decision should not be made without knowing first, what was the Greek religion; and accordingly the envoys proceeded to the city which they called Tzarozorod. In that barbarous name we recognize 'The City of the Czar' or 'King,' the great Constantinople. What it was at that period, the splendor of its ceremonial, both of Church and State, even in the most minute detail, is known to us from the nearly contemporary account (A.D. 987) of the German embassy from Otho. Basil Porphyrogenitus was on the throne with his brother Constantine; and his words, in giving orders to the Patriarch, to prepare for a magnificent reception of the strangers, indicate more than many treatises the importance he attached to the outward show of the ceremonial of the Church, as his grandfather had to the outward show of the ceremonial of the court.—'Let them see,' he said, 'the glory of our God.'—The service was that of a high festival, either of St. John Chrysostom or the death of the Virgin.

"It was in the Church—magnificent even now in its fallen state, then all gorgeous with gold and mosaic—of Saint Sophia. Even had they been as far as Rome itself, they would have seen nothing equal to it. St. Peter, as it now is, was far in the future. Cologne Cathedral was not yet born. The boast of Justinism was still the masterpiece of Christian architecture.

"The Russian envoys were placed in a convenient position. The incense smoked, the chants resounded, the Patriarch was in his most splendid vestments. One incident is preserved in a Byzantine annalist which the Russian chronicler has omitted.—'The Russians were struck,' he says, 'by the multitude of lights, and the chanting of hymns; but what most filled them with astonishment, was the appearance of the deacons, and subdeacons issuing from the sanctuary, with torches in their hands;' and, as we happen to know from an earlier source, with white linen wings on their shoulders, at whose presence the people fell on their knees and cried,—'Kyrie Eleison!' The Russians took their guides by the hand and said ·—'All that we have seen is awful and majestic, but this is supernatural. We have seen young men with wings, in dazzling robes, who, without touching the ground, chanted in the air Holy! holy! holy! and this is what has most surprised us.' The guides replied (and the Byzantine historian repeats it without changing the tone of his narrative, even in the slightest degree) :—'What! do you not know that angels come down from heaven to mingle in our services ? '—' You are right,' said the simple-minded Russians ; 'we want no further proof; send us home again.'

"It is a striking instance, of the effect produced on a barbarous people, by the union of religious and outward magnificence; and, the dexterity with which the Byzantine courtiers, turned the credulity of the Russian envoys to account, is an example of the origin of many of the miracles of the middle ages; not wholly fraud, nor wholly invention, but a union of the two; a symbolical ceremony taken for a supernatural occurrence, and the mistake fostered, not by deliberate imposture but, by the difficulty of resisting the immense temptation to deception, which such mistakes afforded. A like confusion supports to this day the supposed miracle of the Holy Fire at Jerusalem.

"As in many similar cases the results far outlasted the sin or the weakness of the first beginning.—'We knew not,' said the envoys on their return, 'whether we were not in heaven ; in truth, it would be impossible on earth to find such riches and magnificence. We cannot describe to you all that we have seen. We can only believe that there, in all likelihood, one is in the presence of God, and that the worship of other countries is there entirely

eclipsed. We shall never forget so much grandeur. Whosoever has seen so sweet a spectacle
will be pleased with nothing elsewhere. It is impossible for us to remain where we are.'

" The rest of the story may be shortly told.
With some few Eastern touches, it is not unlike
the national conversions of the West. Vladimir,
still in a state of hesitation, besieged the city of
Cherson in the Crimea, and, like Clovis, vowed that
he would be baptized if he succeeded. He then
sent to demand from the Emperor Basil, the hand
of his sister Anne in marriage, under the threat of
doing to Constantinople as he had done to Cherson.
With some difficulty Anne was induced to sacrifice
herself to the barbarian prince, *in the hope of avert-
ing so great a danger and effecting so great a good.*
Her sister Theophano, had already been established on the throne of the German Otho. She
acquired a more lasting fame *as the channel through
which Christianity penetrated into Russia.*

" He was baptized accordingly at Cherson, and
then issued orders for a great baptism of his people
at Kieff. They also hesitated for a short time. But
a like argument, combined with the Grand-Duke,
convinced them also. The huge wooden idol
Peroun was dragged over the hills at a horse's tail,
mercilessly scourged by twelve mounted pursuers,
and thrown into the Dnieper, where it was guided
and pushed along the stream till it finally disappeared down the rapids, in a spot long afterward

known as the Bay of Peroun. The whole people of Kieff were immersed in the same river, some sitting on the banks, some plunged in, others swiming, whilst the priests read the prayers.—'It was a night,' says Nestor, 'wonderfully curious and beautiful to see; and when the whole people were baptized each one returned to his own house.' The spot was consecrated by the first Christian Church, and Kieff, which already, as we have seen from old traditions, had been the Glastonbury, became henceforward the Canterbury of the Russian Empire."

Vladimir, unlike the ordinary savage, was more brutal than benighted. He was able to discriminate between the creeds with oriental cunning. With usual designing avarice, and cupidity, he accepted the Christian religion, only to gain the hand of the beautiful Anne, and to add grandeur to his court, and to glorify his reign.

From the very incipiency of his development, primitive man has thus been led by the things that satisfy his corporeal cravings. We find the savage to-day intellectually in his infancy, steeped in the vices of generations—a demon in brutish instincts —a combination of childlike simplicity, and unmeasured ferocity. What may be to the savage, virtue is to civilized people often an enormity. And *vice versa;* for example, the naked Indian maiden blushes when her necklace is removed, regarding it to be an indelicate exposure of her person.

It is an indubitable and acknowledged fact that

the savage is attracted to advancement only by those things which appeal to his senses. " The first step toward teaching a savage is to feed him : the stomach satisfied, he will listen to instruction, not before."

Mr. Duncan grasped, and grasped intelligently, the true science of civilization—he learned the insistent needs, and pliant capacities, of the savages. We have seen how effectually he provided for these needs, and trained these capacities.

CHAPTER VI.

THE CRISIS.

CHRISTIANITY, humanity and civilization seemed to triumph over all this region, when, suddenly, in the autumn of 1881, an unrighteous storm of persecution, gathered in a quarter altogether unlooked for; soon, it broke over Metlakahtla in fury; and, has continued to rage ever since, with cruel asperity; at this moment, it threatens the settlement with destruction.

This, all because Mr. Duncan, above all things dared to do his duty, to his God, and to his people, despite the intrigues of his foes.

Mr. Duncan, left England as a missionary layman, and he is a missionary layman still. He was expected, and urged to take Church of England orders —even the title of Bishop was open to him—but his labors being so richly blessed as a layman, he, refused to change his degree. His answer to the Bishop of Columbia who urged him was :—that he feared that Church orders would prove to him, what Saul's armor was to David; only an encumbrance, and therefore, he preferred keeping to the use of the sling and stone.

During more than twenty years of Mr. Duncan's missionary efforts, the Church Missionary Society under whose auspices he was working, unceasingly praised him, and his methods, and, the Society even went so far as to issue circulars,* to its missionaries advocating evangelistic work, on the very plan then being carried out by Mr. Duncan, and whose success no doubt, influenced them greatly in issuing these circulars.

It was not until after the death of the great Henry Venn, who, as secretary of the Society, had guided its affairs, for so many years, always heartily approving of and encouraging Mr. Duncan in his methods of evangelistic and secular work, that it became manifest that the Society's directors differed from Mr. Duncan in their views of mission work, and methods of conducting it. The present bigoted incumbent, only assumed the secretaryship † a short time before the rupture which I shall describe in this chapter.

It was after this melancholy change in the *person-nel* of the leadership, and, not until then, that *the Society gave evidence of a gradual, though marked change in its policy.* Its aims which heretofore had been broadly evangelistic, now soon became deeply colored, and circumscribed with ecclesiasticism.

Mr. Duncan was always perfectly frank in his re-

---

* See Circulars, Chapter VIII., this volume.
† Another gentleman now dead had filled the brief interim.

ports to the Society. His observations, and analysis of the people with whom he had to deal, caused him to avoid, from the first prompting, or leading them in conformity with the elaborate service of the Church of England, which was the Church of the Society; and the Church of which Mr. Duncan was himself a member. He persistently declared that his going among heathen, was to save sinners, and not to glorify the Church; to lead them to a pure life, not, to teach them dogmas.

Several years ago, the Society became impatient and insistent for a closer resemblance in the Metlakahtla Church service, to that of the Church of England; and for those statistics from the mission, which are deemed to count for so much in publications, but, which in reality are often fictitious and misleading.

We have in following Mr. Duncan's work come to understand, that one, of the principal characteristics of his teaching; and one, of the secrets of his success, was *simplicity*. He cared solely for the sound and healthy growth of the work. The Society, now apparently imagined the Indians to be advanced Christians, but he knew, he was still dealing with Indians, he had found steeped in barbaric atrocities, and many of whom, he knew to be still mere babes in religious comprehension. The Society, conceived that the forms and ritual of the Church, were safe, and suitable for the Indians to follow; but, Mr. Duncan, as he grew in experience, saw more and more clearly, that the distinctive dress of the ministers and Bishops, as well as the order of Service of the Church—especially in the administration of the Lord's Supper,—were calculated to bewilder, rather than edify the Indians with whom he had to do, in their present stage of progress.

Besides, he found in their inordinate passion for spirituous liquors which was universal, a special danger in offering them wine as a sacrament. Furthermore, it was a difficult dilemma to reconcile, the deviation of church requirement, from the prohibitory state law, which imposed the penalty of imprisonment upon any Indian who even touched wine, or other liquors.

They would naturally query to themselves, how is it, that the church law is at variance with the Queen's law ? The Queen says *no !* The Church says *yes !*

Mr. Duncan gave this subject a great deal, of serious, and anxious consideration. And often discussed it with his church elders, and the more advanced native brethren ; explaining to them the full significance of the rite :—they seriously apprehended the effect upon their weaker brethren, who might depend upon the sacrament, as a charm to take away sin, and afford them a passport to heaven. And one might naturally expect, that many of the yet unconverted natives would regard the partaking of the sacred fluid, as a covert manner of indulging, in that which was forbidden them by law, even if a non-spirituous wine was used. Furthermore, Mr. Duncan was dealing, with men who had but recently been converted from cannibalism, and we may readily understand that the introduction of a rite, which in the performance, assumed to be the partaking of the body, and the blood of our Saviour, was a matter which required the utmost caution. One can but recall that "the Roman heathens ascribed to the early Christians, that the sacrament was a cannibal's feast."

To those who had formerly regaled themselves at banquets of human flesh, how fine would be the point of distinction, and moral consideration, between the *emblem* which was assumed to *represent* the substance ; and the *real* substance, to partake of which, they were now taught, was a most atrocious sin. They who had tasted human flesh in their days of heathenism, benighted as they then were, would have recoiled with horror, at the bare thought of consuming, even by emblem a part of one of their gods !

It must be apparent to all, that Mr. Duncan sought above all things the spiritual welfare of his converts, and would be the last one to withhold from them, anything essential to their salvation, and with his knowledge of their minds and dispositions, and the stage of their development, he was better able to judge of their spiritual requirements, than were men in London, who had never even seen them. Yet, recently these perfunctory dictators, had presumed to square them, by a procrustean, ecclesiastical rule, and insist upon the introduction of an elaborate eucharist; representing that without such, Mr. Duncan was giving the Indians but a " *mutilated Christianity* " and " *false teachings !* "

In the minds of many of the most distinguished Christian authorities, the celebration of the Lord's Supper, is more honored in the partaking of *the real invisible*, but all potent, spiritual essence of Christ; than in the actual consumption of an emblem; though it is generally admitted that where there are no impediments, the observance of this sacred rite is most desirable.   Participation in this rite should be reserved for mature minds, with full consciousness of its import, and the act should be one of intelligent, personal free will.   The Christian world has recognized this fact, in the abandonment of the administration of the sacrament to infants.

On this subject, the late Dean Stanley,—accounted the most learned ecclesiastical authority of our day,—spoke very plainly.   It is well known that he held as paramount to forms, and ceremonies, the rescue of the human soul, and the dissemination of true Christian religion, in whatsoever manner, it was most effective in its application to those especially *to be saved.*   I quote him freely, and with a feeling of great reverence, for I owe to his lucid expositions, a fixed belief in the harmony of the Christian religion with modern science.   Dean Stanley thus, speaks of the sacrament.

"Not a single church now communicates in the form in which it was originally given. . . .

"It has been well said by a devout Scottish bishop,* in speaking of this subject: 'We should not expect to arrive at the secret of Hamlet by eating a bit of Shakespeare's body; and so, though we ate ever so much of the material bones or flesh of the Founder of the Eucharist, we should not arrive one whit nearer to "the mind which was Christ Jesus."' . . .

"They who believe in the singular mercy and compassion in the Parable of the Prodigal Son, or in the toleration and justice due to those who are of another religion, as in the Parable of the Good Samaritan, they, have or have not partaken of the sacrament, have thus received Christ because they have received that which was the essence of Christ, His spirit of mercy and toleration. . . .

"These three things then, the lifting up of the heart in words of devotion to God, *the performance of kindly and useful deeds, to men, and the dedication of self*, are the three things by which the Supreme Goodness and Truth, according to true Religion, is pleased, propitiated, satisfied.

"In the great exemplar and essence of Christianity, these three things are seen in perfection. . .

"The constant under-song of better spirits from the earliest times, which maintains with regard to

---

* Bishop Ewing.

both sacraments, not only that, in extreme cases, they may be dispensed with, but that, their essence is to be had without form at all. . . .

"The most Protestant of all the statements on this subject in the English Prayer Book is itself taken from an earlier rubric to the same effect in the mediæval church. 'If man . . . by any just impediment do not receive the sacrament of Christ's body and blood, the Church shall instruct him that' [if he fulfil the moral conditions of Communion], '*he doth eat and drink the Body and Blood of our Saviour Christ to* his soul's health, *although he do not receive*, the *sacrament with his mouth.*' Such a concession is in fact the concession of the whole principle. . . .

"The moment that door is opened, for the moral consideration of what is due to mercy and humanity, the whole fabric of the strict sacramental system vanishes, and reason, justice, and charity step in to take their right place."

Mr. Duncan always looked forward hopefully to a time, when it might be safe to introduce the Lord's Supper, and once wrote the Society, suggesting a modified form, thinking that at an appropriate moment, a simple emblematic form of evening-meal, or, social feast, might be adopted which would resemble the original repast; that is to say, not administered by a priest: but, the Society wanted the celebration to be carried out with full detail, ceremony, and vestments, as in the Church of England.

Therefore, all things considered, it is obvious that they could not agree.

In respect to Baptism, Mr. Duncan, perceived the necessity for carefully guarding this rite, and keeping the Indians under lengthy probation. He had taught them that Baptism might be compared to a label on a can of salmon, to signify, and vouch for the quality of its contents. The Indians are now surprised to see sectarians running eagerly to clap on the label of baptism, without much regard whether the candidate's life corresponds with the label, or not.

Only a short time ago a Bishop of the Society on his way up a river—in a single day converted, and baptized a sick Indian Chief of a heathen tribe, who had while in health stoutly refused Christian instruction. After a short interview—the chief yielded to the Bishop's advice, handed over his medicine-rattle,—and accepted baptism, as he wanted, he said, to be saved—meaning the healing of his body. The Bishop flourished the rattle before the Indian spectators as a trophy, and then went on his journey; congratulating, himself on what a graphic article he could write of the incident, for his missionary publications. But, now for the sequel. After the Bishop's departure the baptized invalid's sickness increased. Being, therefore, disappointed, he consulted some of his people, as to what he had better do. They blamed him for giving up his medicine-rattle to the Bishop. His superstitious fears became aroused, and, he resolved to demand its restitution, and to return the water of baptism to the Bishop. A cup of water, was accordingly placed in readiness near his bed. In a few days the Bishop on his return called to see the sick man. Instead, however, of receiving a friendly greeting, he was met with a sullen ill-tempered demand for the medicine-rattle. In vain the Bishop remonstrated by telling the baptized Shaman, he was now a Christian. The savage's demand was repeated with a clamorous threat, and finally, the rattle was returned to him.

As the Bishop left, the dying Indian threw after him the cup of water, saying at the same time.— " take back your baptism," and, followed it with violent imprecations.

Bishop Ingham, in his fearless and flat-footed, charge to the missionaries at Freetown, West Africa ; in referring to the rotten condition of affairs brought about, by greater efforts to enroll names, and establish the church, than to purify and elevate the converts, he says it :—" has shown up a mass of iniquity with which our present rules of discipline entirely fail to deal. The church is responsible for binding as well as loosing. It is evident that, amongst church members, church officers, and communicants, there is much undiscovered iniquity. The church must wash her hands of this state of things ; and *we hope to enforce, as a beginning, some stricter discipline as to the sacraments of Baptism and the Lord's Supper.*"

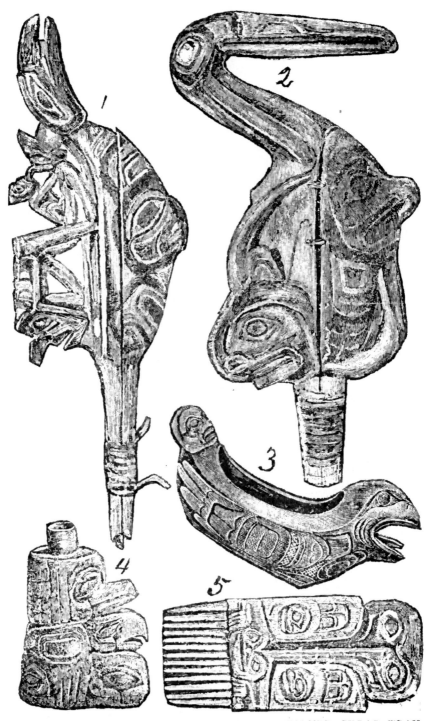

I AND 2, CARVED MEDICINE-RATTLES; 3, CARVED CEDAR TRAY;
4. CARVED PIPE: 5, CARVED COMB.

The inconsistency of baptizing unreformed savages, is further illustrated in the incident of the landing of the missionary priest, Father Bolduc at the Songhee village Camosun (now Victoria) before the establishment of the first trading post. After addressing Chief Tsilathach and his people for half an hour, he invited them to be baptized.

Tsilathach replied, "baptize our Enemies!—do not baptize us, a priest who came before you some years ago baptized many of the Kwanthmus and Cowichins, and they all died !"

The fact was, that a plague had visited the coast immediately after, and the association, was only natural to these superstitious people.

It is told of an old barbarian Chief, who when he was baptized kept his right hand out of the water, that he might still work his deeds of blood.

How necessary all this proves to us the reservation of this rite to the truly converted. But this necessity, is *now* apparently ignored by the Society's agents. It is a twofold sin to deceive a fellow-creature, into the belief that there is a magical power, of purification, and salvation, in the mere observance of the ceremony of baptism; and it *is distinctly a deception*, to turn this symbolic Christian ordinance, into a magical rite, to invest it with powers it does not, and never did possess.

It is only after satisfactory probation, that members of the Metlakahtla congregation are baptized and admitted to full membership,—baptismal rites

being administered by an ordained clergyman*—
thus, the sacrament is made more impressive as an
emblem in its original significance to cleanse, to
purify.

Mr. Duncan, regards the duties of a missionary
as purely evangelistic, and not ecclesiastical. He
believes that to insure the best results, every Christian congregation gathered out of Heathendom;
should begin its history as a free, and independent
branch of Christ's Church, in *unity, and in sympathy, with all* evangelical Christians; but, allowed
to develop naturally on Scriptural lines, and adopt
that kind of church order, most in harmony with the
native mind. Whereas, the Church Missionary
Society, rigorously demand, that all converts to
Christianity through its agency, shall be stamped
as members of the Church of England, conform to
its exacting ritual, and adopt its spirit of exclusive-
ness. It did not recognize with Burke, that " The
cause of the Church of England is included in that
of religion, not that of religion in the Church of
England." Here, we are confronted with that spirit
of bigotry, that has wrought havoc with freedom of
conscience in all ages. At the time of the Reformation the Protestants declared that its issue was
founded on this:—"that the Bible is a sufficient
guide for every Christian man. Tradition was rejected, and the right of private interpretation as-

---

* See Chapter III

sured. It was thought that the criterion of truth had at length been obtained."

But, alas such was not to be. Calvin in roasting Servetus to death over a slow fire at Geneva—for daring to express his religious convictions,—bore witness that human ecclesiastical prejudices, still suborned true godliness. Narrow-minded hierarchy, has clogged the wheels of Christian religion, from the first. The utter absurdity, and the dire consequences of most of the ecclesiastical conflicts, strikes with amazement every student of history. For instance, the unseemly ecclesiastical quarrels of the fourth century, affecting the co-eternity of Trinity; some claiming that there was a time when the Son did not exist, that, as a necessary condition of the filial relation the Father must be older than the Son. The opponents argued that they had been for all time co-existent; the latter faction was victorious at the Nicene Council, which anathematized all who should say, that there was a time when the Son was not, or that before He was begotten, He was not.

This contest led the pagans of Alexandria, to amuse themselves by representing on the Stage the Father and Son as twins—but worse than this for Christianity it led to the establishment of Mahometanism.

In the stubborn conflict of blind dogmatism with the progress of knowledge, the true spirit of Christianity has been ruthlessly hampered. Christianity, if it serves its parleyed purpose, should ever go hand in hand, with knowledge, to the betterment of mankind.

It has been well said that, in the annals of Christianity the most ill-omened day, was that, in which she separated herself from science, and antagonized intellectual progression.

If the lives, time, temper and wealth expended in establishing dogmas and carrying on cruel persecution, in the name of Christ, had been devoted to propagating, teaching, and exemplifying the great central truths of Christianity, with their attendant blessings, how much more exalted might have been to-day, the intellectual condition of the universe; and how much larger portion of mankind, would know and worship God, in honesty, and in truth. Christianity has not been maintained, because of its divisions and creeds, but has survived, in spite of them.

" Look at the Bible on the one hand, and History on the other; see what are the points on which the Scriptures lay most emphatic stress; think how much of the sap and life of Christendom has run to leaf, and not to fruit; remember how constant is the protest of Scriptures, and, we may add, of the best spirits of the universal Church, against preferring any cause of opinion, or ceremony to justice, holiness, truth and love; observe how constantly and steadily all these same intimations point to One Divine Object, and One only, as the centre and essence of Christianity." (Dean Stanley).

Prof. Max Müller, undoubtedly the most renowned scholar for his erudition, not only in the science of languages; but, in the science of religions, in one of his lectures on this subject says :—

"We want less of creeds, but more of trust; less of ceremony, but more of work; less solemnity, but more of genial honesty; less of doctrine, but more of love. . . .

" The fundamentals of our religion are not in these poor creeds; true Christianity lives not in our belief, but in our—*in our love* of *God and in our love of man founded* on *our love of God.* . . .

" Men fight about religion on earth; in heaven they shall find out that there is only one true religion, the worship of God."

Lord Macaulay on his return from India to England, said: " I have lived too long in a country where people worship cows, to think much of the differences which part Christians from Christians."

This is a practical, reasoning age, and though we cannot by exact science, or cold reason, solve the mysteries of the Infinite, yet, we may measurably judge of things tangible or apparent.

It is hardly in accordance with the spirit of our age, to inflict torture upon those scientists, who throw new light upon old mysteries, even if they do not exactly correspond with our interpretation of Bible science; we should to-day feel little sympathy with a movement that choked off the progress of intellect, or the revelation, of new arts,

and sciences. It is not many ages since all the
horrors of the inquisition threatened those who
dared vouchsafe evidences, to show that the world
was round, not flat—not square!

Yet, this is an age of anomalies. In our day we
see the greatest light thrown upon the Book of
God, the highest cultivation of the intellect, the
greatest religious freedom, and yet, some of the
most shameful cases of ecclesiastical persecution.
That zealot,—Lord Penzance of England a relic of
the dark ages, posing as a nobleman in this age of
reason, has within the last four years exercised his
hereditary, or so-called divine right and power, by
thrusting clergymen into prison, and keeping them
incarcerated for months, because they deviated from
the prescribed formulas of the Church in their services, or, perhaps burned too many, or, too few
candles upon the altar!

In comparison with this, it is refreshing to read
the following resolution, passed by the Protestant
Episcopal National Convention, at Chicago, October
15, 1886.

" The House of Bishops, takes the opportunity to
assure the House of Deputies, of its profound sympathy with the spirit of their resolution. This
House, declares its hearty respect, and affection, for
all who love the Lord Jesus Christ in sincerity, and
at this time, especially for their fellow-Christians
assembled in this city, as the National Council of
Congregational Churches in the United States.

This House, also, avows its solemn purpose, under the guidance of the Holy Spirit to promote, with the concurrence of the House of Deputies, some practicable plan for bringing before all our fellow-Christians in this land, the duty to our common Lord and Saviour of terminating the unhappy divisions, which dishonor His blessed name, and hinder the triumph upon earth, of His glorious kingdom."

There is nothing objectionable in the mere matter of variations in Church organizations, names, manner of conducting service, or, differences in beliefs. It is the proselyting spirit, the attempt to force arbitrary dogmas upon others, and the consigning to perdition those who disagree with them, that is un-Christlike, pernicious and debasing.

I respect all religions, and creeds, that contribute to the unfolding, and elevation of mankind. I personally have no secular, or sectarian prejudices, which could prompt me in a trifling spirit, to hold up in derision the sacred religion of anyone. I am neither orthodox nor heterodox in my beliefs.

"When I list to such bigotry, and witness such coercion; I yearn to wield the invisible broad sword, and sharp sword of *Supreme Justice*, and cleave between brambled heterodoxy and orthodoxy a broad swath, as a thoroughfare for right doing, and well-being for all humanity: A swath, from pole to pole, over which the white, the black, the red, the yellow, enfranchised; untrammelled; might safely traverse toward the light through all existence, *without jostling one another*" (M. French Sheldon).

I believe there is grace in all religions, and that righteousness and holiness belong exclusively to none. I make this plain, that I may not be misunderstood when I would impugn those men, who degrade true holiness, by cant, and hypocrisy. True piety is revered by all, sectarianism is the bane of Christianity.

It is the misfortune, but not necessarily the fault of a church, that among its representatives appear Asses guised in Lions' skins, and Wolves in Sheep's clothing. However, if when the bray, or treacherous fangs reveal the truth, and then the church persistently insists, that the Ass is a Lion, and the Wolf is a Sheep, can we wonder that the world mocks ?

Atheism, is mainly fed by the revulsion caused by sectarianism, tinged too highly, with canting hypocrisy. Honesty in religion, is, as essential, as honesty in business.

When the highly educated people of civilized countries fail to comprehend the creeds, and doctrinal distinctions; how, can the infant mind of a benighted savage, be expected to grasp them ?

If one teaches the savage that this, or that rite, or ceremony, is essential to his salvation, how is he shocked, and thrown into confusion, when the prelate of another creed comes along, and proves to him by the Bible, that his previous teachings are all wrong,

and gives him a new plan of redemption! This
divine, is followed by another who condemns the
teachings of his predecessors, and as conclusively
proves his theories, by the selfsame book, of the
white man's God.

The savage, bewildered by these polemics, dis-
credits all. The central truth has been so obscured
by dogmas, that he sees before him only uncertain
trails ; even the white men straggle and do not
agree, as to which one leads to heaven ; how then
can he, poor groping savage, with inferior intellect
decide, when the wise men are confounded ?

He relapses into heathenism, returns to the religion of his fathers, worships the gods that have
piloted them to the happy hunting ground ; or perhaps like M'tesa the Emperor of Uganda, to whom
Stanley broke the light of Christianity, pure and
simple, and left him pleading,—in his own words—
" Stamlee, say to the white people, when you write
to them, that I am like a man sitting in darkness,
or born blind ; and that all I ask is that I may be
taught how to see, and I shall continue a Christian
while I live."

M'tesa received missionaries cordially until in a
competitive contest,—rivalling that held before
Vladimir—by their wrangling, over distinctions in
creeds, and nationality, and by contradictory teaching, he became convinced, that they knew no more
of the true way, than did he. In his distraction, he
turned to his ancient worship for consolation, and

in propitiation for his apostasy, is said, to have committed most horrible acts.

Thus the missionaries themselves, by greater loyalty to sect, than to God, by greater loyalty to nation than to humanity, turned back, to the most atrocious heathenism, and barbarism; this willing convert to civilization, and Christianity, and his seeking people.

" I have for years thought," wrote that distinguished authority Bishop Patterson—" that we seek in our missions a great deal too much to make *English* Christians. . . . Evidently the heathen man is not treated fairly, if we encumber our message with unnecessary requirements. The ancient Church had its selection of fundamentals." . . . Anyone can see what mistakes we have made in India. . . . Few men think themselves into the state of the Eastern mind. . . . We seek to denationalize these races, as far as I can see; whereas, we ought surely to change as little as possible—only what is clearly incompatible with the simplest form of Christian teaching and practice. I do not mean that we are to compromise truth . . . but, do we not overlay it a good deal with human traditions!"

The mistakes in the East have been repeated, in nearly, every part, of the mission world.

" Let missionaries preach the Gospel again as it was preached when it began the conquest of the Roman Empire, and the Gothic nations; when it had to struggle with powers and principalities, with time-honored religions and triumphant philosophies, with pride of civilization and savagery of life—and yet come out victorious. At that time conversion was not a question to be settled by the acceptance or rejection of certain formulas or articles ; a simple prayer was often enough : '*God be merciful to me a sinner.*'

" Among uncivilized races, the work of the missionary is the work of a parent ; whether his pupils are young in years or old, he has to treat them with a parent's love, to teach them with a parent's authority ; he has to win them, not to argue with them. I know this kind of mission work is often despised ; it is called mere religious kidnapping ; and it is said that missionary success obtained by such means proves nothing for the truth of Christianity ; that the child handed over to a Mohammedan becomes a Mohammedan, as much as a child handed over to a Christian missionary becomes a Christian. All this is true; missionary success obtained by such means proves nothing, nothing for the truth of one Creed " (Max Müller).

" The Indians have their own myths, it is true ; but they are eminently spiritual; and we should not condemn them because they are so constituted as to demand rational solutions of whatever is presented to them as truths. They read intelligently the writing of the Great Spirit in all exterior nature, as well as in the human soul.

" The tints of the flower, the cells and fibres of the leaf, the granules of the rock, and the veins of the wood, are poems—hymns—sermons—not of unmeaning and lifeless words, that fall coldly on the ear, like flakes of spring-snow, only to dissolve and pass away, but living utterances of that great Interior Life, which in all they see, and hear, and know, they recognize, and honor and adore. This great sentiment of praise pervades the whole character of the true Indian. It informs, it inspires, it exalts him. Think then how impossible it must be for him to exchange this august worship, that has grown with his growth, and strengthened with his strength, for any of those dogmas, which are so far from satisfying Christianity itself, that they have cut into the very heart of the Church, dividing it into hostile factions, armed with deadly hate against each other, until history in almost every age, has been dyed crimson with the blood of the faithful " (Beeson).

Efforts were made to tempt Mr. Duncan to submit to, and accept the Society's dogmatic views. A *mere hireling*, might have yielded, but Mr. Duncan, who had sacrificed everything for the service of his God, *was decidedly not a mere hireling;* besides, his experience and observations had fortified him in his convictions.

He had seen in abandoned mission stations, the failure of sectarian methods. He had seen the hollow work sectarians can produce—alike, hurtful to the teacher, and the taught. He had observed how men, who worked for the fame of their Church party, wrote too frequently exaggerated reports, to please; although they spared themselves both the time, and trouble to dig deep—do genuine work, and wait patiently for results.

Apropos of which W. H. Dall, narrating his experiences on the Yukon River, during his extensive exploration in Alaska, makes the following cogent remarks, after attending the services of a well-meaning missionary, the sermon being rendered into a jargon by an interpreter :

" In the evening the Indians, old and young, gathered in the fort-yard and sang several hymns with excellent effect. Altogether, it was a scene which would have delighted the hearts of many very good people who know nothing of Indian character; and as such will doubtless figure in some missionary report. To anyone at all who understood the situation, however, the absurdity of the proceeding was so palpable that it appeared almost like blasphemy.

" Old Sakhniti, who has at least eighteen wives, whose hands are bloody with repeated and atrocious murders, who knows nothing of what we understand by right and wrong, by a future state of reward and punishment, or by a Supreme Being—this old heathen was singing as sweetly as his voice would allow, and with quite as much comprehension of the hymn, as, one of the dogs in the yard.

"Indians are fond of singing; they are also fond of tobacco, and for a pipeful apiece you may baptize a whole tribe. Why will intelligent men still go on talking three or four times a year to Indians on doctrinal subjects, by means of a jargon which cannot express an abstract idea, and the use of which only throws ridicule on sacred things, and still call such work spreading the truths of Christianity?

"When the missionary will leave the trading-posts, strike out into the wilderness, live with the Indians, teach them cleanliness first, morality next, and by slow and simple teaching lead their thoughts above the hunt or the camp, then, and not until then, will they be competent to comprehend the simplest principles of right and wrong. The Indian does not think in the method that civilized men adopt; he looks at everything as 'through a glass—darkly.' His whole train of thought and habit of mind must be educated to a higher and different standard before Christianity can reach him.

"The Indian, unchanged by contact with the whites, is in mind a child without the trusting affection of childhood, and with the will and passions of a man."

Mr. Duncan, not yielding to the Society's domination, in the course of time its attitude became imperious, and feeling that his honesty of purpose was at stake; he determined to resign his post, and surrender his Mission to other hands, that would mould it, as the Society wished; while he would seek a fresh field of labor among unreclaimed, heathen tribes.

This was distinctly signified to the Society, and, it is well known, that again and again, it endeavored to fill his place with an ordained man ; or at least by someone likely to take orders.

At one time, Mr. Duncan entirely abdicated the mission at Metlakahtla to an ordained clergyman, sent out by the Society, and had only been absent a few weeks, preparing for a new mission, when Metlakahtla was thrown into a state of dreadful confusion ; and the organization wellnigh wrecked, by the unwise ecclesiastical enthusiasm of the new missionary ; the effect of whose methods, upon many of the still superstitious minds, was to create a sort of fanatical cyclone. Some were led in the fever of their delirium, to declare that they witnessed miracles ; beheld, and held converse with the Holy Spirit ; and that angels hovered about the village.

This man in his blindness, was actually congratulating himself, on the work of the Holy Ghost, but when the news of his foolishness reached Victoria, there was a general demand that Mr. Duncan should instantly return, and save his life's work from utter destruction. He did return, but, it was with great difficulty that he succeeded in eliminating the results of a few weeks' misdirected, fanatical zeal.

The Society thanked Mr. Duncan, very heartily

for his timely interference; and Bishop Bompas, whom they sent to Metlakahtla just after this incident; severely censured the clergyman for his indiscretion, and expressed the fullest approval of Mr. Duncan's course.   Although, the Bishop had come with the intention of introducing the Lord's Supper, he saw by the recent proceedings, that these people, yet, needed careful, and judicious, management and guidance; and deemed it extremely precarious, and inopportune to initiate the administration of the sacrament during his stay.   In this decision, he was but in accord with Mr. Duncan's well-matured judgment; though, recently it has been falsely intimated' by the Society that Bishop Bompas was only prevented from introducing the rite, by Mr. Duncan's resistance.

A succession of failures nullified the Society's plans to relieve, Mr. Duncan, and necessitated his remaining from year to year.

Finally, the northern part of British Columbia; —containing but three ordained clergymen of the Church of England—was created a Bishopric.

The Bishop of New Caledonia, made Metlakahtla his headquarters, and at first wrote glowing effusive accounts of the work there.

In establishing himself, he asserted his authority not, with Christian dignity, but in a pompous, arrogant and offensive manner.   He took care to distinguish the importance of his caste, by conspicuously parading his sacerdotal vestments, before the

Indians; and claiming the title of "*My Lord*" from all. His deportment forcibly reminds one of H. M. Stanley's pen-picture of another ecclesiastical potentate.

"The Bishop in his crimson robe, and with his sacerdotal title, "Missionary Bishop of Central Africa" (why he should be so named I cannot conceive), has reached the bourne of aspiring priesthood, and is consequently ineffably happy. But this High Church (very high church indeed) prelate, in his crimson robe of office, and in the queerest of all head-dresses, seen stalking through the streets of Zanzibar, or haggling over the price of a tin-pot at a tinker's stall, is the most ridiculous sight I have seen anywhere outside of a clown's show. I, as a white man, solemnly protest against the absurdity. A similar picture to the Bishop, in his priestly robes and a paper cap, in a tinker's stall, is the King of Dahomey, in a European hat with his body naked, promenading pompously about in this exquisite full dress. Whatever the Bishop, in his blissful innocence, may think of the effect which it produces in the minds of the heathen, I can inform him that, to the Arabs and Wangwana who have settled in Unyanyembe, he is only an object of supreme ridicule; and also, that most of his pale-faced brothers entertain something of the same opinion.

"Poor, dear Bishop Tozer! I would fain love and admire thee, were it not for this exhibition of extreme High-Churchism in a place like Zanzibar!"

Dr. David Livingstone, who was very much incensed at this sort of mock mission-work, commented very pungently upon the self-same Bishop.

"The excellent Bishops of the Church of England, who all take an interest in the 'Central African Mission,' will, in their kind and gracious way, make every possible allowance for the degeneracy of the noble effort of the Universities into a mere Chaplaincy of the Zanzibar Consulate. One of them even defended a *lapsus* which no one else dared to face; but whatever in their kind-heartedness they may say, every man of them would rejoice to hear, that the Central African had gone into Central Africa. If I must address those who hold back, I should say: Come on, brethren; you have no idea how brave you are till you try. The real brethren who are waiting for you have many faults, but also much that you can esteem and love. . . .

"Some eight years have rolled on, and good Christian people have contributed the money annually for Central Africa and the 'Central African Diocese' is occupied only by the lord of all evil. It is with a sore heart that I say it, but recent events have shown to those who have so long been playing at being missionaries; and peeping, across from the sickly Island of their diocese on to the mainland with telescopes, that their time might have been turned to better account."

A CHIEF LYING IN STATE.

Dr. Livingstone likens the Bishop of Central Africa, to a man of similar buffoonery sent to the Sandwich Islands, after a very successful, missionary work, had been established there, by American missionaries.

"A Bishop they got, who, in sheer lack of good breeding, went about Honolulu with a great paper cap on his head, ignoring his American brethren, whose success showed them to be of the true apostolic stamp, and declaring that he was the only true Bishop.

"Of all mortal men, missionaries and Missionary Bishops ought manifestly to be true gentlemen."

Henry Venn, the late distinguished, secretary of the Church Missionary Society, speaking from vast experience, was wont to say, that translating a missionary to a Bishop, bred trouble and ruined the man's usefulness.

Had the Bishop of New Caledonia clad in his showy vestments, accompanied our Saviour on a visit to savage tribes, the Redeemer would have in all probability been ignored for His simplicity of apparel ; as was the case with a certain clergyman, of many frills, who, some thirty years ago, on his way to the North Pacific, called at Honolulu, donned his best cloth, arrayed his valet in glittering livery, and gained audience with the King, who rushed past the prelate, and grasped the hand of the valet, mistaking,—because, of his magnificence, —the slave for the master !

The superstitious mind of the savage naturally attributes magical powers to priestly vestments. Mr. Duncan, had always found it necessary, to avoid peculiarity of dress, as any oddity, was regarded as a symbol. One explorer in writing of British Columbia, makes mention, of a priest who when unable to visit a tribe, sent his oddly shaped hat, and the people fell down and prayed to it, as to an idol!

It is not the gown of a judge, but the justice he dispenses that commands respect, and elevates him in our estimation.

It is the invisible *toga virilis*, that makes *the man*, whatsoever his rank in life.

I for one, admire the vestments of the clergy. I enjoy the ceremonies of the most elaborate ritual, they are to me beautiful, picturesque, and I fain would have them remain in the church service whenever, and wherever, their true value and significance is understood; but, their introduction to superstitious savages, ever has been, and ever will be, fraught with jeopardy, to genuine Christianizing work. Attractive vestments, and ceremonies signify to a groping savage, a hidden meaning, meretricious, and calculated to distract him from the real essentials of salvation.

"'You have' says Faustus to Augustine, 'substituted your agapæ for the sacrifices of the pagans; for their idols your martyrs, whom you serve with the very same honors. You appease the shades of the dead with wine and feasts; you celebrate the solemn festivities of the Gentiles, their Calends, and their solstices; and, as to their manners, those you have retained without alteration. Nothing distinguishes you from the pagans, except that you hold your assemblies apart from them! Pagan observances were everywhere introduced. At weddings it was the custom to sing hymns to Venus!'

" Let us pause here a moment, and see, in anticipation, to what a depth of intellectual degradation this policy of paganization eventually led. Heathen rites were adopted, a pompous and splendid ritual, gorgeous robes, mitres, tiaras, wax tapers, processional services, lustrations, gold and silver vases, were introduced, the Roman lituus, the chief ensign of the augur, became the Crozier " (Draper).

Ecclesiastical Vestments. " The antiquarian investigation of this matter," says Dean Stanley, " is not in itself devoid of interest. It belongs to the general survey of the origin of usages and customs in the early ages of Christianity. The conclusion to which it leads is that the dress of the clergy had no distinct intention—symbolical, sacerdotal, sacrificial, or mystical; but originated simply in the fashions common to the whole community of the Roman Empire, during the three first centuries.

" The Christian dress as we have indicated, was intended in its origin, not to separate the minister from the people, but to make him, in outward show and appearance exactly the same. . . .

" Unless it can be shown that they were sacerdotal in the second or third centuries, it is wholly irrelevant to allege that they became sacerdotal, in the 13th or 19th centuries.

"Whatever sacerdotal, or symbolical, or sacramental associations have been attached to them may be mediæval, but certainly are not primitive; and *those who wish to preserve the substance of the primitive usage should officiate, not in the dresses which are at present worn in Roman, Anglican, and Non-conformist Churches, but in the every-day dress of common life*—in overcoats, or smock-frocks, or shirt-sleeves, according as they belonged to the higher or inferior grade of the Christian ministry.

"There may be reasons against ecclesiastical vestments of all kinds. But the fact of their being modern is not itself against them, unless we insist on making them essential as containing ideas, which they do not, and never were intended to, symbolize." . . . .

"This leads us to another obvious conclusion. If there be no intrinsic value in these vestments, then, whether the law forbids them or enforces them, the same duty is incumbent on all those who regard the substance of religion above its forms, namely, that *on no account should these garbs, whether legal or illegal, be introduced into churches or parishes where they give offence to the parish or the congregation.* The more any clergyman can appreciate the absolute indifference of such things in themselves, the more will he feel himself compelled to withdraw them the moment he finds that they produce the opposite effect to that which he intended them to have. On the necessity of such a restriction, it is a satisfaction to believe that many even of those whose opinions rather incline them to these peculiar usages, would more or less concur."

In these outspoken views of Dean Stanley many other great church dignitaries acquiesce.

The well-known Church of England journal " *The Rock*" London Nov. 14th 1879, in a leading article titled, " *Do Lord Bishops help or hinder Foreign Missions ?* " told such plain truths, that certain church dignitaries raised a perfect tempest over it. I quote the following, from the article :

" The Standard recently informed us that the Archbishop of Canterbury in an address, mentioned that he had recently been present at a consecration of four Bishops, three of whom were appointed to foreign Sees—viz., Jerusalem, Travancore, and a place in the extremity of North America, and one for East London.

" His Grace, observed that he looked upon the consecration of these Bishops as " fairly representing the wide field, which was now open for missionary effort throughout the world.

" From this and his subsequent observations, it was evident that in the estimation of the Primate the appointment of an English Bishop to any region on the earth's surface, was equivalent to taking possession of that region for missionary enterprise, and an earnest of the success which a mission, duly sustained by English liberality is sure to achieve.

"Now this view, however natural to the mind of an Archbishop is unfortunately open to objections from reason, and from fact. In the first place, it is very questionable whether the presidency of a prelate of the English type over a foreign mission, may not act as a serious hinderance to the spiritual work altogether. There are two agencies which must never be lost sight of in the preaching of the Gospel among uncivilized people.

"First, the most perfect freedom of action and second, the complete absence of all cut and dry forms, and systems of service.

"The *modus operandi* while exactly suited to place, people and circumstances, should in the first instance, be too irregular, to admit of its being subject to episcopal control in our sense of the term. With such irregularity, and simplicity, English prelatry must ever be coming in collision.

"Moreover, experience has amply proved that the attempt to transplant English episcopacy into foreign mission fields has proved a failure. From the time that Bishop Selwyn was sent out to preside over the New Zealand See, to the present hour the difficulties attending the experiment have been, more and more apparent. It has been truly said of Bishop Selwyn's episcopate in New Zealand, that *it paralyzed the mission work there.* At this we

need not feel surprised. . . . Yet as an en-
thusiastic New Zealand admirer said, he was not,
as he was called in England a Missionary Bishop
'for his influence with the natives was never much,
save as the head of the Church of England, in New
Zealand '—that is, as we understand it, he represented the Church of England, but not the religion
of the Lord Jesus Christ, and by so doing he, as
far as in him lay, undid the work of the humble
missionaries who for years before Dr. Selwyn's arrival, had so successfully labored in the Gospel with
the simple object, of bringing the natives to a knowledge of salvation, through a crucified and risen
Saviour.

"Unfortunately this seems to be the case with
almost all so-called Missionary Bishops. They go
out, not, so much to labor in the work and doctrine,
as to represent the Mother Church, and in their
several dioceses to set up as close an imitation as
possible of the ecclesiastical system at home, with
all its paraphernalia of cathedral capitular bodies,
church dignitaries, rubrical rites, liturgical services,
and the like, utterly out of place—these are in a mission station, and far more calculated to produce disturbing complications, than to promote the work of
evangelization. Take for example, the very discreditable relations at present existing between the
Bishop of Grahamstown (Dr. Merriman), and the
Very Rev. F. S. Williams, dean of St. George's
Cathedral, there, arising out of a question of pre-

cedence in reference to the cathedral of which Dr.
Williams is dean. The Bishop claims the right to
preach there, as well as in every church in his diocese at his discretion. To this the dean demurs,
and on Sunday April 27th last, actually ousted the
Bishop from the Cathedral pulpit, by preaching
himself after he had received formal notice of his
episcopal superior's intention to preach.

"For this and other alleged acts of insubordina-
tion and contumacy, Dean Williams has been tried
in his absence, condemned and sentenced to a
month's suspension from his office; but to these
proceedings he pays no attention. Upheld by his
people, he flouts the Bishop and treats the sentence
of the episcopal court with contempt. So much
for the absurdity of attempting to set up the Church
system in the wilds of South Africa!

"Is then the Arch-Bishop of Canterbury prepared to say that the state of things at the Cape—
where the Bishop's experiment has been fully tried
—is calculated to advance the cause of Christian
missions? or that cathedrals and their appendages
—which we believe are regarded as indispensable
to the dignity of a Bishop—are more likely to serve
the cause of Christ, or of Satan?

"The fact is the prelacy, after the lordly type
with which we are favored at home, is something
worse than an absurdity, when aped in the colonies
or other fields of foreign labor. Here we are habituated to mitres and croziers, black silk aprons,

looped up hats, knee breeches, and buckled shoes.
They form the bijouterie of a pampered church,
and represent not the humility, and poverty, of the
lowly Jesus, but—the wealth, and dignity, of the
proudest empire upon earth.

"Although we have become habituated to the
doctrine of apostolic succession, we cannot shut our
eyes to the egregious folly, of reproducing such mon-
strosities abroad. The notorious cases of Doctor
Mylne and Coppleston—the Bishops respectively
of Bombay and Colombo—are sufficient to prove
this; for in what have their episcopal labors consisted, but, in thwarting the work of the Church
Missionary Society, and so entangling the relations
between the Society and the Church, that is *their*
dioceses simple mission work or Church-of-England
principles! And then consider the positive iniquity
of subordinating an evangelical mission to a Romish Bishop!

"No: if we must have Bishops in our colonies
and foreign missions—and we admit that without
them an Episcopal Church would be an anomaly—
let us have them without the bawbles, and ecclesiastical frippery, that surrounds them at home. Let
us wait till a Church is formed by the simple preaching of the Gospel, and then from among the laborers in the field, select the one most pious, intelligent,
laborious, and unassuming, to superintend the others,
not as a *lord* over them, but as a shepherd, *primus
inter pares*, who will share their labors, counsel them

in their difficulties, correct what is evil, encourage what is good, and in the exercise of a wise and loving judgment heal all dissensions that may arise, and watch against every species of error that satan may introduce. Let such a man eschew the episcopal habits and the episcopal vestments. No up-turned hat, no apron, no kneebreeches, no buckles, and no rings; and above all, no mitre, no crozier and no cathedral with its episcopal throne, and its train of Church dignitaries and artificial services. Let the heathen be taught to despise, and to mourn, the gross folly of assuming the title of *my Lord*.

"As a follower of his Divine Master, he will find his place among the most humble, and like Him he will have power in his office and in his work. Under his superintendence no complications will arise with committees of religious societies of England. He will have no pretensions of personal dignity to protect, and they will not desire to supersede him in the highly important office which he fills.

"As it is the sacerdotal lordlings intruded under the title of 'Bishops' into colonial and dominion Churches, who are now doing so much mischief, and giving so much trouble, it is evident that the whole system of foreign Church patronage, must undergo revision and amendment, if sect prelates sent out is not to become the centre of a discreditable collision between Bishops appointed by one authority, and clergy appointed by another. The evil is obvious; and is assuming formidable dimensions, nor will matters ever improve, according to our judgment, so long as genuine Christian laborers are subjected to the absurd pretensions, of those who are more concerned about their episcopal dignity, than about the interests of Christ, or the salvation of souls."

I hold in no disrespect the title of Bishop; this title has been, and is, honored by many very great men, but it has also been, and is, dishonored by many most unworthy men. We all in our hearts respect an exalted title, when that title represents the measure of greatness of its possessor : but, far better be a grand man, devoid title, than a void man with a grand title.

After having made various excursions from the direct points at issue to show my readers that Mr. Duncan is sustained in his course of action, by the most learned authorities, and by men whose experience, and study of savages, and mission, and educational work, lend peculiar force to their views, I return to the theme of my story.

The Bishop of New Caledonia, soon began in an overbearing, pragmatic manner, to interfere with the work of Mr. Duncan, and others : then he attempted to provoke contest with the missions, which, other denominations were busy establishing for the North Pacific Indians. Continuing in his high-handed course, his outrageous interference with one of the Society's missionaries, led the Society to check him ; and, in order to avoid further complications, the Society authorized all of its missionary staff in the diocese, to meet yearly, for conference on mission affairs. In July, 1881, the first conference was convened at Metlakahtla, and consisted of three clergymen, and three laymen.

The Bishop, who had by his indiscretion rendered himself somewhat obnoxious, conspicuously absented himself, from the conference of which he was chairman.

Feeling that a crisis had now arrived, in the working of the mission at Metlakahtla, Mr. Duncan, determined to place the responsibility of the dilemma upon the Conference, and to stand by the issue. He reminded the Conference, that he was a layman, and that the Society wanted an ordained man in his stead : and asked, *in view of these facts, whether they, would advise him to resign his connection* with Metlakahtla; since it would seem impossible, as well as unnatural, for anyone to supersede him, while he remained in the mission.

The Conference, in Mr. Duncan's absence, unanimously agreed upon the following resolutions :—

" The Conference having heard Mr. Duncan's statement, and knowing the value of his labors, and experience, not only to the work at Metlakahtla, but also to the Church Missionary Society's missions generally, in the North Pacific field; *unanimously, decline to advise Mr. Duncan to resign."*

The question of resignation being thus disposed of ; another question naturally arose ,—namely· How the difficulty involved in his remaining at his post could be met ? Therefore, he asked the Conference, whether it, was prepared to advise the Society, to allow Metlakahtla to assume its independency—work out its own destiny,—and *bear its own expenses?* The majority, of the Conference; resolved, to advise the Society *to constitute Metlakahtla into a lay mission, and leave the work in Mr. Duncan's hands, without clerical supervision:* the minority, wanted to give the mission its *full independence.*

These resolutions aroused the wrath of the Bishop, and through his prompting, the Society in London was led to take very hasty action in the matter. The Society wrote a letter to Mr. Duncan *inviting* him home for conference, and on the same day (as it afterward appeared) wrote another letter *disconnecting* him from the Society, and calling upon him to quit his work at Metlakahtla ;—this second letter was sent, not direct, but under cover to the Bishop. Crossing these letters was one from Mr. Duncan, to the Society in which he had stated his views on the position of affairs. The Society's letter of invitation was received by Mr. Duncan, while he was at Victoria, some 600 miles distance from Metlakahtla; and, just at a moment when business matters of great importance to the community, demanding his personal attention, rendered it impracticable, for him, to immediately comply with the Society's request.

He wrote at once, explaining how he was situated, and alluded to the letter, he had recently posted, and, which when received would probably render his presence in England unnecessary. In any case, he only asked to *postpone* his visit to England, until he should again hear from the Society.

On Mr. Duncan's return from Victoria to Metlakahtla, the Bishop, with absolutely indecent haste, and in a defiant, officious manner, demanded, an interview, and rudely thrust into Mr. Duncan's hands the "*Enclosure*,"—actually before the steamer which had brought Mr. Duncan and the letter, had left the harbor—the "*Enclosure*," which finally disconnected him from the Society, and thus unceremoniously severed a connection of twenty-five years duration !

However, the Bishop, in his ill-concealed impatience to get rid of Mr. Duncan, had flagrantly overstepped his commission. He *had been instructed by the Society to give the "Enclosure" to Mr. Duncan, only in case, Mr. Duncan, absolutely refused* to visit England. The Bishop knew from Mr. Duncan's own lips that he had not refused. On the receipt of Mr. Duncan's letter explanatory, of his position, the Society also knew full well he had not refused ; therefore, the Society at once addressed a letter to the Bishop with instructions *not* to give him, the "*Enclosure*." These instructions designed to obviate a rupture, came too late ; the overweening Bishop, had done the mischief beyond reparation.

The Bishop realizing the gravity of the crisis he

A DRUMMER OF THE METLAKAHTLA BRASS-BAND.

had precipitated, deemed it well to start at once, to England; and, attempt to mollify, by plausible misrepresentations, and quasi-evidences, the richly deserved censure which he had earned, and feared, from the Society. Also, with the view of strengthening himself in his purpose to undermine Mr. Duncan's influence.

The Bishop succeeded, it would seem by subsequent events, in justifying, his unprincipled course in the eyes of the Society.

As soon as the Metlakahtlans became aware of what had happened, they were deeply incensed, and unanimously and heartily entreated Mr. Duncan not to forsake them, but remain at his post, and carry on his work as heretofore.

In connection with this incident occurs a fair example of the Bishop's artful system of conveying false reports to the Society; his process of making history. Since the rupture the Society has shown an unhealthy thirst for this sort of startling fiction, and has drunk it in, with avidity; and, has published gross charges; and, has pronounced judgment, without testing its witnesses, or giving the accused a hearing:—carefully, refraining from publishing the written statements of the Metlakahtlans, while they gave wide circulation to the false charges made against them.

The following is the Bishop's written account of the meeting of the Metlakahtlans, when they petitioned Mr. Duncan to remain.—

" At one of the public meetings Mr. Duncan put the question, ' Will all on the *Lord's* side hold up their hands.' All held up their hands. Then he *artfully* said—' All on the Bishop's side hold up their hands.' Imagine their *surprise* at being thus *ensnared*. Several afterward told me that they did not know, that Mr. Duncan was the Lord, or they would not have raised their hands."

When the Bishop's veracity was challenged and this statement proved to be a barefaced falsehood, he made an apologetic quibble.

The true account of the meeting is substantially the subjoining.

Immediately on learning of the Bishop's action the Metlakahtlans called a meeting, at which assembled every native in the village who was able to attend ; even, the aged, the decrepit, the sick, all, came to deliberate upon this crisis and voice their sentiment.

We may well understand, that these people, knew beyond a question, to whom, they were indebted, for their past development, and felicitous condition, and to whom, they could best trust, their future guidance.

It was but a brief session. Their hearts seemed to throb in unison, stirred by fealty and reverence for their benefactor. There was no prolonged harangue, but, a few short speeches ; pointed, earnest, touching.

Then, the Chairman put the question, will you

have the Bishop, or Shim-au-git* (Mr. Duncan) as your leader?

When Mr. Duncan's name was put to the assemblage, every soul voted for him to remain. The Bishop received not a vote. *Mr. Duncan was not present* during their deliberations or voting.

After these proceedings, Mr. Duncan was sent for, and on entering the crowded assembly, he, was beckoned to a seat. He said not a word—great silence prevailed. An Indian arose, and assured him in the name of the people, that he was unanimously entreated to remain amongst them.

When the Indian had finished his speech, he, called upon all present to testify to the truth of what he had said, and to show Mr. Duncan how they had voted before they had sent for him. Every soul stood up, and held up their hands that he might see, and be convinced of their unanimity.

When the meeting was asked to show him how many wished to retain the Bishop, not an one stood up, not an hand was raised, not an aye was uttered!

Mr. Duncan then briefly, acknowledged their unanimous call, and assured them that he accepted.

The officers of the Society, now say that Mr. Duncan should have ignored this call, and have left Metlakahtla, and that,—"The real secret of his not acting in this straightforward manner lies in the

---

* Shim-au-git simply means chief or master, and is the name by which they designate Mr. Duncan.

power he had gained over the Indians. His word was law, and he did not wish to vacate the commanding position among them, which he had attained."

This man, whose unsparing immolation of self, in his sedulous efforts, in rescuing this flock from barbarism, saw that to save his life's work from utter destruction, he must yield to their appeal, and stand manfully in the breach, and protect them from the impending calamity. He who had braved the terrors of attempted assassination; and had stood out so uncompromisingly against the Shamans and cannibal chiefs, the slave and liquor traders; and had not flinched in the loathsome presence of the plague, was not found wanting in *this*, the hour of their supreme trial and peril.

CHAPTER VII.

COERCION AND TURMOIL.

AN agent of the Society, who remained at Metla-kahtla after the rupture, without a following, and without missionary work to engage him; recognized the unanimity of the Indians; and *openly* avowed his intention to respect such; but, with shameful duplicity *secretly* schemed to destroy the harmonious union.

About four months after the crisis, this agent abetted a secret conclave, of three or four Indians, who had been chiefs under the old tribal arrangement; but, who had lost their prestige through the advancement of civilization. These chiefs, came to believe that by allying themselves, to his faction, he could afford them a grand opportunity to reassert their importance. Therefore, they renounced their allegiance to the body of Metlakahtla Christians, and were eagerly received as genuine adherents, to the Church Missionary Society.

The conduct of these Indians, however, is not so much to be wondered at: it is the conduct of the Society's agent that is so astonishing. He well knew what these men were aiming at. He was also aware that one of them, was a convict sent by the Governor-General of Canada to Metlakahtla, to be kept under surveillance; another, he knew had often been sent away from the settlement for treachery: and, that neither of these men were actuated by any religious conviction, or, love for the Society, but, simply and solely, by spite and ambition. Yet because they would afford a foothold for the Society, and a covering for the Bishop's discomfiture, they were received with open arms, and their praises trumpeted to England as " Great and mighty chiefs." " The most Godly of the chiefs " and " Faithful adherents."

The Bishop, returned to Metlakahtla, soon after this discreditable movement had taken shape, and at once assumed leadership. Flaunting the Society's indorsement of his course, in the face of the community; he endeavored to cow all into submission to " his Lordship "—by boasts of the greath wealth, and power of the Society, accompanied with expressions of contempt for their *puny benefactor*. He held out temptations with one hand, and intimidation with the other.

The following in a nutshell, is the essence of what the Bishop proclaimed :—Why, that, lone insignificant little man, is helpless,—he can never stand against the great, and powerful Society, that commands, an annual income of a million dollars. I can crush him without an effort—Come to my fold and you shall want for nothing—I will teach you the

truth the *only* truth—Your old teacher is a *misleader*
—He has taught you false doctrines—Your only
way to salvation is to follow me.

The Bishop, immediately began to put in execution his designs for disrupting the Metlakahtlan
community. His tactics were as follows:

I.

On the very day of the rupture, " His Lordship"
tried to bribe the native teacher David Leask, by
offering him the addition of £50. a year to his salary
of £100, if he would forsake Mr. Duncan's leadership and accept work for the Society under his
orders. David knew nothing of the rupture at the
time of his interview with the Bishop, but suspecting from the Bishop's words and manner that something was going wrong, stoutly rejected his overtures.

II.

On the Bishop's return from England, the Indian
Council of Metlakahtla sent him a letter. The
Bishop assumed the air of offended dignity,—met
the messenger, took the letter from his hand, and,
without opening it tore it up, then threw the fragments down and stamped them under foot. A
second letter, was then sent to him by the Council.
This time the Bishop called the messenger into the
house, led the way to the fire, took the letter, and
threw it into the flames.

III.

The morning after the Bishop's return the school-master,—an Englishman—who had been employed and paid by Mr. Duncan from his own private funds since the severance from the Society; stepped into Mr. Duncan's office just before the time for opening school, and announced, that he had been informed, that the Government had authorized that the school should be placed under the Bishop's control, and, therefore, he had accepted work under the Bishop. Straightway without an hour's notice, and with this argument, in his mouth, which was afterward proven to be *utterly false*, the unprincipled white man, corrupted by the Bishop, quit his duties in Mr. Duncan's school, and immediately joined the Bishop's staff. Mr. Duncan having no one to occupy the deserted post,—had to conduct the school himself with the assistance of a native.

IV.

A few days after this, the native assistant was missing from her duties in the morning. In the afternoon she appeared, and on being interrogated, confessed that she had been away on the Bishop's Steam Yacht. It was evident that her allegiance also was being tampered with. On being rebuked for her conduct, she threw up her position, to be employed by the Bishop at an increased salary. Thus these two school teachers by the

Bishop's intrigues, and their own unfaithfulness deserted Mr. Duncan's large school, without any warning, and dropped into the easy employment of conducting a school of some ten or fifteen children.

V.

These attempts to cripple Mr. Duncan's, school being completed the Bishop's next design was to cramp the Metlakahtlans' resources. Since Mr. Duncan's severance from the Society, they had to rely mainly for means to carry on the Mission, upon the profits derived from the village store, in supplying goods to the neighboring tribes, and on the industries which had been mainly created by Mr. Duncan's money and labor. Therefore, to imperil the continuance of the industries, and render the store unremunerative, was not too contemptible, a thing for the Bishop to attempt. However, to make his steps, in this direction appear plausible, *false statements* were published. The public was told, that the adherents to the Society, were not allowed to trade in the village store, on equal terms with other Indians, and were insulted by Mr. Duncan's people; therefore, the Bishop was obliged to have a store of his own. The sanction and capital being obtained from the Society, the Bishop at once opened a shop in the mission-house, in which he resided; and having no risks to run, or expenses to bear he could well afford to put his business on a basis, which would prove ruin to any competitor's store. The success of this underhanded scheme demanded this unbusiness-like basis, therefore, his goods were offered at prices which left no profit whatever.

The Bishop entertained great expectation from this trading project, as it served to draw non-adherents, to his house for trade; and enable him to suggest to the Indians, how much they were being cheated by the other store; and, also it afforded the means of gratifying his few adherents, with loans of goods, a privilege they soon took advantage of, and freely became his debtors. The Metlakahtlans themselves saw the trap and despised it. But the Bishop did succeed in his object, in so far, as he lessened their income, by securing considerable of their business from neighboring tribes; yet though weakened by this process they yielded not.

VI.

The next step the Bishop took, was to bring the secular arm to his aid.

In 1882 the Indians, after having sought and obtained legal advice, decided to remove *their own* village store* from proximity to the house where the Bishop resided.

The Bishop incensed at this read the riot act, and sent such a *false* and alarming report to Victoria,

---

* See Mr. Duncan's refutation in Appendix.

that the Government was induced to despatch a man-of-war to Metlakahtla.

At the time there was no British ship available, therefore, an application was made to Washington, and the services were obtained of the United States Revenue Cutter, "*Oliver Wolcott*" and in due course arrived at Metlakahtla with two magistrates on board.

A large number of the supposed rioters including Mr. Duncan, was summoned ; but to the complete dismay, and, mortification of the Bishop, the magistrates, after investigation declared there had been no riot, hence dismissed the case.

This false alarm cost the Province it is said $7,000. What it cost Metlakahtla cannot be told ; but no one has ever heard of the Bishop's even being rebuked, either by the government, or by the Society, for the injury he had wantonly caused.

VII.

Before the arrival of the "*Oliver Wolcott*" to quell the so-called riot, a fresh case occurred, which the magistrates were called upon to deal with.

The Bishop's party desiring a drum, had discovered one in the possession of an Indian, and procuring the cash from the Society's agent concluded a purchase. It soon *transpired*, that the Indian had no right·to sell the drum, as he only shared its ownership, with six or eight others. His aggrieved partners, after ascertaining the disposition made of their joint property, applied to Mr. Duncan as the resident magistrate for redress. Wishing to avoid making it a case for the courts to settle, he wrote to the agent, informing him of the circumstances, begging him to investigate the matter, and do what was right. The agent, however, refused to comply, demanding that the aggrieved Indians, should sue the offender; but, promised the drum should not be used till the rightful ownership was settled by law.

A few days elapsed, when this promise was broken. A boy was seen on the road about to use the drum. Two of the joint-owners immediately took possession of it, and the boy complained to the Bishop. The Bishop issued at once warrants of arrest, and threw the two men in the lock-up; informing them that they would be held prisoners for three or four days, or, until the ownership of the drum, was decided by trial.

As soon as the Bishop's action became bruited about in the village, there was a general outcry against the injustice, of thus consigning men to prison, before, they had been examined; and a meeting was held by the Indians, of which Mr. Duncan knew nothing till it was over. The Indians decided to ask the Bishop, to accord the accused men an immediate trial, and with that intention started for his residence. Espying the Bishop on the road they awaited his approach. One of their number, an old man, accosted him, saying, " Why do you not try the two men before putting them into prison?"

The Bishop deigned no reply, but passed on. Another man then stepped up to the Bishop, and putting out his hand touched him on the shoulder, for the purpose of signing him to stop for an interview, and repeated the question. The Bishop suddenly turned upon him with raised fist and struck him with all his might. The Indians who were standing about fearing the man might retaliate immediately cried out, "Don't strike back, but appeal to the law." Thus entreated the man restrained himself. Another Indian standing hard by cried out, "Shame on the Bishop!" and the Bishop dealt him a blow and put himself in the attitude of a combatant. This was more than the Indians could endure, and the Bishop was the recipient of some blows, which, he said in court, kept him from his usual avocations for three days. Had it not been for the timely interference of the Native Constables, doubtless the Bishop would have been roughly handled, for his passionate and uncalled for attack. After the mêlée was over, which the Bishop's overt acts had provoked, the exasperated Indians at once set the two imprisoned men at liberty.

When this case came before the magistrates, the Bishop testified that the old man who first accosted him "struck" him on the face. Subsequently, before a commissioner's court the Bishop declared, the old man simply placed his hand before his (the

Bishop's) face. The word "struck" which was *false* was omitted. It is significant to notice, whatever the old man did he was not indicted—only maligned—but, the man whom the Bishop had "struck" but who, did not retaliate was fined on a point of technicality, because he had touched the Bishop's shoulder. The other Indian who was first. struck, by the Bishop, and then returned the blow was also fined.

The Indians wanted to appeal the case to a higher court, but the wary magistrates to shield the Bishop's conduct, put the fines so low that appeal was inadmissible.

The drum, on account of which, the whole trouble had arisen, was duly returned by the magistrates to the rightful owners; and nothing was done to the two men who broke prison, as their arrest and confinement had been illegal.

VIII.

His Lordship resorts to firearms! The Bishop by a course of intrigue, nagging and brutal violence had so irritated the Metlakahtlans that, it was only with difficulty that Mr. Duncan restrained, these men, who in the state, he found them a few years before, would have avenged such wrongs with bloodshed. The school-house which had been built for the community, on ground belonging to the community, with funds, a part of which only was con-

A NATIVE VIOLET.

tributed by the Society,—was taken possession of by the Bishop and turned into a rival church. The Indians galling under many indignities, gave notice to the Society's agent, that, as the building was not being used for the purpose for which it was originally erected, it must be moved to closer proximity to the mission house. The agent did not heed this notice, and the Indians took no further steps.

But the Bishop, intimating, that he had information that on a certain night, the Indians intended to take possession of the building, determined to fight. He armed himself with a Winchester rifle,—filled the magazine with bullet-cartridges, and with the white school-master, he had inveigled, he spent the night in the school-house, having however, previously warned his own party not to approach the building lest he might mistake them for his enemies. Whether or not, the Bishop if he had been given a chance would have taken as many lives, as his repeating rifle contained bullets—is best known to himself. No shooting occurred, for the reason, that no attack was even contemplated. The Bishop's night watch, first became known to the Metlakahtlans when in early morn, he was seen sneaking out of the school-house with the Winchester rifle under his arm. As might be supposed the news quickly spread throughout the village, and subsequently to the surrounding tribes; and, the indignation it kindled, is not likely to soon die out.

IX.

Next, the Bishop and the agent of the Society came into collision with the Metlakahtla Council, by backing one of his party in an act violating a by-law of the village. Since the founding of Metlakahtla, no one had been allowed to erect buildings, without consent of the community as represented by the Council. This regulation, had been strictly observed and had proved highly beneficial in many ways. The Bishop ignored the Council, and sustained one of his followers, in an extension to a building on communal ground, in defiance of the by-law. The man was warned to desist, but he flouted the warning, and like his master, seemed ready to defend his position by acts of violence. His courage however failed him, when the Indians walked in a body, and quietly took down, the few scantling he had erected. The Bishop or his assistant forwarded a basely exaggerated report to Victoria, and in due course,—as usual,—a man-of-war was despatched to Metlakahtla :—This time bringing the Superintendent of Indian affairs, and, an Indian agent recently appointed.

These gentlemen first endeavored to get Mr. Duncan, to co-operate with them, in making the Indians believe that they had committed a grave offence against the law; but, that if they would now accept the Indian agent, and come under the yoke of the Indian act, then by-gones should be by-gones. Mr. Duncan refused to identify himself with these gentlemen and their mission, and so the law was put in force. Summonses were served without the slightest opposition.

All was going on satisfactorily in the crowded court, till the Bishop appeared, and was seen whispering in a confidential manner, to one of the magistrates; when, as if an earthquake had shaken the building, the Indians all suddenly rushed out, leaving the bewildered magistrates, vainly shouting for order. Both Indians and magistrates went straight to Mr. Duncan's house,—the one to tell, and the other to ask why, the panic had occurred.

Mr. Duncan straightway succeeded in showing the Indians, their imprudence, and persuaded them to apologize, and return to Court. The magistrates took good care to keep the Bishop from again interfering and violating the rules of justice by acting both as plaintiff and adviser to the bench.

The trial resulted in the magistrates calling upon the accused, to enter into their own recognisances to keep the peace,—that, was all,—but the Indians refused, offering rather to surrender their liberty, and be kept in custody till their case could be heard in the Supreme Court before a Jury at Victoria. The magistrates declined to keep the Indians in custody and so nothing whatever was done.

The man-of-war departed, but the Indian agent remained to endeavor to bring the Indians under the Indian Act, and induce them to accept his services as agent. Discussions between the agent and the Indians followed. They told him, that the Indian Act, was adapted to Indians while they were ignorant, and wild; but was not suitable for Indians in their condition of enlightenment. They asked why, the Government had not sent an agent to them, twenty years ago, when his services were needed, and why the Government wanted to degrade them, and impede their progress, by putting them under such a yoke as the Indian Act, at this stage of their advancement. They compared the system of an Indian Agency, to a small shoe, suited for a child's foot; and reminded him that their feet were now, the feet of men,—hence the shoe he had brought them was obviously too small.

The agent saw clearly he was not wanted, and returned to Victoria the first opportunity that offered.

X.

The rights of the community to their land being challenged, and infringed upon, and the Bishop continuing to aggravate the people upon every conceivable pretext, the Indians determined to have their legal rights, defined, and established The school-house was still being used as a rival church, and a centre for a party of bribed deserters, who with their ruler openly avowed their inimical intentions, to undermine, and destroy, the community.

No attention having been paid to the Metlakaht-lans' notice to remove the building, and their rights being defied; after fully discussing the subject in council, they determined to take possession of it. Quietly and *in the day time* they carried out their resolution. The Bishop filed an information against seven Indians, who were supposed to be the main actors : charging them with riotously and tumultu-ously breaking into, injuring, and taking possession of a church—the property of the Church Mission-ary Society of London. The Indians were tried, but, the evidence against them failed in every particular, to substantiate the indictment, but the magistrate in his zeal to support the Bishop, over-stepped the law and committed five out of the seven men to take their trial, if called for, at the next assizes at Victoria. The men refused to give bail and were therefore sent in custody to Victoria, —600 miles from their homes. On arriving there, they were told the Grand Jury had not only thrown out the "Bill" against them, but, had expressed the utmost astonishment at the conduct of the magistrate. His animosity had been so obvious, and his actions so illegal, that, had the case con-cerned white men instead of Indians, he would no doubt have been called up to suffer a severe pen-alty.

The Indians had the satisfaction of being released, and the village the gratification, of having resecured the school-house for their children.

XI.

Close upon the heels of this trial came a man-of-war with three Commissioners, to inquire into the troubles at Metlakahtla. One, of the three Commissioners, was the very magistrate, who had just committed the five Indians before alluded to, for trial, and the other two, were his bosom friends,—hence, no wonder the commission proved a farce; and the proceedings in court, only, an exhibition of how constituted authority, may be prostituted, to serve personal or party spite. It would be but an act of justice to the Indians, if the proceedings of these Commissioners were exposed. Their course was iniquitous in the extreme, from the moment of landing they sided with the Bishop; at the same time assumed a severely hostile attitude toward Mr. Duncan, and, endeavored to persuade his people, that he, had been giving them "*bad teachings.*" The following is cited from the Church Missionary Society's report of the Chairman's address, and will indicate the tenor :—

"Nothing could have been more admirable than the *tact,* and *patience,* with which the Commissioners treated the Indians who came before them, and *explained to them, what they thought necessary.* Thus, at the commencement of the proceedings, the chairman, Mr. Davie, addressed them (through an interpreter) as follows :—

'We wish to tell everybody why we come here.

Somebody has told the Government that the Indians of Metlakahtla have behaved badly, and that other Indians say they will do the same as the Metlakahtlans.

'The Government does not believe the Metlakahtla Indians are bad themselves. The Government think the Indians *may have had bad teachings, that the Indians would not do bad things unless* they *had bad teachings.*

' *We are told* that at Metlakahtla people have been struck; that threats have been made; that houses have been taken by force; that people have been told to leave, and threatened with violence if they remained. All this is wrong. *We think the Indians would never do such things out of their own hearts.*

' *We are also told* that a church was pulled down at Kithralta. This is wrong.

' *We are told*, it would not have been pulled down, had not bad example been set by Metlakahtla.

' *We are told* the bad Indians of Queen Charlotte Islands tell the good Indians there, that they will do the same as at Metlakahtla; that those bad Indians say if one of them be put in jail at Massett, they will pull it down. All this is wrong.

' *We are told the Metlakahtlans say all the land belongs to the Indians. This is not true. White men who teach this are false to both Indians and whites. We will tell you the truth about the lands. First, all the lands belong to the Queen.* . . .

'White men who tell the Indians otherwise are false both to Indians and whites, and make trouble.

. . .

'*We are told* the Indians laughed at Dr. Powell and laughed at the gunboat. This was wrong and very foolish. Dr. Powell is the chief Indian Agent. He is the agent appointed by the Canada Government to take care of the Indians, and *look after their lands.'*"

The commissioners in their report say.—"'In justice to Bishop Ridley and the Church Missionary Society, which has numerous missions in the North-West, it is proper to say that the few Metlakahtla Indians associated with them, have not been parties to any of these disturbances, *nor have the missionaries of that Society, so far, as the Commission could learn, advocated the notion of the Indian title*, with the *exception of Mr. Woods, a layman,* whose action *has met with the disapprobation of Bishop Ridley*. The disturbances and disquietude have, to a considerable extent, grown out of a desire on the part of the majority of Metlakahtla Indians (who undoubtedly are in a great measure subject to Mr. Duncan's influence) to have what they have been educated to call unity, and to expel from Metlakahtla any person, or any sentiment, not in accord with the will of the majority.'"

As an example of the perfidy rife, I will cite one of the principal cases brought before the Commission by the Bishop, who sought to brand the Metlakahtlans with a dark crime, but, fortunately the *truth* came out.

Under oath the Bishop testified that a short time before, he had been fired upon,—it *was night—the shot passed through a window close to him—he distinctly heard the report of the gun,*—he had chased the two villains in the dark, half way down the village, but was outrun, and on the following morning the bullet was found upon the floor of the room. When surprise was expressed by the Commissioners that these facts had not sooner been made public,—the Bishop on his oath—declared he had kept the villainous act perfectly secret even from his own party,—as its publicity would only have affected the public mind for evil. The truth is, Bishop Ridley did not want the alleged tragedy investigated. It served his purpose best to keep it shrouded in darkness and mystery. How sorely chagrined he must have been, when the droll facts became known, and *it was proven that he had not been fired at—* that *no shot had been fired at all*, therefore, no report could have been heard by him:—but a young man of the Bishop's own faction, in sport had tossed a small pistol-bullet at the wall of the Bishop's house, for the purpose of startling a young girl he saw at a window. The bullet slipped from his fingers, and had gone instead through the window of the room in which the Bishop, happened to be at that moment !

The Bishop, when asked to produce the bullet,

stated he could not find it then, though he had
kept it for some time.

It was, a shallow but convenient quibble; for,
had he produced the bullet it might have told a
tale against either or both the Bishop's veracity, and
his common-sense.

Then, as to the secrecy the Bishop claimed he had
observed; it was ascertained, that on the morning
following the alleged tragic event, the Bishop informed his adherents of the occurrence, and offered
five dollars to anyone who should give the names of
the "two villains." When this reward was offered,
the man who had thrown the bullet was present, and,
but for shame would have confessed, and claimed
the money. The Society's reports of the Bishop's
evidence before the Commission assert,—" In only
two matters were his statements successfully contradicted "—one of these,—his declaration under
oath, that Mr. Duncan had made a certain statement; the other, wherein he took oath, that he had
distinctly heard the report of the rifle at the time
he, claimed to have been fired at. In both instances,
his testimony was proved to be *utterly false*. The
Society aver he was successfully contradicted in
only two of his sworn statements. A thing to boast
of in a Christian Bishop, who should exemplify
truth. The deduction consequent upon the aforesaid, seems to emphasize the melancholy fact, that
the greatest sin, is in being found out! It is not
surprising that this fictitious shooting case, has

made "His Lordship" the laughing-stock of the whole coast.

XII.

In the autumn of 1885 during Mr. Duncan's absence in England, another sinister attempt was made by the Bishop, to bring the Metlakahtlans, into trouble through the machinery of the law. "His Lordship" had spared no effort to undermine, and ruin the business of the Metlakahtlans co-operative stock-company village-store; upon the profits of which the community mainly relied for supporting their institutions. His shop trick was partially successful, inasmuch as, he did draw from the communal store a considerable amount of the trade of neighboring tribes and, of a few villagers. Seeing the need of resorting to some means for *self-preservation* the Council decided to levy a fine upon any member of *their* community, who should purchase goods at "His Lordship's" shop. Shortly after, it came to the notice of the Council, that a young woman had violated the by-law. The fine was collected without the slightest remonstrance, moreover this same young woman, was sharing the privileges and benefits of the community, and it was a matter of her own option, whether she should remain or leave.

The very reason for the first exodus of these Christians from Fort Simpson, and their coming to Metlakahtla, was to form a Christian community, membership of which might be attained by converts from any of the many surrounding tribes. Those who came were to give up their tribal and other distinctions, and live as one people, united, and binding themselves each one to follow the rules laid down, from time to time, by the Council. So that unity and cohesion, was the basis and protection of the settlement. The coming of each was voluntary. His stay was voluntary, and he could leave if ever he found the rules irksome. They wished to live as brethren united in all things.

The Bishop, on hearing of the action of the Council took special pains to work up a case for the magistrate; in which he succeeded after some delay, and considerable trouble. The magistrate, eager as before to serve the Bishop, and especially in any way that would punish the Native Council; again acted unjustly and overstepped the bounds of his jurisdiction. He committed two Indians to prison, but as soon as their case came up before a Judge of the Supreme Court—they were set free. The magistrate's illegal proceedings were so glaring, they could no longer pass without resentment. A lawyer was instructed to bring action against him for damages, but the magistrate, managed to slip out of the way, by going to California; remaining out of reach of the law for six months :—after which time, no action, according to law could be instituted against him.

Although, the case was dismissed on a technical

point of law the Judge before whom this appealed case was tried, declared it was fully within the rights of a Society or Community, to enact such rules and levy fines,—just as clubs and other similar organizations regulate their members, and membership by a system of laws and fines.

The Church Missionary Society, in its reports concerning this case, dilate at length, upon the lamentable idea, that the young woman, was an orphan, and paid the fine to save herself from prison ;—these statements are absolutely false, and their falsity, is well known to its Bishop.

In this manner, " His Lordship" continued the unholy siege against Metlakahtla.

My only reason for so circumstantially detailing these cases, is that they have been so outrageously misstated, and enlarged upon in the Society's inflated reports. It is a curious and suggestive fact that the Society's publications which had indorsed, and lavishly eulogized Mr. Duncan's work, up to the date of the rupture, thenceforth, veered completely around ; and from that moment have spared no opportunity to basely traduce him, and discredit his work !

There is no enmity so bitter, as love turned to hate. The Society from profuse honeyed adulation turned upon Mr. Duncan, and stung him with the venom of a scorpion.

The Society had suddenly changed its tone to-

ward the mission, although no change had occurred
in the work, only a metamorphosis in *the relationship.*

"His Lordship's" reports will afford us a little
insight into his methods of mission work. On one
occasion he tells how he conquered the medicine-
men at one of the Mission Stations—they disturbed
him by their noise, and he—"stepped quickly up to
the chief performer, I took him by the shoulders and
before he could recover his self-possession had him
at the river's brink, assured him I should assist him
further down next time."—This shows what a gentle mild mannered man was this Bishop, though the
Society has already assured us of this, in speaking
of the delicate manner in which Mr. Duncan's connection with the Society was severed " after much
loving correspondence" that,—"All who know the
Bishop must have been sure that he would have
done it most gently and lovingly."

The Bishop, however, is versatile and shows variety in his affectionate methods. He reports, his
charge to a native assistant, in this wise.—"'May
I go down and hold service?' 'Yes go and be
gentle as Jesus was' I said. 'May I take a bell?'
'Yes take a small one because you have only a
little knowledge."'

How touching, is the comparison between the
manner in which the Bishop caressed the shaman,
and the precept he offers the native teacher.

In writing of the Metlakahtlans taking possession of the school-house, he informs us how our old acquaintance—" Paul Sebassah,* the *great chief*, has since told me, he had made up his mind, to recover the church or die in the attempt. When he came, with the rest, to report the seizure, he could scarcely speak for half-suppressed rage. I saw danger impending, and was at my wits' end until his speech was ended. I was then expected to speak, so I said, ' Let us pray for guidance.' This subdued his anger. God has indeed *sanctified*. I dreaded the effect of our armed watch, we were urged by the magistrate to maintain. It for a time stirred the blood of the men, but prayer conquered again."

We have already observed how ingeniously the Bishop, can pirouette words in such a manner, as convey novel versions of incidents, quite foreign to facts. There is something remarkably thrilling about the so called " graphic passage " written by the Bishop, about three months before the rupture while taking up the coast his little steam yacht " *Evangeline* " (was the name a foreboding to the peaceful settlement ?) : I quote this, merely because so much has been made of the incident to prove the great *courage*, and *heroism*, of this lordling who faced the *grave dangers*, of the North Pacific. His Lord-ship delivers himself thus :—

" It is now 10.30 and *my turn* to be on deck.

---

* See Chapter II.

The moon shines brilliantly on a glassy sea. The Indian at the helm is singing ' Rock of Ages ' but he must go to bed! The only other person on board is the European engineer who is fast asleep. We must go on until we reach the Skeena to-morrow morning as there is no harbor that I know nearer. There we shall (D. V.) spend Sunday and go on to Metlakahtla Monday morning."

The inference of the reader with nothing more explicit, is that the Bishop in his little steam yacht was voyaging from Victoria to Metlakahtla, with only two men, and that there is no harbor for anchorage known to him, hence, he must navigate the vessel during the lone midnight hours, while his paltry crew were off duty How brave all this looks on paper till illuminated by truth. The unsentimentalized facts are, that, the " *Evangeline* " was attached by a stout hawser to a large steamer, employed in the coast trade, and the lesser craft was being towed at a fine rate. There was no duty for the Bishop to perform, as the two men found no hardship in alternate watches, for they were merely called upon to hold the helm. It is preposterous to suppose that the captain, would have asked or accepted the Bishop's pilotage, even if the Bishop had been versed in navigation. There was a calm sea, and a bright moonlight, and no obstacles to an all-night cruise; for the captain was perfectly familiar with the harbors dotting the coast line.

The Bishop had heralded that he should (D. V.)

spend the Sabbath at Skeena, and on Monday voyage thence to Metlakahtla. However, it best suited his own convenience to proceed with flags flying into Metlakahtla on Sunday afternoon. The Metlakahtlans were astounded by the Bishop's conduct, as there was no necessity whatever, for this violation of the Sabbath,* which seemed to demonstrate to the natives his contempt for the teachings, they had received, and, seemed to indicate that he was not so bound. It discovers the key to the man, and his writings, and is a specimen of his capability for disguising the truth.

With blind conceit, the Church Missionary Society loses no opportunity to make virulent tirades upon, and to read lessons to the Roman Catholic Missionaries, and denounce the very follies, of which it is itself guilty. The Church of Rome has its faults, and has made its mistakes as has every church.

True, the Roman Catholic Church will ever have to bear the blame, for the inhuman methods adopted to Christianize the Spanish American countries, but we must not forget that at the same time, the Protestants were committing quite as grave errors. As a consequence of the methods adopted by the Roman Catholics in Mexico, Central and South America, it will require many years for those countries to reach an age of religious reason.

---

* See Chapter III., re Metlakahtlans observance of the Sabbath.

While I was travelling in Ecuador some years since, I was told by an Indian the following incident, which indelibly impressed itself upon my mind : A party of priests borne on the backs of Indians went as missionaries amongst the Napa's —a tribe on the eastern slope of the Andes, that had never acknowledged the authority of the Spanish invaders—soliciting them to accept the religion of the cross, like the other nations, who after the fall of Atahualpá humbly accepted the yoke of oppression ; but these heathens, shook their heads and laughing in derision, said, pointing to the slaves bearing the Jesuits: "And carry you on our backs? Oh no! We don't want a God that will transform us into beasts. Our God is the Sun, he smiles upon us, gives us light, and makes men of us, not dogs!"—What a moral is herein embodied.

Notwithstanding the many mistakes of the Church of Rome, it has numbers of devoted, self-sacrificing missionaries in various parts of the world, who could give the Church Missionary Society points in true practical mission work, which elevates, reforms, rescues. The success of missionary work, is far more dependent upon the quality, and adaptability of the individual missionary, than it is upon the name of the society that sends him out.

A full history, and exposure of the Church Missionary Society's proceedings, in their North Pacific missions during the last five years, would not only unfold a sad picture of ecclesiastical arrogance, and religious intolerance; but, would prove, that lamentable incompetency now presides over the affairs of the Society at headquarters. It cannot be possible that the supporters of the Society really know, the true state of affairs, or, how shamefully their funds are being frittered away in carrying on a cruel persecution, against a little struggling native community, in retaliation for the rejection of a bigoted Bishop, who tried by foul means to get rule over it; and refusal to adopt elaborate formulas of service, which were illy-adapted to its requirements.

It has best suited the purpose of the clique in control to smother the real facts, and endeavor to justify, in the eyes of the members of the Society, the iniquitous course pursued by the Bishop, and its officers, by publishing gross misrepresentations.

Not less than fifteen persons (counting the wives of six) have left the Society's work there during the last four and a half years, of whom seven were from the Bishop's station at Metlakahtla, and seven from the Skeena River. The Society's publications have disguised the real facts, and attributed the failures mainly to ill health; but in truth, disgust at the confusion into which the mission work has been thrown, is the actual cause of most of the resignations.

The demoralized state of the Society's work through the unwise, and overbearing, conduct of the Bishop, is not confined to Metlakahtla, or to the Skeena River: their agents are no longer well-

received by the natives anywhere on the coast, and
in one place have actually been driven away. On
the Nass River the Society's mission work is death-
stricken; on Queen Charlotte Island it is ready to
collapse; at Alert Bay there is no progress,—and
yet, the Society continues publishing magnified reports respecting these places.

Though the natives are literally alienated from
the Society's agents, who have fallen into such bad
repute—the Society evidently does not want to believe it is so, and, therefore, goes on attributing its
own distresses, and every act of opposition taken by
the people against their agents, to the direct, or the
indirect prompting of Mr. Duncan.

Even the destruction of the Church by the Kith-
ratla Indians at their own village, the Bishop had the
audacity to ascribe to Mr. Duncan's direct orders.—
Whereas, the Bishop well knew it was the outburst
of long pent up anger, in the Indians which led to
the mischief, and, that, their anger was generated by
his own indiscreet proceedings, and afterward augmented by the insolent conduct of a native teacher
he sent to them.

The Metlakahtlans are not less human in their
feelings, in their impulses, than are white men.
they had been taught to throw off the yoke of their
old superstitions, and were enjoying the fullest measure of religious liberty, profiting spiritually and materially; delighting in carrying the message to the
yet heathen tribes: But, how soon was this scene

changed ; when the Lordly white Shaman of the Church cast a pall over them like, the black plague. In his own life, they saw the contradiction of what they had been taught, was true, and right, and good. They had at first regarded their *benefactor* as a supernatural being, but, as they became enlightened they recognized in him the mortal man, but, one who lived in all honesty, the precepts he taught them ; as his life in mingling with them, became to them human, the grandeur of his nature became intensified in their eyes ; —his words were truths, his ways were just, wise, patient and consistent.

Can we wonder at their resentment, when these people found this Bishop who outrivalled the Chilkat chieftains in his imposing vestments, overturning those things, which had proved their salvation, brutally assaulting men after the manner of a bully,— corrupting their weaker fellows by lavish expenditure of the Society's funds,—maligning, and bearing false witness against them, and, against he who had led them out of darkness, and who had never failed them in the hour of trial,—inciting the Government to despoil them, of their land, harassing them with trumped-up charges in the law courts, and by means of false alarms, bringing frowning men-of-war to terrorize them ?

Is it surprising then, that they rejected and resisted this Bishop ? Rather we must wonder more at the patience, with which they endured his insults, and assaults so long.

Instead of inciting these people Mr. Duncan, often found it most difficult to restrain them, and had they been white men it is doubtful if he could have succeeded.

The Society has called Mr. Duncan's rule over the Metlakahtlans, autocratic: *truly, his rule is autocratic*, but, it is *the autocracy of love*.

The Society formerly fully endorsed, and approved in every particular, Mr. Duncan's methods of religious, and secular work; but, though his plan of action continues unchanged, the Society now, reviles him and in direct contradiction to its own previous assertions, and in the face of the overwhelming testimony I cite in Chapters III. and IV. it, now unblushingly gives vent in print to such preposterous expressions as this;—

"The true secret of Mr. Duncan's failure, has been his, permitting the material, and secular part of his employment, to supersede the spiritual."

Failure, the Society calls the result of Mr. Duncan's work; it is *such a failure* as most men would envy him!

Furthermore, the Society congratulates itself that "the great object of the Church Missionary Society is, not to make men expert in the practical, industries of life, but to make them wise unto salvation."

By what means the Society "tries to make men wise unto salvation," and, how well it has succeeded we have abundantly seen, in the course of events at Metlakahtla. "By their works shall ye judge them."

E. Ruhamah Scidmore "*Alaska*" Boston 1885— in a highly interesting chapter on the Metlakahtla Mission thus pictures the situation of affairs :—

"Mr. Duncan is one of the noblest men that ever entered the mission field. . . .

"It was with real regret that we parted at the wharf, and it was not until we were well over the water that we learned of the serpent or the skeleton in this paradise. Though Metlakahtla might rightly be considered Mr. Duncan's own particular domain, and the Indians have proved their appreciation of his unselfish labors by a love and devotion rare in such races, his plainest rights have been invaded and trouble brewed among his people. Two years ago a bishop was appointed for the diocese, which includes Fort Simpson, Metlakahtla, and a few other missions. . . . Bishop Ridley, disapproving of Mr. Duncan's Low Church principles, went to Metlakahtla and took possession as a superior officer. Mr. Duncan, moved from the rectory, and the bishop, took charge of the church services. In countless ways a spirit of antagonism was raised that almost threatened a war at one time.

"The whole stay of the Bishop has been marked by trouble and turbulence, and these scandalous disturbances in a Christian community cannot fail to have an influence for evil, and undo some of the good work that has been done there. *Mr. Dun-*

can, made no reference to his troubles during the morning that we spent at Metlakahtla, and his desire that we should see and know what his followers were capable of, and understand what they had accomplished for themselves, gave us to infer that everything was peace and happiness in the colony. *One hears nothing but praise of Mr. Duncan, up and down the coast,* and can understand the strong partisanship he inspires among even the roughest people. His face alone is a passport for piety, goodness, and benevolence anywhere, and his honest blue eyes, his kindly smile, and cheery manner go straight to the heart of the most savage Indian. His dusky parishioners worship him, as he well deserves, and in his twenty-seven years among them they have only the unbroken record of his kindness, his devotion, his unselfish and honorable treatment of them. He found them drunken savages, and he has made them civilized men and Christians. He taught them trades, and there has seemed to be no limit to this extraordinary man's abilities. When his hair had whitened in this noble, unselfish work, and the fruits of his labor had become apparent, nothing could have been more cruel and unjust, than to undo his work, scatter dissension among his people, and make Metlakahtla a reproach, instead of an honor to the society which has sanctioned such a wrong. An actual crime has been committed in the name of Religion, by this persistent attempt to destroy

the peace and prosperity of Metlakahtla and drive
away the man who founded and made that village
what it was. British Columbia is long and broad,
and there are a hundred places where others can
begin as Mr. Duncan, began, and where the bishop
can do good by his presence. If it was Low Church
doctrines that made the Metlakahtla people what
they were a few years since, all other teachings
should be given up at mission stations. Discord,
enmity, and sorrow have succeeded the introduction
of ritualism at Metlakahtla, and though it cannot
fairly be said to be the inevitable result of such
teachings, it would afford an interesting comparison
if the Ritualists would go off by themselves and
establish a second Metlakahtla as a test."

It is perhaps, to the Society's credit, that it has
remained loyal to its Bishop, who has shared in its
follies, and in its disgrace, but, the following quotation from its reports reads like a farce, to those
who know the truth :—" It is only just that we
should pay our frank and hearty tribute to Bishop
Ridley who for the last five years has amidst no
ordinary *danger*, obloquy, and discouragement, *fearlessly* maintained the Society's position, at Metlakahtla."

Had the Bishop been actuated by high-minded,
principles, he would have retired from Metlakahtla
in obedience to the unanimous voice of the people,
in 1881 ; or, to the respectful letter they in public
assembly sent him in 1882. He chose, rather to

treat the request with defiance, and contempt, and began a contest which has gone on increasing in intensity, and bitterness, up to the present time.

Similar appeals to the Society were utterly disregarded. The plea that there was no other place to which the Bishop could go, is but a shallow subterfuge.

And now, *after nearly five years of intrigue, and lavish expenditure of the Society's funds, some twelve or fifteen families, form the Bishop's party.*

Judging from the number of missionaries employed by the Society at Metlakahtla, sometimes, as many as eight (male and female) and how much it has cost to *coddle*, and *bribe their adherents and coerce the Metlakahtlans ;* the sum total of expense borne by the Society, since the rupture cannot be less than £6,000 or about $30,000.

The amount paid to Mr. Duncan, for his services during a period of more than twenty years, and which resulted, in the creation of the successful, self-supporting Christian village of Metlakahtla, was about £3,000, or $15,000. That is to say, about one-half the amount the Society has squandered in coercive schemes, and efforts to destroy the Metlakahtla Christian Union since 1881.

It is estimated that since the rupture, the Government of Canada has, at the instigation of the Society's agents, spent upwards of £6,000, or $30,000 of the public funds, in coercing and terrorizing the Metlakahtlans with men-of-war : add, this to

A NATIVE HOPEFUL.

the Society's outlay, and we have a total of $60,-
ooo.

It is beyond comprehension, that the citizens of
Canada sit quietly by, and see their treasure thus
wasted in perpetrating cruel outrages upon their
fellow subjects.

Consider, how hardly money is obtained for missionary purposes, and that according to the Society's
own published statement, *the poor of England contribute more, than five times as much to its funds,
as the opulent nobility—!* Think of the poor dis-
tressed creatures, who in self-commiseration, divide
their scanty meals, and stint their own home comforts, to contribute pennies to save the souls of
heathen peoples, whom they regard as more unfortunate than themselves,—illustrating forcibly how
a touch of nature makes one wondrous kind.—
Surely, it is an outrageous shame, that a Society
drawing the penny dole, and widow's mite, for the
alleged purpose of rescuing, the pitiable heathen
from their savagery, should be guilty of squander-
ing such an amount of these precious funds, to
propagate, in the name, of Christ a work of malicious persecution! Not to win to Christ, but to
glorify a pompous Bishop, and pull down the work
of an honest Christian layman, because he dared,
to cast his lot with the people, whom he had by
his own fidelity, and genius, raised from the lowest
state of barbarism to a fair state of civilization.

CHAPTER VIII.

CASTING THE TOIL.

As the truth about the Society's blunders at
Metlakahtla, and, generally on the North Pacific
Coast, was becoming known in England, and scan-
dalizing it; the committee resolved to send out two
trusty members, to report upon the troubles and
vindicate its course. With exceptional candor it
admits, that "The feeling in British Columbia ran
high, and, on the whole seems to have been adverse
to the action of the Society."

Mr. Duncan was in London at the time, and
only reached Metlakahtla after the meetings and
interviews between these gentlemen, and the Indians, were over, and he had but an hour's conversation with them there. Their report, published
by the Society, is certainly one of the most remarkable documents, ever issued by a religious body.
It abounds in barefaced falsehoods, and many of the
statements not wholly false, are such distortions of
the truth, as to make them equally discreditable.
The real authors of the fiction in this report would
put Munchausen to blush.

The Deputation, which was received cordially,

and treated courteously, began its work by attempting in an insinuating manner, to prejudice the Metlakahtlans, against their leader ; and, to corrupt them into secession, by holding out to them the old bribe; namely, the Society's enormous wealth, and power; and promises, or intimations of special benefits, if, they would but join the Bishop's party.

To give force to their attitude, the Deputies argued : "The Church Missionary Society, is intrusted with *more money than any other society* in England." "The money last year was *over a million dollars.*"

Soon, this invidious course excited suspicion, and doubt in the minds of the Metlakahtlans, as to the honesty of purpose, of their inquisitors ; and, having so often been falsely reported by the Bishop ; and, in the Society's publications, they wisely resolved to commit all communications to writing. However, this precaution, has not saved them from these prevaricators, whose verdict was a foregone conclusion.

A detailed reply, to this unique report is being prepared by Mr. Duncan for the members of the Church Missionary Society; as there is ample evidence, both verbal and documentary, for the complete refutation of the statements therein contained. A brief reply, by the Rev. Robert Tomlinson, will be found in the Appendix of this volume.

The Deputation did not hesitate to take advantage of Mr. Duncan's absence, by seizing the opportunity, to make a most cowardly attack upon his character, before a full assembly of the Metlakaht-lans. However, Mr. Duncan's inner life, and the whole truth regarding the case in point, was too well known to his followers, to afford any success in this dastardly attempt. First, I quote from the Society's report of the Deputation's work,—

" It is very distressing to read that ' Mr. Duncan represents all the funds that pass through his hands as his personal property, and the Society was prac-tically ignored. In fact, there is clear evidence that on one occasion he distinctly told the Indians that the Society had never sent him, or supported him, or given him anything.' *No doubt he would explain this to mean that both the impulse to come, and the support in the work, came from a higher source ; but this explanation would not be likely to suggest itself to the Indian mind.*"

The first two statements, are utterly false; the italicized portion, is a " loving and affectionate " sneer, quite in accord with its whole treatment of this matter.

After profuse protestations, of the deep interest, the Society felt in the Metlakahtlans welfare, the Deputation launched the following charge.

" Mr. Duncan, was paid a salary by the Society, year by year, from 1857, when he came out to you, at Fort Simpson, to 1881, when his connection with the Society was severed. The Society, also sent out money besides this for the expenses of the Mis-sion ; *according to the rules, and to the actual prac-*

tice of the Society, all money given for the Society's Mission belongs to the Society, not to the Missionaries ; all such money is subject to the control of the Committee, it makes no difference whether the money is paid into the Society's treasury in London, or given to any of its agents for special purposes, or to any Missionary by friends at home or abroad for any branch of the work carried on by the Missionaries.

" Mr. Duncan, collected money from the friends of the Society, and as he tells us, from others also. But as our agent he collected that money for our Mission; if he had not been our agent, the money would not have been given for our Mission, and he had no authority to collect for any other. The following is one of the Society's rules. ' Every individual connected with the Society in its different ' missions, in whatever department of labor, shall keep a detailed, and accurate account, of the funds placed at his disposal, in the form that may be pointed out to him ; and shall regularly transmit such accounts to the Parent Committee, or to their representatives at the Mission, at such period as may be specified for that purpose.'

" Mr. Duncan then ought to have accounted for all money received by him for this mission, whether for Church, school, sawmills, or other purposes (The Cannery was established after the severance, and does not therefore come under the rule). Part of the expenses of the other works came from trade profits ; but these profits belong to the Society,

since the industries were part of the Society's mission-work for your benefit. Mr. Duncan's good
management made them more than pay their expenses. If there had been loss on the whole work,
the Committee would have acknowledged their responsibility for making up that loss."*

The Metlakahtlans knowing the absolute falsity
of the accusation, and realizing, the manifest unfair-
ness in thus attacking Mr. Duncan, in his absence;
when the Deputation might easily have brought up
the charge when it met him in London, in the presence of the officers of the Society, and when access
to his reports and accounts could have been had—
they were extremely indignant, and several present
expressed their feelings by leaving the room at the
close of the address.

The Rev. Robert Tomlinson replied to the address, charging the Deputies with making a cowardly
attack, with the intent to injure Mr. Duncan in the
eyes of the people, and he *characterized the charge
as a base, and groundless slander.*

The Deputies replied they imputed no motives.

Mr. Tomlinson, declared, that it was not a question of motives, at all. Their words contained a
charge of fraud, or, breach of trust, on the part of

---

* In the Appendix, is a full statement of the facts connected with
the secular fund, written by Mr. Duncan at my request; wherein
he completely refutes these charges which were originated by the
Bishop.

Mr. Duncan. And he, would not sit there, and hear an honored servant of God thus slandered.

Two days afterward the Deputies, proposed to Rev. Mr. Tomlinson that they should withdraw part of what they had said. This he would not accept. The following day the Deputies endeavored to allay the irritation their indecent assault had caused by making to the Metlakahtlans the ensuing written statement.

"*We have no suspicion whatever that Mr. Duncan misused, or in any way misapplied the funds intrusted to his care. On the contrary, we believe that he used them strictly, and wisely, for your benefit, and in a manner probably which the Society would heartily approve.*"

The Deputies pleaded that it was quite possible Mr. Duncan, was not acquainted with the rules, and perhaps he was not even asked for any accounts.

Rev. Mr. Tomlinson replied.

"As you have adopted this formal manner of contradicting what to the people and myself, seemed to be the plain meaning, we gladly accept your interpretation. At the same time, I cannot help feeling, surprised, and grieved, that on a point of so much importance, you are so ignorant as not even to know whether the Society asked for any accounts, and that without taking the least pains to enlighten yourselves, you gave utterance in a public meeting to a statement, which had you examined into the matter, you would have known to be *unfounded*.

And shortly afterward Rev. Mr. Tomlinson sent
the following additional statement to the Deputation :

" The ground which you appear to take as regards the accounts is :—' That the rule of the Society required Mr. Duncan, to render accounts of
the money he collected for the Church, the Stores,
the Industries, as well as other operations of the
missionary.' You speak of the rule of the Society,
but you do not say when it was made or how long
it has been in force. If the rule was in force when
Metlakahtla was founded, then the whole conduct
of the Committee and Secretaries of *the Society for
over twenty years in approving of these works and
industries, and yet never once asking for accounts of
expenditure on them, while they regularly received,
and accepted, the accounts for all the Society's money
expended during those years, shows that the rule did
not refer to such industries at all.*"

What more could be required to expose the pu-
sillanimous spirit of this Deputation. In their address opening the discussion, the Deputies evaded
the subject of the existent troubles between the
Society and the Native Christians—and, placed
the burden of the split, on Mr. Duncan's shoulders.
Falsely representing, that it was brought about, by
a *change* in Mr. Duncan's mind, and method—
ignoring the truth—*the Society's change*, and *not*
Mr. Duncan's.

The Metlakahtlans had suffered too bitterly by

the petty warfare carried on, with the Society's
funds, and sanction, not to know their real grievances ; so, the smooth-tongued flattery of the Deputation was lost upon them. In their reply, the
Metlakahtlans, indulged in no evasive terms but
went directly to the point. They knew, that the
Society failing in its attempts through its emissaries,
to bribe them, or corrupt them, had endeavored to
rob them, of land which they had inherited from
their fathers, and their fathers' fathers ; and which
was as veritably theirs, as was the freehold of an
Englishman in England !

Furthermore, they knew, that for the past five
years the Society, in carrying on its work of malicious persecution, had resorted to numerous, unprincipled methods, to destroy their Christian independence, and force them, to adopt its elaborate
rites, and ceremonies ; and to submit to a Bishop,
whom they deemed by his daily deeds, unworthy
to wear *the cloth.*

This Christian community, had been formed for
the moral protection of those who had renounced
their evil ways : they were a happy, prosperous,
people, and had found the bond of union, an invaluable safeguard. What wonder then, when a serpent came among them, endeavoring by all manner
of iniquitous devices, to undermine and rupture
their union, that they acted upon their rights in
protesting against the presence, in their midst of
this instigator, and his band of pampered hirelings,

which he had made instruments for fomenting discord among them. The very primal principles,
union, *peace*, and *piety* upon which the Community
was organized, were being nullified, and by whom ?

They knew that their weaker and more venal
native brethren, who had succumbed to the corrupting fund, would hardly have defied the rules of
the village to which they had pledged themselves,
but, for the instigation and backing of the Society's
representatives, who, treated the village rules with
contempt.

The Metlakahtlans, called the attention of the
Deputation to the fact, that the Society, had refused their request that a deputation should be
sent out to investigate the troubles, when they first
began, but rather had attempted to force them into
submission. The Society's first steps, they thought,
should be to right the wrongs it had inflicted.

In their letter replying to the Deputation's
address, they expressed themselves as follows :
" We wish to bring before you in a few words
the real state of the case, which you have not so
much as referred to in your speeches, and to ask
the Society two questions.

" Metlakahtla, including the two acres, was Tsimshean land and the site of an old village, before
ever Mr. Duncan left England. The first Tsimsheans who wished to serve God showed this place
to Mr. Duncan as a good site for an Indian village.
There never was the smallest idea of taking it or

any part of it from us. *We were willing and glad for the Missionaries of the Society to occupy the two acres as long as we felt they were working for us, but we never supposed the Society would try and take these two acres from us, and claim them because they had their buildings on them, any more than we supposed that Mr. Duncan would want to take from us the pieces of land on which he erected the saw-mill and other works.* We were no parties to the arrangement between the Government and the Society about the two acres. *We feel that the Society is not working for us any longer, but is opposing and hindering us,* and we wish them to move off our land. We ask the Society this question : Will the Society in consideration of our prior claim to the land, and our earnest request, give up their claim and yield to this our unanimous wish?

" The reason for the first Christians leaving Fort Simpson, and coming to Metlakahtla to form a Christian community of members from any of the many surrounding tribes, was, unity. *Those who came were to give up their tribal and other distinctions, and live as one people united, and binding themselves each one to follow the rules laid down from time to time by their Council.* So that unity was the basis of the settlement. The coming of each was voluntary, his stay was voluntary, and he could leave if ever he found the rules irksome.

" Before the separation, the Society told us *they wished to make some changes* and bring us into direct connection with the Church of England. *We did not want these changes, and when the Society found we did not want to change they dismissed Mr. Duncan because he would not try to make us do what they wanted. We all, without any exception asked Mr. Duncan to stay here among us.* After some months, a few separated from us. They had a right to leave us if they chose, but not to remain at Metlakahtla, after they had separated from us, because they had promised to be one with us. It is not that these few have left us that causes the trouble, but that they are being supported by the Society in doing what they ought not to do.

"What we wish to ask the Society is this. Will the Society refuse to hear our earnest entreaty, and in opposition to our unanimous wish, continue to support the direct cause of the dissension, and dis-union among us, or will they not rather listen to our prayer, and withdraw their support, and thus put an end to the trouble, and enable us to return to the old paths, and again enjoy that union which was such a blessing to us, and those around us?

" From the people of Metlakahtla and signed for them by

"DAVID LEASK, SECRETARY."

The Deputies continued their invidious course, and met the frank, open statement, of the Metla-kahtlans, with another bid ;—they seemed prepossessed with the idea that all men were purchasable.

They *indicated their belief in the success of the Bishop's schemes for impoverishing the Metlakahtlans*, by intimating that as they were not supported by *a society*, the permanence of the present Native Christian organization was doubtful ; hence, felt it incumbent upon the Society's agents to remain in their midst, for, the Society—so solicitous for their welfare,—might at any time have to again assume the responsibility of their support.

In their report to the Society, the Deputies held out this hopeful prospect of the Metlakahtlans' capitulation. "Notwithstanding the special inducements Mr. Duncan offers to the Indians in the form of remunerative employment, which are not great, the Mission may yet, under God's blessing bear the fruit of which at one time it gave so much promise."

Observe the artfulness of the Deputies' words, addressed to the Metlakahtlans in reply to their letter.

"You say that the Society is not any longer working for you, but is opposing and hindering you. And you wish them to move off the land.

"You have separated yourselves from the Society, you have, of course, a perfect right to do so if you choose. But the Society does all it can for your benefit, and will go on working for your benefit still. It does not hold Mission Point only for the benefit of those who adhere to it. It is bound to do all it can for them. But it is bound to hold

Mission Point, and does hold it, *for your highest benefit* also. It held it at first, that the word of God might be introduced among you. It holds it now, in order to offer you the *full* benefit of the religion of Christ, which has so happily *begun* to take root among you. For instance—you have been *deprived* hitherto of the Lord's Supper. This is one of the greatest privileges of the Christian Religion, and every true Christian has a right to it. While *your* Christianity is in this and other respects *imperfect*, the Society cannot feel that its work of establishing the Gospel among you has been completed. Many of you do not at present care to accept the ministrations the Society offers to you. But that does not set free the Society from the *duty* of putting within your reach an *unmutilated* Christianity. Further the Society cannot lose sight of this, that at present *you are not, as far as they know, supported by any society. Thus they do not see any guarantee that the present state of things will be permanent among you. They feel therefore, that they may* at any time have to take up again that responsibility for the support of the Gospel among you which they bore for so many years."

Then with amazing audacity, and deliciously naïve arguments, they endeavored to convince these poor people, that they had no rights to their inherited land, except by the charity of the crown! Alas! Christianity, what ignoble acts, are cloaked 'neath the amplitude of thy snowy mantle.

INFANT'S AERIAL TOMB.

Next followed a letter from the Metlakahtlans, which is born, of a spirit pregnant with that love of civil and religious liberty, that is ever intensified by tyranny and oppression.

METLAKAHTLA, May 4th, 1886.

"DEAR SIRS :—In your first interview with us *you would have misled us into the belief, that you had come from the Society, seeking reliable information* to enable them to decide upon a course of action. Your second communication, shows us that this was not the intention of the Society, for they had already made up their minds as to how they would act in the only two matters which really concerned us and them, and stood in the way of peace being restored. So that any discussion of matters in conference, would have been so much waste time.

"You tell us the Society will not give up the two acres, and you refer us to some ' decisions,' as you are pleased to call them, but what are in reality only the opinions of individual Government officers, and then boldly assert we can have no claim on these two acres. *The God of Heaven, who created man upon earth, gave this land to our forefathers, some of whom once lived on these very two acres, and we have received the land by direct succession from them. No man-made law can justly take from us this the gift of Him who is the source of all true law and justice. Relying on this the highest of all titles, we claim our land and notify*

*the Society, through you its Deputies, to move off the
two acres.*

" But you tell us it is not only to maintain the
Society's claim of the two acres, that they refuse to
leave Metlakahtla. They wish to continue the division among us. The Society, you tell us, cannot
sanction the principle adopted by us, that ' Religious unity is necessary to civil unity,' and even dare
tell us that this principle is contrary to God's word.
How you can reconcile this last assertion, with the
history of God's people of old, as recorded in God's
word, and with other portions of the blessed scriptures, we are at a loss to imagine. You stand forth
as the champion of disunion, civil and religious.

" Ever since the disruption, *we* have been credited
with being the cause of the existence and continuance of the dissension among us. Now, at last, the
truth has come to light, and it is clear to all men
that to the Society, and to the Society alone, belongs
this proud distinction. For by leaving Metlakahtla
the Society can at once, and, completely put an end
to the dissension. For unity we came here. For
unity we remain here. And for unity we are prepared to contend to the last. God inclined our
hearts, while we were still in the midst of the strifes
and divisions at our old heathen villages, to accept
this principle. God has blessed us acting on this
principle, and God will help and defend us contending for this principle.

" You say we have departed from the Society.

We never, by any promise or agreement, joined the Society. It is quite true the Society sent out and supported our teachers. We remember this and feel grateful to them for it, but this does not bring us into connection with the Society. The money was not the Society's, but the contributions of Christians to God to aid in the spread of his Gospel. *Does the Society for the Prevention of Cruelty to Animals, which is also supported by con- tributions, claim any right over or connection with those animals which, by the help of their paid agents, they have rescued from torture. If not, why should the Church Missionary Society claim any such right in or connection with its converts?*

"Again you speak to us as if we had left the Church of England. We were not asked to join the Church of England when we came to Metla- kahtla, nor when we came forward for Baptism. Though we were visited at various times by min- isters of that church* who baptized many of us, yet none of these asked us to join the Church of England. The first time we were asked to join the Church of England was when the Society de- cided that the Lord's Supper, must be introduced among us, *with the ceremonial of the Church of England.* At once we objected to join the Church of England, or any other denomination, preferring to be an independent Native Church, with power to

---

* Several Bishops, an Archdeacon, a Dean and other clergymen of the Church of England. See Chap. II.

regulate our ceremonies in accordance with God's word, and as best suited our needs. Our statement in our former letter, that the Society proposed to make changes and bring us into direct connection with the Church of England, and that it was the attempt to force this upon us, which caused the disruption, is simply in accordance with the facts, and your attempt to explain it away, only shows how ignorant you are of these facts, and the position assumed by the Society in the matter.

"You say we have been *deprived* of the Lord's Supper. It is not so. No one has ever done this. The way the Society and its agents have been and are acting has made us hesitate to adopt the rite. Not from forgetfulness of our blessed Lord's Command, but because through love and respect for Him we would not let this His precious gift be mixed up in the controversy. When God, in His own good time, has restored us to unity and peace, we can consider the subject, and introduce the rite among us in the way most nearly according with what is written.

"Again, you tell us that because we are not in connection with any other society, you see no guarantee that the present state of things will be permanent. We see the highest guarantee in such beautiful promises as that which was a source of such comfort to St. Paul, when he says : ' My God shall supply *all* your need,' and while we recognize the truth that God often uses human means, have the highest warranty of scripture that He is not only *not* dependent on them but sometimes even refuses to use them. *Your reflection on Mr. Duncan's conduct while in connection with the Society, excited in us a feeling of painful surprise, that two Christians sent out by a Christian Society, could come all the way from England, and in his absence, try to damage the character of one whose service God has so signally acknowledged.* In your letter of yesterday you have, we are happy to say, explained a part of what you originally said, but you still cling to your unfounded assertion that we are indebted to the Society, and not to Mr. Duncan, for the existence of the various industries established among us. We *know* better, and so your assertion goes for nothing.

"*You say the Society still cares for us and is anxious to do all it can for our benefit. How has it shown its interest in us? By bringing ships of war and Government officials to overawe us, by dragging us before courts and magistrates, by fining and imprisoning some of us, by upholding and supporting everything they have seen to be objectionable to us, and by refusing to do any one thing we asked for. We do not call this love and care, but, persecution.*

" By distinctly refusing to give up our land or remove from Metlakahtla, the Society has taken away the need to further discuss matters, and we wish this letter to close the correspondence.

" We believe the time for conferring about or discussing matters has passed, and the time for deciding how best we can obtain the object we have in view has arrived.

" From the people of Metlakahtla and signed for them by

"DAVID LEASK."
Secretary.

This letter was accompanied by the subjoined formal notice :

METLAKAHTLA, BRITISH COLUMBIA,
May 4th, 1886.

To the Church Missionary Society of Salisbury Square, London, England, its Deputies, Agents, and all others who may have power to act for it.

NOTICE

We, the people of Metlakahtla hereby notify you to move off and leave that part of the village site of Metlakahtla, commonly known as Mission Point, as we cannot consent to you occupying this portion of our land to be a continued source of disquiet and annoyance to our village.

For the people of Metlakahtla,

(Signed)

DANIEL NEASHKUMKGEN
JOHN TAIT
ROBERT HEWSU
THOMAS NEASHLAHPSP.

The Society unblushingly publishes the following statement to Christian England :

" When the mission was, in its infancy, removed from Fort Simpson to Metlakahtla, the Indian chief at whose suggestion the change was made, gave the Society the piece of land on which his own house was built; and the principal mission buildings were erected on it." There is not the slightest grain of truth in this statement, as can be fully, and irrefutably proven.

The Society likewise avers, that, "there was moreover no place to which the Society's adherents, could be removed, and a new settlement founded." This is too preposterous for serious consideration, as it is well known, that there are innumerable favorable sites, offering equal advantages, and that there are abundant fields for mission work, untouched in British Columbia.

The Rev. Robert Tomlinson addressed, the following letter to the Deputies :

METLAKAHTLA, May 4th, 1886.

" DEAR SIRS : In the accompanying letter of the Indians, I find the statement that ' they had never been asked to join the Church of England.' It might well be a question how this could be consistent with the fact, that from the first, they had been under the instruction of those who were members of the Church of England, and sent out by the

Society as such. As one who was for many years a missionary of the Society, and for some eleven of those years the only ordained missionary attached to the Society's North Pacific mission, I would beg leave to lay before you some quotations from the Society's annual letters to the missionaries, from which it will appear that such a result was not only compatible with consistency on the part of the missionaries, but even in direct harmony with the views of the Society at the time. These quotations are marked A. B. C., and are from the annual letters of 1876, 1877, 1878. To these I add an extract from a letter of mine to the Committee dated Ankiht-last, August 28th, 1882, written before I left the Society. It is marked D. This extract is but an epitome of the principles which actuated me while in connection with the Society. Nothing was introduced which was in any way contrary to the doctrine and practice of the Church of England. While at the same time we always considered the native Christians had a right to choose whenever they wished to do so, such rules, orders, and ceremonials as were consistent with the word of God and for their benefit.

"Of course it was understood that whenever they did so they would be forming themselves into an Independent Native Church, and must not count upon further help from the Society.

"We followed the example of the Apostle Paul. Himself a member of the Jewish Church, and sent out by that Church, but establishing Independent Native Churches at the various scenes of his labors.

"Yours sincerely,

"ROBT. TOMLINSON."

QUOTATIONS.

Church Missionary House, London,
September, 1876.

ANNUAL LETTER TO MISSIONARIES.

A.

" The time seems to have come when Native "Christian independence may be still further "extended, when the Native Church may not "only draw still less upon European resources "than it does at present, but when by assum- "ing a more distinctly native character, it may "exercise a more powerful attraction on the "heathen population by which it is surrounded. "We would therefore suggest that Missionaries "should represent this subject to their native "brethren, especially to the leading Laymen "amongst them. Let the idea become familiar "with them, let the Lay delegates of the "Church Councils have it frequently brought "before them and should any circumstances "arise indicating the advantage of Church inde- "pendence let the Church Committees and dis- "trict and federal Church Councils at once take "action. *A general request from native Chris-*

"*tians in any Mission for an independent native*
"*Church would be irresistible.*"

Church Missionary House, London,
October 1st, 1877.
ANNUAL LETTER TO MISSIONARIES.

B.

" But while as members of the Church of England
"the Committee and the Society generally
"desire to act in strict obedience to the laws of
"that Church, as well as in conformity to its
"spirit they must protest against the same
"restrictions being imposed on those Native
"Christians in various foreign countries, whom
"it has pleased God to bring to the profession
"of faith in Christ through the Society's in-
"strumentality.

"What the Committee wish to see in these con-
"verts is not submission to the Church of
"England, but the desire for, and ultimately
"the attachments to, *an Independent Native*
"*Church.*

"The Society's object is the Glory of God in the
"evangelization of the heathen and not the
"aggrandizement of the English Church. At
"the same time they regard it as more honor-
"able to the Church of England to be the
"Mother of independent children *than to be the*
"Mistress of subject communities."

Church Missionary House, London,

Oct. 1st, 1878.

ANNUAL LETTER TO THE MISSIONARIES.

C.

'This independence of European help will neces-
"sarily involve independence of coercive Euro-
"pean control. Of this we must not be afraid.
"Our object is *not* the extension of the English
"Church. In many fields such an object would
"be unattainable. . . . The connection
"therefore between the Church of England and
"those native congregations which have been
"formed through the labors of the Church
"Missionary Society's Missionaries must be
"regarded as provisional and temporary. The
"ultimate relation will resemble, probably,
"that which is cherished in the Protestant
"Episcopal Church of the United States, fra-
"ternal or even filial affection, but not the
"smallest approach to subordination."

Ankihtlast, August 28th, 1882.

LETTER OF REV. R. TOMLINSON TO C. M. S.
COMMITTEE.

D.

'My effort among these poor people from the first
"has been to teach them the simple Gospel, to
"lead them to study their Bibles, to encourage

" and help them to rise out of their physical as
" well as moral degradation, and to advance
" their temporal interests. I studiously avoided
" drawing their attention to Church or Secta-
" rian divisions or dissensions, and aimed chiefly
" at uniting them in the closest bonds to fight
" against heathenism and those temptations
" which their position exposes them to."

In these circulars, we have the most positive evidence of the *Society's change of policy* which no
amount of quibbling can explain away   From the
very beginning of his Mission work, Mr. Duncan
had faithfully reported to the Society his methods,
and it, manifested its approval. These very circulars were without a doubt measurably prompted
by Mr. Duncan's successful procedure.

The Society states in one of its publications :—	Why does the Society *contradict itself* a year later in the same publication ?
"May, 1885 :	Sept , 1886 .
"*Almost up to the time of the separation*, there was no reason to suppose that the Mission was other than a Church of England one "	" It had been *long* known to the Committee that the Mission which had been so favorably begun was not being carried on according to the principles which they upheld, or in a way which they could approve."

Who is responsible for the falsifying of its own
statements?

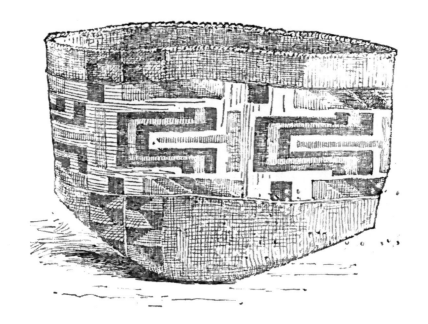

GRASS-WORK BASKET.

Finding itself thwarted in all other attempts to coerce, or bribe, the Metlakahtlans into submission to the Bishop's mandate, the Deputation, devoted itself to the humane act, of urging the Dominion Government to treat them as wild savages, and force upon them the Indian act, and the pernicious system of Indian agents. Pointing out, that this would effectually, put a stop to Mr. Duncan's " influence for *evil over the Indians.*"

After returning to England, the Deputies in order to justify themselves and the Society, attempted to discredit, the views expressed in the letters they had received from the Metlakahtlans, by declaring that they were *made to* state thus and so, by their white teachers, and not allowed to speak freely of their own accord. Why did not the Deputies challenge there, and then, these letters, while yet at Metlakahtla? Be it remembered, that Mr. Duncan was in England at the time. They know that their statement is false, and that those letters do faithfully represent the views of the Metlakahtlans, hence this falsehood is as cowardly as, their attack upon Mr. Duncan in his absence, and, of a piece with such.

To further justify the Society in its offensive conduct, the Deputation, makes a most malevolent attempt to rob Mr. Duncan's work of its lustre, it does not hesitate to assert, that :—" Looking below the surface the state of education is very low." . . . " We found that but *a small proportion of the*

Indians know English and those few far too imper-
fectly—to use with profit an English Bible." . . .
" We have observed the mode of teaching, and the
actual work, and are convinced that they are not
calculated to promote scriptural knowledge and
spiritual life." . . . " The ordinances of religion as instituted by Christ Himself not being
properly administered."

" The Deputation heard of no gatherings for
prayer or for mutual edification, and there are no
signs of missionary zeal among them, nor any attempt to make known the truths of the Gospel to
their heathen fellow-countrymen."

The Deputies thus give the " lie direct " to those
distinguished clergymen, explorers, and others,
whose personal corroborative observations, I have
quoted in Chapters III. and IV. A proud and
noble thing, for two high-minded gentlemen to lend
themselves to such sneaking falsehoods. As to the
standard of education, I need only refer to the reliable testimony which I have quoted.

During the Deputation's stay in the village, the
Metlakahtlans held their regular services of prayer
which however, it seems the Deputation, did not
see fit to attend. The statement in regard to
native missionaries, is also, a wicked falsehood,
as previous evidences prove ; and at the very
time of the Deputies' visit, money was being subscribed by the Metlakahtlans, from their scanty
incomes, to bear the expenses of two native mis-

sionaries, whom they were sending out to heathen tribes.

A statement quite in accord with the foregoing, is that,—"Another extraordinary regulation was that a demand was made on each person who adhered to the Society, for the payment of thirty dollars, which sum, it was *alleged*, had been given by Mr. Duncan, from his own money, to nearly every householder as an assistance in building his house. *One person paid this amount while others declined;* but there can be no doubt that this enactment served as a strong inducement with many to remain, on Mr. Duncan's side. There is no excuse for such an unwarrantable demand having been made."

This assertion is barren of a single grain of truth. No such demand has ever been made! No one has ever returned such money! No one has ever had an opportunity to decline! Alas, Ananias, thou hast been usurped.

Had the object of the Deputation been to make an *honest* investigation, to learn, and convey the *truth*, to the benevolent contributors to the Society's missionary fund in England, one would have naturally expected it, to have ascertained:

1st. The real cause of the rupture, and how it was brought about.

2nd. Whether, or not, the Metlakahtlans had really, and honestly been unanimous, in voting for Mr. Duncan as their leader.

3rd. If, Mr. Duncan had misled the Indians, and, if so, how.

4th. If the Bishop's party was genuine.

5th. Whether the Society was really promoting, or injuring Christianizing and civilizing work, by remaining at Metlakahtla after the people had requested its withdrawal.

6th. Whether, or not, there was any truth in the charges trumped up by the Bishop, and *not* based on the financial secretary's statement respecting Mr. Duncan's accounts, before they made their public accusation.

7th. Whether, or not, Earl Dufferin's declaration to the Indians, that they had a title to the land was right and just, before inciting the present Government to rob the Indians of their land, without compensation, or treaty.

As we have seen, the Deputation did nothing of the sort. It assumed from the first that the Society, the Bishop and his party, were *right*, and that Mr. Duncan, and the Metlakahtlans were *wrong*. It resorted to whatever schemes and intrigues, it thought most likely to succeed in discrediting Mr. Duncan, and whitewashing the Society's and the Bishop's disgraceful acts. On returning to England the *report* was accepted by the Society's officers as highly satisfactory, and the faithful emissaries were heartily thanked. The Society is made by its officers to announce that Mr. Duncan whom they had treated with such *loving kindness,* " could not even if he had wished and requested it, which he has not, be received back into connection with the Society." Forgiveness impossible! The Bible precepts—the Lord's prayer, forgive us as we forgive, the Prodigal son—notwithstanding : what mockery of Christianity, justice and truth! Who the transgressor, who the judge?

Mr. Duncan with gentle mien, has stood firmly and steadfastly, in his devotion to the grand cause for which he, sacrificed a lucrative post, with every prospect of an affluent and commanding position, in England; to accept a paltry £100 a year, and encounter untold hardships and dangers. He held to his purpose of rescue, in the midst of the dark and bloody scenes of his early experience, as, true set as the needle to the pole. He met unswervingly, face to face, the foes of his adopted people ; he ministered tenderly to the wants of the little children, the aged, the decrepit, or the dying brave, who wrestled for the retention of the lamp.

When the legitimate foes had been conquered, and when the fruits of his labors seemed ripening, revealing the signs of an abundant yield, there came an intolerant scourge to devast and lay all to waste. He then, fearlessly threw himself athwart the path, to check the portentous evil as best he might.

The Society in its anxiety to pull down Mr. Duncan's work, has basely intimated, that he seeks gain and glory. How false this is must be evident to all who know the facts. Not only has he dedicated his life to these people, with marked abnegation but every penny of his possessions as well!

The report of the Deputation vindicated the Society in the eyes of its officers—truth was hoodwinked—the sword of justice warped—the poor Indians defrauded—a noble layman's spotless character assailed—the mission's benefactors in England deceived and betrayed!

CHAPTER IX.

THE LAND QUESTION.

THE bitterest was not yet. The Bishop backed by the Society, had aggressively resorted to all manner of devices, to undermine and encompass the ruin of the Metlakahtlan Christian Union. He had even wantonly charged them with crimes of which they were guiltless. His incessant and aggravating persecutions wore them to the quick. They felt that they could no longer endure the presence of this serpent in their midst; for, he spread only strife, and contention, where there should reign peace and harmony.

With a love of home native to all humanity, they with one accord resolved to appeal to the Government for relief from their oppressors. For, had not Canada been renowned for her generous and humane conduct, toward her aboriginal subjects? and, had not Lord Dufferin with much emphasis assured the Metlakahtlans, that their rights should be respected, and their interests guarded by the Queen and the Government? Surely, thought they, the Government will come to our rescue when it knows our wrongs.

Hence the Metlakahtlans laid their grievances

before the Superintendent of Indian Affairs, and through him, before the Government. The Superintendent apparently sympathized with the complainants and expressed his hopes, of a speedy restoration to peace in the settlement. In his annual report of 1884 to the Dominion Government he writes as follows :—

" I am exceedingly sorry to state that serious trouble and the most unhappy religious rancor still exists at Metlakahtla, dividing the Indians and *causing infinite damage to christianity in adjacent localities,* where sides are taken with one or other, of the contending parties. The retirement of either, or both, would seem the only solution of the difficulties ; and if the latter alternative, is not desirable, and as *fully nine-tenths of the people are unanimous and determined in their support of Mr. Duncan,* the withdrawal of the Agents of the Society to more congenial headquarters, would, I think, be greatly in the interests of all concerned."

In Canadian politics there is strong evidence of the existence, and powerful influence of, the log rolling system, and that cowardice, which is born of political fatuity,—the truckling to the Church and other parties, just as some American and English politicians, without actual sympathy, flirt with the Irish party, the Catholic party, or the Labor party—seeking only political ends and fearing to initiate or support, acts of public justice, until they can make political capital thereby.

Regarding, first, its own political security, the Government took no steps whatever, to carry out the recommendations of the Superintendent of Indian Affairs, but pursued a vacillating course, relying upon the chance, of one of the parties subjugating the other. It is well known that individual members, did so far evince the courage of their opinions, as to privately express in not very complimentary terms, their contempt, for the Bishop's conduct, and wish him out of the way,—but, officially it appears they feared to deal with him.

The Metlakahtlans being thus disappointed in obtaining redress, where they had been led to look for, and expect it ; naturally enough turned their attention to their rights in the soil : for were not they the sole owners of the land at Metlakahtla ? and, was not the Bishop a trespasser in their village, against their will ? Hence, they notified him to remove from their property in so much, as, he had no legal footing thereon.

No sooner had the Metlakahtlans taken this position, for the solution of their difficulties, than at once the Government was up in arms, to quell the natural assumption.

And now it was that, the mean, and cowardly silence which the Provincial Government, had, hitherto maintained toward its Native subjects, in reference to land matters, had to be broken. The concealed injustice was now proclaimed ; and, the Natives *to their dismay, were told, that they had no rights in the land whatsoever ; but that the Queen,* *owned, as well as ruled, all the country of British* *Columbia, not excepting even the village site of Met-* *lakahtla !* To back up this appalling announce- ment the Government sent a party of surveyors, especially, to Metlakahtla, to survey two acres in the village, to be alienated from the Natives and secure such to their bitter enemy, the Church Mis- sionary Society. The Natives stood amazed at seeing and hearing all this ; for had they not heard from the lips of Earl Dufferin, when Governor-Gen- eral of Canada, of the goodness, and sympathy of the Queen—and how safely they might confide their interests to her keeping. The question with them arose, who were they to believe—Lord Dufferin when speaking in the name of the Queen, or, the Provincial Government ? Were they to throw aside their long-treasured trust in the justice of British Law, and bow submissively, at once to glar- ing avarice, and cruel wrong, announced and enact- ed in the name of law ?

In their perplexity the Indians sought and ob- tained the advice of an eminent lawyer at Victoria ; and his opinion was, " that Indians cannot be mo- lested in the possession of lands occupied by them prior to the advent of white men unless in pursuance of treaties duly entered into by them."

Before, the above opinion reached Metlakahtla, it was shown to the Provincial Executive Council, and they requested it might be kept from the knowledge of the Indians, and they promised to hand over the two acres of the village-site to the Metlakahtlans, if the Dominion Government would ask them to do so.

It being supposed from this, that the two governments were about to adjust matters without having recourse to law, it was therefore, thought best that the Indians should not immediately be made acquainted with the lawyer's opinion. They were told what the Provincial Government had offered, and in order to facilitate an amicable arrangement, the Metlakahtlans deputed three of their members to go to Ottawa, in the summer of 1885, and lay their complaints personally before the Superintendent-General of Indian Affairs. This trip covering *a journey of seven thousand miles*, involved expenses very large for so poor a people to bear, yet, they cheerfully made the sacrifice, so anxious were they to have the wonted peace, and the prosperity of their settlement restored.

The results of their appeal to Ottawa, were regarded by the Indians on the return of their Delegates, as satisfactory; inasmuch as Sir John Macdonald had *promised* to communicate with the Church Missionary Society of London, and ask or advise that Society to withdraw its agents from Metlakahtla; and, also he assured them, that all their other grievances should be adjusted.

While in Ottawa with the Delegates Mr. Duncan, at the request of the Deputy Minister of Indian Affairs, drew up an outline of a new policy for the management of the Native subjects in British Columbia, by which in his opinion the difficulties which had arisen with the Natives, would effectually be removed, and peace, and loyalty, restored.

No exception was taken to Mr. Duncan's recommendations — only, that the Deputy Minister, thought it would be difficult to find a man qualified to carry them out.

During an interview, Sir John Macdonald intimated that he would be glad to have Mr. Duncan appointed Government agent, to be responsible for the management of the Northern Section, of the British Columbian Indians. Mr. Duncan manifested his readiness to accept the position provided the Indians were accorded their rights, in conformity with the suggestions he had filed with the Government, and he called the attention of the ministers to the anomalous condition of the land question, in the Province, and quoted opinions of Government authorities from Sessional papers, and Blue Books of Canada.

The Minister of Interior, Mackenzie's Government, writing from Ottawa November 2, 1874, to the Government of British Columbia, says :—

" *A cursory glance at these documents (from Indian Commissioner and others) is enough to show that the present state of the Indian land ques-*

tion in our territory west of the Rocky Mountains
is most unsatisfactory—and that it is the occasion
not only of great discontent among the aboriginal
tribes, but, also of serious alarm to the white settlers. . . .

"The guaranteeing the Aborigines of British
Columbia, the continuance of a policy as liberal as
was pursued by the Local Government seems little
short of a mockery of their claims. IF THERE HAS
NOT BEEN AN INDIAN WAR IT IS NOT BECAUSE
THERE HAS BEEN NO INJUSTICE TO THE INDIANS,
but because the Indians have not been sufficiently
united. . . .

" In laying the foundation of an Indian Policy
in that Province on the same permanent and satisfactory basis as in the other portions of the Dominion—the Government of the Dominion, feel they
would not be justified in limiting their efforts to
what under the strict letter of the Terms of Union,
they were called upon to do. They feel that A
GREAT NATIONAL QUESTION like this,—a question
involving possibly in the near future an Indian
war, with all its horrors, should be approached in
a very different spirit, and dealt with upon other
and higher grounds. . . .

" The policy foreshadowed in the provision of
the 13th Clause of British Columbia Terms of
Union, is plainly, altogether inadequate to satisfy
the fair, and reasonable demands, of the Indians.
To satisfy these demands, and to secure the good·

19

*will of the Natives—the Dominion and Local
Governments must look beyond the terms of that
agreement; and be governed in their conduct toward the aborigines by the justice of their claims,
and by the necessities of the case."*

It should be noticed in reference to the foregoing
quotation from the Blue Book, that the Minister
of Interior of Canada, is complaining to the British
Columbian Government, of the gross injustice to
the Indians, in regard to their land rights, which
the terms of Union embodied, and, he is demanding that a just, and liberal policy be inaugurated.

So anxious had the Administration, under Sir
John Macdonald, been to get British Columbia into
the Union with Canada, that so little a matter as
justice, to the aborigines was apparently lost sight
of, and the Provincial Land Grabbers had all their
own way.   Had it not been that the Mackenzie
Government, on succeeding to power soon after,
put a check upon—the cruel robbery of the aboriginal subjects which had already been sanctioned,
would no doubt have been enforced by the Dominion.   Happily however a change of Administration came in time to avert this calamity, and
the Minister of Interior, boldly unmasked, and denounced the wrong.   It is certain that no Cabinet
Minister in his official capacity, would have had the
effrontery, to use the language, which this Minister
of Interior did, had he not been convinced, that

the evil he was denouncing, was an outrage on humanity.

Now for the facts, which had met the eye, and raised the indignation of this Minister. In British Columbia there were at that time about 30,000 whites and about the same number of aborigines. The Country is nearly three times as large as England—Ireland—Scotland and Wales combined— viz., 218,375,200 acres—yet out of all this immense territory all the land the 30,000 whites agreed to allow the 30,000 natives,—the ancient and original inhabitants of the soil—was a miserable *two acres per capita*, or in the aggregate something less than ten miles square !! It can scarcely be believed that there are men living in this 19th century, under the Christian rule of Queen Victoria, who could be guilty of planning such a scheme of wholesale robbery in the name of law and government. Yet such men hold up their heads in British Columbia, and find ardent supporters in the Church Missionary Society of London, and its lordly Bishop !

Next may be given some quotations from a Report written from the Department of Justice in Canada, and signed by both the Minister of Justice, and the Deputy Minister, dated Ottawa 19th Jan. 1875.

"Nor can the undersigned find that there is any legislation in force in British Columbia which provides reservations of land for the Indians. . . .

"No surrenders of lands in British Columbia

Province has ever been obtained from the Indian tribes with one exception. . . .

"Any reservations which have been made have been arbitrary on the part of the Government, and without the assent of the Indians. . . .

"There is not a shadow of doubt that from the earliest times England has always felt it imperative to meet the Indians in Council and to obtain surrenders of tracts of Canada as from time to time, such were required for the purposes of settlement. . . .

"It is sufficient for present purpose to ascertain the policy of England in respect to the acquisition of the Indian territorial rights, and how entirely that policy has been followed to the present time except in the instance of British Columbia."

The above quotations speak for themselves.

Earl Dufferin, Governor-General of Canada, delivered the following speech on the Land Question at Government House, Victoria, B. C., September 20, 1876:

EARL DUFFERIN'S SPEECH ON THE LAND QUESTION.

"From my first arrival in Canada I have been very much occupied with the condition of the Indian population in this province. You must remember that the Indian population are not represented in Parliament, and, consequently, that the Governor-General is bound to watch over their welfare with especial solicitude. Now we must all admit that the condition of the Indian question in British Columbia is not satisfactory. Most unfortunately, as I think, there has been an initial error ever since Sir James Douglass quitted office, in the Government of British Columbia neglecting to recognize what is known as the Indian title. In Canada this has always been done: no Government, whether provincial or central, has failed to acknowledge that *the original title to the lands existed in the Indian tribes* and the communities that hunted or wandered over them. *Before we touch an acre we make a treaty* with the chief representing the bands we are dealing with, and *having agreed upon and paid the stipulated price*, oftentimes arrived at after a great deal of haggling and difficulty, *we enter into possession, but not until then do we consider that we are entitled to deal with a single acre.* The result has been that in Canada our Indians are contented, well affected to the white man, and amenable to the laws and Government. At this very moment the Lieutenant-Governor of Manitoba, has gone on a distant expedition in order to make a treaty with the tribes to the northward of Saskatchewan. Last year he made two treaties with the Crees and Chippeways, next year it has been arranged that he should make a treaty with the Blackfeet, and when this is done the British Crown will have acquired a title to every acre that lies between Lake Superior and the top of the

Rocky Mountains. But in British Columbia—except in a few places where under the jurisdiction of the Hudson's Bay Co., or under the auspices of Sir James Douglass, a similar practice has been adopted—the Provincial Government, has always assumed that the fee simple in, as well as the sovereignty over, the land, reside in the Queen. Acting upon this principle they have granted extensive grazing leases, and otherwise dealt with various sections of the country as greatly to restrict or interfere with the prescriptive rights of the Queen's Indian subjects. As a consequence, there has come to exist an unsatisfactory feeling among the Indian population. Intimations of this reached me at Ottawa two or three years ago, and since I have come into the province my misgivings on the subject have been confirmed. Now, I consider that our Indian fellow-subjects are entitled to exactly the same civil rights under the law, as are possessed by the white population, and if an Indian can prove prescriptive right of way to a fishing-station, or right of any other kind, that that right should no more be ignored than if it were the case of a white man. I am well aware that among the coast Indians the land question does not present the same characteristics as in other parts of Canada, or as it does in the grass countries of the interior of this province; but I have also been able to understand that in these latter districts, it may be even more necessary to deal justly and liberally with the Indian in re-

gard to his land rights, than on the prairies of the
North West. I am very happy that the British
Columbian Government, have recognized the necessity of assisting the Dominion Government, in
ameliorating the present condition of affairs in this
respect, and that it has agreed to the creation of a
joint commission for the purpose of putting the interests of the Indian population on a more satisfactory footing. Of course in what I have said I do
not mean that in our desire to be humane, and to
act justly, we should do anything unreasonable or
Quixotic, or that rights already acquired by white
men should be inconsiderately invaded or recalled,
but, I would venture to put the Government of
British Columbia on its guard against the fatal
eventualities which might arise should a sense of
injustice provoke the Indian population to violence,
or, into a collision with our scattered settlers. Probably there has gone forth among them very incorrect, and exaggerated information of the warlike
achievements of their brethren in Dakota, and
their uneducated minds are incapable of calculating
chances. Of course, there is no danger of any serious or permanent revolt, but it must be remembered that even an accidental collision in which
blood was shed, might have a most disastrous effect upon our present satisfactory relations with the
warlike tribes in the North West, whose amity, and
adhesion, to our system of government, is so essential to the progress of the Pacific Railway ; and I

make this appeal, as I may call it, with all the more earnestness since I have convinced myself of the degree to which, if properly dealt with, the Indian population might be made to contribute to the development of the wealth, and resources, of the province. I have now seen them in all phases of their existence, from the half-naked savage in a red blanket, perched like a bird of prey upon a rock, trying to catch his miserable dinner of fish, to the neat Indian maidens in Mr. Duncan's school at Metlakahtla, as modest, and as well-dressed as any clergyman's daughter in an English parish, and to the shrewd horse-riding Siwash of the Thompson Valley, with his racers in training for the Ashcroft stakes, and as proud of his stock-yard and turnip-field as a British squire. In his first condition it is evident he is scarcely a producer or a consumer; in his second, he is eminently both, and in proportion as he can be raised to the higher level of civilization will he contribute to the vital energies of the province. What you want are not resources, but human beings to develop them, and, consume them. Raise your 30,000 Indians to the level which Mr. Duncan has taught us is possible, and consider what an enormous amount of vital power you will have added to your present strength."

These words of Lord Dufferin, require no elucidation, they give no uncertain sound, as to the distinguished statesman's views, of the injustice, which has been fastened upon the Indians in regard to their land: but, his eloquent, and powerful arguments, were lost upon the British Columbian authorities. No change of policy has ensued since his visit to the Province, and quite recently the Chief-Justice at Victoria, while arguing on the question of the Indians' land rights, declared, emphatically that the Indians of British Columbia, *have no rights in the land, whatever,* but such as the Crown out of its bounty and charity may accord them ; and added, that all that Earl Dufferin in his great speech had said to the contrary, was only " *blarney for the mob !!* "

Now to return again to what took place at Ottawa. It seemed apparent to Mr. Duncan, and the Indian Delegates—judging from Sir John Macdonald's *promises*—that the Indians' grievances were in a fair way to be settled without litigation, and this decided Mr. Duncan not to return at once to Metlakahtla ; but to give time to Sir John Macdonald to frame the improved policy, for the Native Subjects, for the ensuing parliament, as he had intimated that he would then bring it forward. Mr. Duncan, in the interim went to England, on behalf of the Metlakahtlans. While there he had an interview with the Secretaries of the Church Missionary Society, and learnt from them, that, Sir John Macdonald, had written the letter, he had promised the Metlakahtlans he would write, advising the Society to withdraw from Metlakahtla. Mr. Duncan also met Sir John Macdonald in London by appointment, and during the interview was told by Sir John, that a Deputation from the Church Missionary Society, had waited upon him to discuss the situation, but that he had adhered strictly, to the advice which he had previously offered the Society by letter. Sir John, also assured Mr. Duncan, that as soon as the difficulty with the Society was out of the way, he, would secure for him, the appointment he had alluded to while in Ottawa.

However, it must be distinctly borne in mind that Mr. Duncan was *not* seeking Government employment, but, he had promised only to be responsible for the inauguration of the new policy, which he had drafted, *if*, it was accepted by the Government—as he well knew by accepting the position, and establishing a new era in the management of aboriginal people, he would be conferring a benefit to Indians generally throughout the land.

It would seem however before Sir John Macdonald left London, and after having had a second interview with the representatives of the Society, *he, had changed his mind, and his plans.* Mr. Duncan was informed by one of the Secretaries of the Society, that Sir John Macdonald and the Society, *had come to an understanding.* Which *understanding* it would seem secured to the Society the invaluable services and advocacy of this Minister of State; and insured to him this powerful Church of England Missionary Society's moral endorsement of his iniquitous Indian policy; and the political

LEADER OF THE METLAKAHTLA BRASS-BAND.

support of this Society's Agents, and its, sympa-
thizers in the Church of England party of Canada,
for the approaching general election which must
decide his political fate.

While still in London Mr. Duncan thought it
well as matters had turned; to acquaint the Aborigines Protection Society, with the circumstances
surrounding the Indian land question.   The following is a copy of a letter he addressed to the Secretary of that Society:

"LONDON, 5th March, 1886.

"DEAR SIR: I beg to address you on behalf of
the Tsimshean and other Indian tribes inhabiting
the northern portion of British Columbia, with a
view of soliciting on their account the sympathy and
aid of the Aborigines Protection Society, in connection with the question of their land interests.
From authoritative government documents in Canada it is clearly demonstrable that the Indian land
question in British Columbia is in a very unsatisfactory state, owing as it would seem, to the arbitrary, and unprecedented policy, adopted by the
Government in regard to it.

" It appears that the Imperial edicts, and usages,
which have always defined, and guarded, Indian land
rights in Canada, are by the Provincial Government
of British Columbia, virtually ignored :—the Indian
title is not recognized, nor any treaties with the
Indians made, but an absolute control of all the

lands of the Province is assumed in the name of the Queen, as if the aborigines were a conquered race, and all their ancient inheritance had been confiscated.

"These anomalies have been pointed out to the Provincial Government, by the Minister of Justice, and the Minister of Interior in Canada, in the years 1874 and 1875 (and I might add in 1876 by Earl Dufferin, Gov.-Gen'l. of Canada) but apparently without effect.

"The Indians themselves have till lately been comparatively silent on land matters. Their silence may be ascribed partly, to their ignorance of the Government policy, and partly, because the question had not been directly forced upon their attention by any great encroachment upon their ancient privileges,—owing to the sparseness of white settlers as yet in the North.

"A change however, in this respect has taken place. The Indians are now fully alive to the importance of the land question, and, its bearing, on their prosperity, and social progress. The action of the Government which more than anything else precipitated this change, was their ordering the survey of two acres of land in the centre of the Indian village of Metlakahtla, for the purpose of conveying the same to a religious Society, and thereby asserting their claim to absolute control over the land even in a village-site, in spite of the Indians' protest.

" Though the Indian proprietors were greatly incensed by this overbearing act of injustice, I am happy to say that no violence was offered to the Government servants, who made the survey. The Indians decided rather to appeal to the Law Courts, and trust in the justice of their case.

" Legal advice was obtained from one of the most prominent lawyers in Victoria, who after referring to the Sessional Papers of Canada and Imperial Edicts, says—' Hence, it is I think apparent that Indians cannot be molested in their possession of lands occupied by them prior to the advent of white men unless in pursuance of treaties duly entered into by them.'

" When the legal opinion was shown the Provincial Government, they requested that the Indians might not be made acquainted with it, and offered to hand over the two acres of land to the Indians ; if, the Dominion Government would ask them to do so.

" This concession was evidently only an attempt to shift responsibility on to the Dominion Government, (for so did the Premier of Canada regard it) hence nothing came of it.

" The Indians then determined before invoking the law, to represent their case to the Indian Department, and three Indian Delegates were accordingly sent to Ottawa last summer. The result of this appeal to the Super't-General of Indian Affairs, was to return to the Indian complainants an assurance that their grievances would receive careful attention, and that steps would be taken, which it was hoped would soon remove all causes of complaint.

"It is now about seven months since these assurances were made, but no remedy of the evils complained of, is forthcoming, and I fear there is little prospect of any remedy being found without an appeal to the law.

"I am hoping to return to Metlakahtla early next month, and I should be very glad if on my arrival there I can inform the Indians that the Aborigines Protection Society, had decided to aid them in vindicating their rights, and thus afford them a proof there are in England, those who take pleasure in defending the weak, and helping the poor, without regard to race or nationality.   I remain, Dear Sir, yours faithfully,

W. DUNCAN."

"To F. W. CHESSON, ESQ.,
        Sec'y Abor. Prot. Society,
                London."

To the above letter the following reply was received.

"ABORIGINES PROTECTION SOCIETY,
    6 ROOM, BROADWAY CHAMBERS, WESTMINSTER,
            LONDON, S. W , March 25, 1886.

"DEAR MR. DUNCAN: At a Meeting of the Committee held here a few days ago, Sir Robert Fowler, M.P., Mr. George Palmer, late M.P., for Reading, Mr. Alfred Fowell Buxton and I, were appointed a deputation to wait upon Sir Charles Tupper with reference to the Indian difficulty in British Columbia. We shall wait upon him within the next fortnight, and support the cause of the poor Indians. Very faithfully yours,

F. W. Chesson, *Sec'y.*"
"To W. Duncan, Esq."

The Metlakahtlans received a letter last summer (1886) from the Aborigines Protection Society, informing them that a Deputation from that Society had waited upon Sir Chas. Tupper—High Commissioner of Canada, in London and presented a Memorial to him on their behalf.

For this sympathy and help from the Aborigines Society, the Metlakahtlans seemed very grateful, and the Native Secretary of the Council wrote a letter of thanks to that society.

Before leaving England Mr. Duncan had occasion to address another letter to Sir John Macdonald, of which the following is a copy.

"London, March 24, 1886.
"*The Right Honorable* Sir John A. Macdonald, K.C.B., *Superintendent-Gen'l of Indian Affairs*, Ottawa.

"Sir: I have this day received letters from Metlakahtla, conveying to me information with which I feel it my duty, to make you acquainted without delay.

" From the words and assurances you were good enough to send through the Deputation, which waited upon you last summer in Ottawa—the Indians of the settlement, and neighboring tribes, were induced to refrain from immediately appealing to the Law in vindication of their land claims, and were led to hope that their complaints against the Church Missionary Society Agents, would receive your immediate attention, and, personal intervention.

" It is now eight months since these assurances were received, and, these hopes indulged, but I regret to say the Indians are now complaining even more bitterly, than ever, of the overbearing effrontery of the Agents of the Society.

" It appears that the Bishop has lately read a letter to his few adherents, which they were led to believe emanated from you, and from which they were assured the two acres of the village-site, known as Mission Point, now belong to the Church Missionary Society.

" After this announcement was made—a number of flags were hoisted over the Bishop's house—cannons were fired, and a party paraded the village with banners, and triumphant hilarity. The mass of Indians who will have nothing to do with the Bishop were then informed that the land question, was now settled, by you ; and, that the efforts of the Deputation last summer, had resulted in nothing.

"On being asked however to show your letter —the Bishop admitted, that the letter he had read was not written by you, but Mr. Fenn of the C. M. Society had written it to convey the words uttered by you, at an interview with the representatives of the Society in London.

"I deeply regret these occurrences, and cannot but feel sure that the Bishop has made an exaggerated, and an improper, use of your words, to the Society, and thus, made matters worse than ever to arrange.

"There seems no course open now, which will prove a satisfaction to the Indians but an appeal to the Law, and unless all such offensive prejudging of the case as has been recently enacted be stopped, I fear the Indians will be driven to desperation.

"I am thankful to add that the Aborigines Protection Society, are now in possession of the facts of the case, in which they feel a deep interest.

"Their assistance to bring matters to a right issue is already promised.

"I hope to be passing through Ottawa on my return to Metlakahtla, about the middle of April, when I trust you will favor me with an interview at which I can give you further particulars. I remain, etc.   "W. DUNCAN."

In April (1886) Mr. Duncan left England to return to Metlakahtla. On his way he called at Ottawa but was unable to secure an interview with

20

Sir John Macdonald. Not, therefore, being able to see the Head chief, he addressed a letter to the Deputy of which the following is a copy :

"OTTAWA, April 20, 1886.

"SIR : Being now on my way to Metlakahtla and feeling assured that on my arrival there the Indians will press me for information relative to their affairs, now, before the Indian Department. I am therefore, anxious to lay before you the questions I anticipate they will ask me, and beg that you will be good enough to furnish me with such answers, as I may give them in your name. The questions are as follows.

"1st. Will the Land (Reserve) Commissioner Mr. O'Reilly receive orders to adjust the difficulty between the Tsimshean and the Nass River Indians, in connection with the fishing interests and occupancy of the land on the banks of the Nass River?

"2d. Will the Land (Reserve) Commissioner receive orders to meet the Tsimshean Indians in Council to reconsider and readjust their Reserves?

"3d. Has the Superintendent-General of Indian Affairs given to the Committee of the Church Missionary Society, the authority of his word that the two acres known as Mission Point at Metlakahtla, belong to that Society?

"4th. Is the Indian Department prepared to advise the Government of British Columbia to enter into treaties with the Indians of that Province in regard to Lands to be surrendered by them?

" 5th. Should the Indians of Metlakahtla be compelled to test the legality of the survey of Mission Point made by orders of the British Columbian Government; what, attitude will the Indian Department take in reference to their action?

" 6th. Does the Indian Department permit bands of natives to settle upon lands which are the private property of white men or of Religious Societies—the Indians not having been instructed as to the exigencies involved in their action?

" 7th. Is the Indian Department satisfied with the work and conduct of the Magistrate appointed over the Indians in the Northern portion of British Columbia, and if not are they proposing to remove him? I have the honor to be Sir, your humble and obedient servant, " W. DUNCAN."
"To THE DEPUTY MINISTER OF INDIAN AFFAIRS,
Ottawa."

The Deputy Minister promised to mail an answer to the foregoing letter in a short time.

On Mr. Duncan's arrival at Metlakahtla the Indians pressed him for information on the questions which they had laid before the Government; and naturally enough, were greatly disappointed, when told he had no definite information to give them. However, he, informed them, that he had anticipated their inquiries, and placed such before the Deputy Minister of Indian Affairs, and further, that he hoped the next mail,—some two or three weeks hence,—would bring them the Deputy's reply.

The next mail brought no letter from the Government or the Indian Department : Hence it was that Mr. Duncan addressed a further communication to Sir John Macdonald,—a copy of which is as follows.

" METLAKAHTLA, May 29, 1886.
" *The Right Hon.* SIR JOHN A. MACDONALD, K.C.B., *Supt.-General of Indian Affairs*, OTTAWA.

" SIR : On the 20th ult. at Ottawa I had the honor to submit to the Deputy Minister of Indian Affairs certain questions, which are now engrossing the minds of the Indians in this Section of the Country.

" On my arrival at Metlakahtla on the 10th inst. I found as I had anticipated, the Indians were fully expecting some definite information from me on these questions. All that I could tell them was that the Deputy Minister had promised a communication on the subject, and that I had reason to hope the next mail (about three weeks later) would bring them the desired information. In the mean time, fresh troubles have arisen between the Tsimshean and Nass River Indians, in reference to their land claims, making us look even more eagerly for the promised communication.

" Yesterday the mail arrived but without any let-

ter from the Deputy Minister, and while the Indians were brooding over this fresh disappointment,
they ascertained that the Steamer had brought up
a gentleman to survey Reserves. This led to their
calling a meeting at which I gather, they complained bitterly of the treatment they are receiving
at the hands of the Government, in reference to
their land claims, especially, when they had been
led to expect from *promises* made them through
their Delegates last summer, that Reserves would
be reconsidered and readjusted before being finally
fixed.

"I learn since commencing this letter that the
Fort Simpson Indians, have also taken alarm at the
arrival of the Surveyor and have written a letter to
Metlakahtla calling the Indians to meet them to
consider the situation.

" I do sincerely hope the Government will without delay adopt a course which will result in settling
the minds of the Indians on the land question before some fatal blow is given to the peace of the
Country. I have the honor to be, sir,
" Your humble and obedient servant,
" W. DUNCAN."

Mr. Duncan was non-plussed, that he received no
replies to either of the letters addressed to Sir John
Macdonald, or, to the one, he sent to the Deputy
Minister. Common courtesy alone, would have demanded a respectful answer to these communica-

tions, involving as they did, the welfare of several thousand of Her Majesty's loyal subjects, addressed in a regular and official manner.

What answer could be made, when these people had been cruelly betrayed—the Minister whose duty it was to protect them had played them false; bartered their rights and independence to their designing enemies.

Instead of the Reserve Commission being sent to the Tsimsheans, to readjust his previous incomplete work, as had been promised,—a surveying party was sent to Metlakahtla, in the autumn of 1886,— authorized and paid by the Dominion Government, to survey what it pleased the Government to allow the Indians for a reserve,—*although there had been no treaty, or agreement made with the Indians, for the lands which they were called upon to surrender.*

Naturally enough the Indians were aroused and indignant, at this fresh violation of all right dealing; and after due deliberation, decided to forbid the survey being made—with a view to bring their land matters to an issue. They saw the time had come when their title to the land must be decided; either substantiated, or nullified forever in a court of law. As the news spread, the Indians gathered from various quarters, to join in the protest against the survey.

They quietly but resolutely prevented the surveyors from going on with their work. " The sur-

NATIVE WOVEN MANTLE.

veyor plants his instrument ; the natives take it up.
The surveyor drives a stake ; the natives pull it up.
The surveyor lays a chain ; the natives take it
away."

The Indians however, *used no violence*, though
frequently provoked, by the irritating and insolent
conduct of the surveying party.

The Church Missionary Society, with its usual
high-minded sense of truth, and justice, referring to
this incident delivers itself, as follows :

" With deep regret we have to report the renewal
of lawless proceedings on the part of Mr. Duncan's
Indians at Metlakahtla, under his direct sanction
(acknowledged *by himself*) *if not* (*as is believed*) *at
his instigation*."

In another reference to the Land Question, the
Society publishes the following charge :

" We now come to what is undoubtedly the heart
of the matter. The object of Mr. Duncan, is power :
the desire of the Indians is land. The land question is here, as it has been elsewhere, the secret of
all the discontent, and Mr. Duncan has skilfully
fostered, and worked upon the prejudices of the
people. He has represented to them that the whole
of the land belongs to them, and not to the Government; and the result has been a lawless defiance of
authority."

These are the sort of falsehoods the blundering
officers of the Church Missionary Society, have been
publishing to the world, to cover their own shame

and discomfiture.   Why accuse Mr. Duncan of informing the Indians ?   Did not that distinguished
Governor-General Earl Dufferin, tell them that not
an acre of their land, should be taken from them
until surrendered by treaty, or paid for, at a stipulated price ?   No one familiar with the history of
Metlakahtla, is likely to believe, the assertion that
Mr. Duncan instigated his people, to violence, or
lawlessness.

The officers of the Society, have arrayed themselves on the side of lawless land-grabbers to de-
fraud the poor Natives of their land, and they cannot veil their own infamy, by slandering a man,
whose shoes, they have shown themselves unworthy
to unlatchet.

The facts of the case are, that, in order to prevent
hostile feeling from arising, the Indians not only
reasoned with the Chief of the Surveyors, but, also
showed him the letter, they had received from Sir
John Macdonald, the contents of which implied
that their grievances about land matters, would be
settled before the survey was made.

While affairs were thus pending the action of the
Government, the Metlakahtlans decided for the sake
of clearing up the whole of the land question—to
take formal possession of the two acres of their village-site, which the Government had assumed the
right to alienate.   To this end they built a house
on the two acres and placed men,—*unarmed men,*—
in charge of it ; which action the Church Missionary

Society, has been pleased to describe, as an outrage on the Bishop.

In the absence of the Bishop it says; "About 100 Indians, led by Mr. Duncan's chief lieutenants, broke down the fence surrounding the mission ground, and began to put up the new building. Mr. N—— protested, but was informed they did it expressly to assert their right to the land. The building was soon finished and was then occupied by *armed men.*" . . . On the Bishop's return, "As the steamer's anchor was let go, a boat ran alongside, and one of the Bishop's lads leaped on deck. He brought a scrap of paper" . . . begging the Bishop " not to land, as there would be violence to prevent him coming home. He instantly jumped into the boat and pulled to shore. Crowds of Indians awaited him, but his own people men and women, had come down to the shore armed, and surrounded him as he stepped ashore. The other Indians were cowed and fell back. On reaching his house, he found that during his absence Mr. Duncan's Indians, had erected a building on the Mission ground within a yard of his windows."

The statements that the building was occupied by armed men, and that an armed and threatening mob of Metlakahtlans awaited the Bishop's landing, are utter fabrications, coined in the brain of the Society's faithful Agent.

The Rev. Robert Tomlinson, who was present at the time, thus refutes the Society's report :—"As

regards that portion of the paragraph, which refers to the landing of Bishop Ridley, had it appeared in an ordinary newspaper it might well be
treated as a huge joke, but appearing where it does,
it affords a most melancholy example of the length
to which the agents of the Society, emboldened by
our long forbearance, and silence, are prepared to
go in their endeavor to blind Christians at home,
and to bolster up the indefensible position, of the
Society at Metlakahtla.

"That the building was occupied by armed men
—that there was the smallest idea of preventing the
Bishop's landing—or the least show of resistance,
or any ground for apprehension on the part of
Bishop Ridley . . . or that crowds of Indians
awaited him, or that they were cowed by and fell
back from his armed adherents, is all simply untrue.
Can anything be more lamentably shocking than
that, in giving a simple account, those who were
eye-witnesses and supposed to be above equivocation, much more falsehood, should fall so low?

"Two questions naturally suggest themselves in
connection with this incident.   The first is, whether
the Bishop, by sanctioning, if not directly approving,
of the conduct of the C. M. S. adherents at Metlakahtla, men and *women* coming armed to protect
him, and this be it remembered against those who
had not even threatened him, much less displayed
arms, whether, I say bearing this in mind, the saying 'that Missionary work which once was carried

on by a Henry Martyn is now carried on by a Martini-Henry,' has not passed from a sceptic's sneer to an actual fact ?

" The second, and more serious question is, if the notices of these missions which have appeared in the Society's publications, are so much at variance with the facts they are supposed to relate, what credence can be given to the accounts of the work carried on at other missions of the Society? Has not the time come when the Christian public should demand an opportunity of judging of these facts, other than from the garbled accounts of prejudiced secretaries ? "

Some may question the wisdom of the Metlakahtlans' action in making a test case of the two acres;* but be it remembered, these two acres had been arbitrarily alienated from them by the Government, without compensation, treaty, or surrender by them of any kind whatsoever; and these two acres were, notwithstanding their protest, assigned, to their enemies, who made the premises a centre for disturbing the peace of their village. Furthermore, they were now officially informed that despite

---

* In allowing the Society's buildings to be erected on the two acres—the Indians had no idea of surrendering the land, nor, did they ever consent in any way, shape, or manner, to give the Society a title. They regarded the measures of the Government as solely a formal matter to keep off white trespassers. The Indians themselves, however, had no voice in the arrangement. See pages 260–261.

the legal opinions they had obtained, as well as the assurances, before cited of Earl Dufferin ; the Provincial Government had decided that they had no rights whatever to the soil, and, that though they had inherited it from their forefathers, they were simply objects of charity, and their occupancy of any plots of land set apart for them, was solely by the generous bounty of the crown.

Nor was this all. They saw that even reserve titles granted by the Government were worthless : for, the reserve rights of the neighboring tribes were being ruthlessly violated and set at naught, by the administration. The time was ripe to settle conclusively for all time, their rights as loyal subjects. There was a vital principle at stake, which involved their very homes, the sacred roofs that sheltered them and their families.

This subject of test cases, is not so insignificant as might appear at a glance. Since in civic, and politic history many of the most important events have pivoted upon like tests. John Hampden suffered imprisonment rather than pay a few paltry shillings on the levy of Charles the First, because, his test case involved the rights of Englishmen at large, and his action ultimately brought them relief. The people of England then occupied very much the same position as the Natives of British Columbia do now ; inasmuch, as the Exchequer Chamber had placed at the disposal of the crown, the entire property of the English people ; and the King had his Star Chamber, and High Commission Courts, which filled a place similar to that occupied by certain high-minded justice-dealers, of British Columbia, of the present day.

At the same period, the King gave the Puritans and the Scots a holy cause; just as the Church Missionary Society sustained by the Dominion and Provincial Governments, has given a holy cause to the Metlakahtlans. Even Charles the First's cruel system of terrorizing, and imprisoning, those patriots who dared to resist the unlawful trespass of their rights, has been reproduced. And to make the parallel, complete, Canada has the prototype of Charles the First, in the person of Sir John Macdonald the Prime Minister, of whom it may be said, as of Charles the First:—" his promises were violated without scruple or shame!"

It would seem, that Sir John, not only bartered the inherited rights of the Metlakahtlans to the Church Missionary Society, but, also hired himself out to that body as its advocate. In his report, 1887, as Superintendent-General of Indian Affairs, of the Dominion of Canada, he ignores and says not a word about the correspondence, and evidences of their grievances, placed before him by the Metlakahtlans; nor, does he say a word, about his own official promises which he so wantonly violated, but he proceeds to cover up his infamy, by reiterating statements, which originated with the Society, and which he knows by positive evidences, to be absolutely untrue.

In referring to the Metlakahtlans' protest against
the survey, he says their action was "it is feared,
the result of *evil counsel* given them by those who
should, from the position occupied by them, toward
the Indians, have been their advisers for good instead of for *evil*.   This is all the more to be regretted, in view of the fact that *one* at least if not
more, of those *suspected* of having *used their influence with the Indians to instigate them to the com-
mittal of the acts of lawlessness* above described, was
for many years largely instrumental in promoting
their welfare, and indeed in reclaiming them from
their condition as savages.   But of late years *owing
to chagrin* at the action of the Church Missionary
Society, in whose service the work had been from
the outset carried on, *in refusing its sanction* to certain *changes* inaugurated *or proposed to be introduced* in the ritual of the Church of England at
Metlakahtla, which resulted in the appointment of
Bishop Ridley . . .   bitter antagonism has been
displayed ; the former lay incumbent of the mission, being the leader of a very large contingent of
the Indian population, whose feeling toward Bishop
Ridley and his adherents, has led them to the commission of acts, which cannot even be justified on
the ground of law, much less on that of Christian
amity."

Sir John, knows the history of this contest too
well, to make such a statement through ignorance.
He knows that Mr. Duncan, has not instigated the

Indians to revolt, or to lawlessness; and that the Society and the Government officials alone, have broken the peace, and committed acts of violence.

A more deliberate misstatement, can hardly be conceived than Sir John's, declaration, that the rupture between the Society and the Metlakahtlans, was brought about by the Society's "*refusing its sanction* to certain *changes* inaugurated or *proposed to be introduced* in the ritual of the Church of England at Metlakahtla" by Mr. Duncan. I have placed before my readers in Chapters VI. and VII. abundant evidence, that the *change* has been solely on the part of the Society.

It seems almost incredible that this great Minister of State, should find it necessary to resort, to such petty intrigues against a struggling community; in order to gain his personal ends, and maintain his political position.

Mr. Duncan who would not be a tool in the hands of this man, to rob the Indians, is now pitilessly put upon and slandered by him.

Nearly two months elapsed after the arrival of the surveying party, and no steps having been taken by the Government to bring matters to an issue, Mr. Duncan left for Victoria. On his arrival there, he at once proceeded, by invitation, with other friends of the Indians, to a meeting in the Provincial Secretary's Office. The whole question in reference to the Indians' rights, and the attitude they had taken to obstruct the Survey of their reserve, was fully discussed. It was evident, throughout the discussion, that the Provincial Secretary was in favor of adopting peaceful measures; but his colleagues were for coercion. The Government had in fact, before Mr. Duncan's arrival at Victoria, committed itself to a menacing policy, and, therefore, for its dignity sake, it was hard to renounce such, though shown to be utterly unjust, and uncalled for. A man-of-war was therefore despatched.

The following vigorous editorial from the *Industrial News*, Victoria, B. C., October 30, 1886, shows that the harsh, coercive, measures of the Government, do not find universal approbation amongst the white population of British Columbia:

THE METLAKAHTLA TROUBLE.

"The '*Cormorant*' has been despatched to Metlakahtla to enforce the survey. The day the '*Triumph*' was leaving, word was sent to the Admiral that the premier, the Hon. Mr. Smithe, wished to see him very particularly before the vessel left. The ship was actually detained some little time. The premier drove down with Captain Troupe, and thus obtained the order for the despatch of the bluejackets to coerce the Indians. This matter requires looking into more closely than people might at first imagine. *The whole of this trouble might probably be traced to the Fort Simpson land grab.* Of course anything relating, even so remotely, to that grab, sits very closely to the premier's heart. To secure it to his friends, *he did not hesitate, in the first instance, to infringe his oath of office and, by so doing, bring disgrace upon the high position he occupies.* The cabinet secret which he held, and which was guarded, not only by his honor as a man, but by his oath as a minister, he divulged, to enable his friends to make this grab. It has been called a steal; it is not a steal—it is only a grab, *secured by dishonorable and dishonest means. But while defrauding the province, it seems they moreover have alarmed the Indians.* And this last is the difficulty in the way now.

"These Metlakahtla Indians, thanks to the devotion, perseverance, and wonderful management of Mr. Duncan for thirty years or more, are civilized; they no longer are nomads. These men build houses and live in them, know trades and work at them, till the soil and live from it, and *having been taught the value of a home, they declined to be turned out of theirs.* They are unwilling to allow the surveyors to enter upon their reservation. Is there anything strange in that? *There never has been any treaty between these Metlakahtla Indians and the Government. The Indians are on their own land.* It is not to be supposed that they do not know what a survey is the usual prelude to. Surveyors were very busy over the Indian reservation opposite the city just before it was handed over, at a nominal figure, to Mr. Dunsmuir.

"Surveyors have been busy about Fort Simpson, and their presence was simultaneous with the securing of that grab by the omnipresent Mr. Dunsmuir and others. The Indians, no doubt, are aware of all these facts, and they not unnaturally dread the presence in their midst of these civil engineers and their instruments. Moreover, they have appealed to the Dominion authorities, and asked for a proper and legal inquiry into their case. *They do not pretend to place themselves in antagonism to constituted authority, they only deny the claim made to their land, and ask the hearing every proprietor is entitled to before being dispossessed.* There is nothing unlawful in that so far, and furthermore their application has been granted, and the investigation they demand, promised them. This is the first and most important cause of trouble. Round it, of course, circulate others. A ritualistic bishop, whom nature intended for the more congenial occupation, of superintending the decking of mimic altars by baby-girls, has managed to mix himself up in the matter.

"Mr. Duncan was Christianizing these people, and, what is more important to the State, civilizing them. As soon as they got to know enough to take in the fact that it was their duty to support their clergyman, of course a bishop of the Church of England came to the front to take the living. And for the punishment of the unknown sins of these unfortunate Indians, the choice is said to have fallen on a ritualist.

" All bishops, we know, are high, no matter how broad, or how low they may have been as clergymen. Ritualism means sacerdotal power extended. Now these ill-used aborigines, who, no doubt, have found it difficult enough to master the first principles of the Christian creed, will have an opportunity to exercise their half-awakened intellects over the subtle distinctions, that separate the Ritualist from the Romanist. They will be told of the horrors of the papistical confessional, but advised when in trouble, and the spirit moves them, to seek relief by pouring the full tale of their sins, into the ear of their fatherly spiritual master. The absurdity of the Romish doctrine of transubstantiation, will be impressed upon them, and at the same time, they will be advised to go fasting to the Holy Communion; they will be told that it is not the real presence, but they must think it is, and treat the bread with the same reverence, approach it with the same fear, bow to it with the same fervor as if it were. These pretty little distinctions without differences, these posturings and twistings, genuflexions and eastward inclinations, that they have been taught to look at with distrust, will no doubt be grafted upon them if his lordship has his way, so that in a short time we shall have a population, neither Catholic or Protestant, simply heathens deprived of their idols.

"It is said that Sir Matthew Begbie's name is used as the authority for instructions to the com-

mander of the gun-boat, in the event of the Indians
resisting the survey, to seize Mr. Duncan and bring
him down here and try him for conspiracy It is
somewhat difficult to decide what the Chief Justice
might not say or do.   Before the exposure which has
accompanied the Sproule case we certainly would not
have believed him capable of making such a speech.
Now, we should not be astonished to hear that he
had added· 'and bring him before me, I'll try him.'

"These Indians having appealed to the Dominion authorities for an investigation. *Why is this
survey being forced now ? It is because the Premier
feels that it is absolutely necessary to drive these
men to resistance, and by starting a small Indian
war draw attention from his own dishonorable doings.*   Must Mr. Duncan be cast into gaol and subjected to the tender mercies of such a man as Sir
Matthew Begbie, in order that Bishop Ridley may
enjoy a living, sport a beretta, and teach the Indian
maidens to decorate his altar and attend his confessional ? If the government for a moment imagine
that the people of British Columbia are going to
tolerate anything of the kind, they are egregiously
mistaken. *If there has been any conspiracy, it has
been on the part of those who have combined to rob
the Indians and rob the Province,* and the head and
front of that conspiracy is the Hon. William Smithe,
the Chief Commissioner of Lands and Works, *who
violated his oath of office* in order to enable his asso-
ciates to make the grab."

The man-of-war arrived at Metlakahtla. The Indians were treated as criminals and eight of the supposed leaders arrested, taken to Victoria 600 miles from their homes, and thrown into prison. As to the house the Indians had built on the two acres—the Chief Justice granted an injunction to pull it down, and took occasion at the same time to declare, "*the Indians have no rights in the land*" and to treat the words of Lord Dufferin with scorn and contempt.

In the face of these trying circumstances the Indians controlled themselves both nobly, and bravely; submitting quietly to the mandates of the authorities.

Cowardly prostitution of official trust, is openly charged by the British Columbians, against the authorities; their acts speak for themselves. Nothing is sacred that comes within the snap of the maw of these voracious Land vultures!

Might—asserting its supremacy over right, sends flagrant injustice unabashed to drive the Indians from their homes.

How long will generic differences, be held up as an argument to preclude the Indian, from the capacity of experiencing, that love of home, and country, which is preached up as one of the cardinal virtues of the human family?

From the time of Captain Cook's voyages, nearly every explorer, records the strong attachment of the North Pacific Natives, to their land. They have an emphatic and distinct idea, of personal, and tribal rights of property. Admiral Mayne R.N. reports :—

" On our way we stopped at the northern settlement on Admiral Island, as it had been reported that some Indians had been troublesome there. We found, however, that the Indians had been doing nothing more than to tell the settlers occasionally, as Indians do everywhere, that they (the whites) had no business there except as their guests, and, that all the land belonged to them.

" It appeared to be most desirable here, as at other places, that the Indians should be duly paid for their land."

The official policy of defrauding the Indians, and dividing the spoils, is not a new one in British Columbia, though it has in the past, been conducted with such artfulness, as not to attract much public attention.

The belief that the attitude of the Canadian Government,—toward its Indian subjects has been universally humane, and just, is a popular, but an egregious error. Bancroft writing of the British Columbian Indians says :—

" *The cruel treacheries*, and massacres by which nations have been thinned, and flickering remnants of once powerful tribes gathered on Government reservations, or, *reduced to a handful of beggars, dependent for a livelihood on charity, theft, or the wages of prostitution,* form an unwritten Chapter in the history of this region. That this process of *duplicity* was *unnecessary* as well as *infamous*, I shall not attempt to show, as the discussion of Indian policy forms no part of my present purpose. Whatever the cause, whether from an inhumane civilized policy or the decrees of fate, it is evident that the Columbians, in common with all the aborigines of America, are doomed to extermination."

In illustration of the high-minded sense of justice of the men who are now scheming to rob the natives of their land, I will cite an incident from the career as magistrate of Dr. Helmcken,* one of the present land-grab leaders. While Dr. Helmcken was in the dual employment, of the Government and Hudson's Bay Co. three sailors deserted. Indians were hired to pursue them, with orders to bring them back dead or alive—the Indians shot them down in the forest, and returning produced evidences that they had killed them all, and were duly paid the promised reward.

"Now mark the course of justice pursued by the officers of the imperial government. Instead of proceeding against the instigators of the murder, and arresting the officers of the Hudson's Bay Company, as they should have done, they direct the full force of their vengeance against the natives. *Helmcken, the newly fledged magistrate, cognizant*

---

* Bancroft's History British Columbia, see Appendix of this volume for full account.

of the whole affair, and well knowing who were the guilty persons, and what hand he himself had in it, goes to the Newittee camp, twelve miles distant, and loudly demands the surrender of the murderers. The savages acknowledge the murder, but plead that they were only executing orders. Truer to themselves and to the right than were the white men, they refuse to give up the perpetrators of the deed, but offered to give up the property paid them by the white men for the commission of the crime. This did not satisfy the European *justice-dealers.* Servants of the Hudson's Bay Company. Some one must be punished ; and *as they did not wish to hang themselves, they must find victims among their instruments.* As the *magistrate* was unable to accomplish their purpose, Wellesley sent a force under Lieutenant Burton, in three boats of the '*Dædalus*' against the Newittees. Finding their camp deserted, Burton destroyed the village, and made a bonfire of all the property he could find. The following summer, H. M. S. '*Daphne,*' Captain Fanshawe arrived. Meanwhile the Newittees had rebuilt their village, supposing the white men satisfied with the injury already inflicted. One day while holding a potlach, and being at peace, as they believed, with the white men, the '*Daphne's*' boats, under Lieutenant Lacy, crept into their harbor, and announced their arrival by a discharge of musketry. Men, women, and children were mercilessly cut down, persons innocent of any thought of wrong against their murderers, and their village again destroyed. Then the '*Daphne*' sailed away. Justice was satisfied; and Blenkinsop and the rest of them went about their work as usual."

Who now will question, the propriety of Dr. Helmcken's, sitting in judgment upon the rights of the Natives?

The Indian's bitter cry for mercy, has found no lodgment in the hearts, of the avaricious administrators, who have not only ignored the natives ancient land rights, but, have also ignored official pledges to these poor oppressed, and long-suffering, but, loyal subjects of Queen Victoria.

Again and again, has the bitter cry been wailed, but ever with the same heartless response:

I quote the following extract from an address delivered some time since by the chief of the Nanaimo Indians, to the Governor:

"YOU, OUR GREAT CHIEF: We, the Nanaimo Indians, have long wanted to see you and speak our hearts to you, and we want Mr. Crosby to translate our words. . . .

"*We want to keep our land here and up the river.* Some white men tell us we shall soon have to remove again; but we don't want to lose these reserves. *All our other land is gone, and we have been paid very little for it. God gave it to us a long time ago, and now we are very poor, and do not know where our homes will be if we leave this. We want our land up the river to plant for food. Mr. Doug-*

lass said it should be ours and our children's after we are gone. We hope you, our new chief, will say the same. We have 300 people in our tribe, though a number are away fishing now. Many are old and not able to work, and some of our children, who have neither father and mother, have no clothes. We hope you will be kind to them. Our hearts are good to all white people, and to you, our great chief. We hope you will send our words to the great Queen. We pray that the Great Spirit may bless her and you. This is all our hearts to-day."

Similar prayers are being offered to-day by outraged natives on every hand; sacred pledges to them have been violated, their lands, illegally seized, and sold, in spite of their protests. They have found the Indian agents to be in league with the trespassers, and partners in the profits. From the Government, if answers come at all, they are couched in artful phrases, or words without meaning. They are granted,—from their own inherited land—such meagre reserves as suits their iron-handed masters, with intimations "that beggars should not be choosers," and that gun-boats, or artillery will answer remonstrances; thus, making bitter oppression more bitter.

As if to afford these despairing Indians further evidence—if such is needed—of the insecurity of tenure they hold over reserves set apart for them in British Columbia—it has lately come to their knowledge; that Sir John Macdonald on his visit to Victoria in the summer of 1886, took upon himself to sell the Indian reserve in the vicinity of Victoria, for $60,000, or about one quarter of its value, to a wealthy citizen of the Province. In this transaction the Premier, did not even consult the Indians who owned the reserve.

If then the Superintendent-General of Indian Affairs, can when it pleases him, dispose of an Indian reserve, which was settled by solemn agreement, and legally defined by documents many years ago,—signed and sealed—as was the reserve just sold—how much easier will reserves set apart arbitrarily by the government, without any legal document intervening, be at the mercy of his will?

Dr. Powell, the present Dominion Superintendent of Indian Affairs for British Columbia, wrote the following letter to Mr. Duncan, shortly before the rupture:

"BRITISH COLUMBIA INDIAN OFFICE,
VICTORIA, August, 1879.

"SIR: Referring to my recent visit to the village of Metlakahtla, may I beg to convey to you my acknowledgments for the kindness, courtesy, and co-operation with official duties you were good enough to extend to me while at the mission. I cannot conclude without heartily congratulating you on the wonderful effects of your arduous mission labors among the Tsimsheans for the last twenty years. I consider that you have performed a great and noble work in reclaiming from ignorance and barbarism a most *useful, contented,* and *law-abiding* community, the effect of which is not confined to your own locality, but is felt and highly appreciated by all the Northern tribes.

" At Queen Charlotte's Island, . . . I found your name highly respected, and an ardent desire generally prevalent among the Hydahs to participate in the great reforms you have been chiefly instrumental in creating among the Tsimshean Indians.

" Personally, I wish you every success, and I shall not fail to acquaint the Honorable Superintendent-General, with the *loyal* feeling, and great progress in civilization, I saw so fully exhibited among the Indians during my brief and pleasant sojourn at Metlakahtla. I have the honor to be, sir, your obedient servant,

" J. W. POWELL.

" *Indian Superintendent* "

Since then Dr. Powell has soiled his hands by collusion with the land grabbers, even participating in the spoils. It is obvious that he now feels it incumbent upon himself, to justify the recent outrages, by making the following statements in his report to the Dominion Government; *statements, which he knows beyond a question to be absolutely false.*

He says —" The most violent efforts have been made by Mr. Duncan's adherents to seize the property and drive the Bishop thence. Threatening notices, riotous assaults, and every kind of intimidation, have for the long period which has since elapsed, been tried in vain, and the place has only been held, it would appear *vi et armis.*" . . .

The Metlakahtlans " have taken possession of the jail, or provincial lock-up, holding the keys and they do not hesitate to impose fines, or imprisonment, upon any whom their boycotting system cannot reach."

To this he adds several other misstatements, which originated with the Society's Agents, and have appeared in the Society's publications. Had Dr. Powell desired to tell the truth, he had every facility for testing the Society's charges ; the slightest investigation of which, would have proved them to be without foundation.

The authorities, are evidently startled by the indignant outcry of the Indians, which is reaching them from nearly every quarter of British Columbia, in regard to the land robberies ; and seeing, that an Indian war, or, a popular outburst, now threatens, Dr. Powell endeavors to shield the Dominion officials, first by manufacturing a case against the Metlakahtlans, and then throwing the entire blame of the threatened uprising of the Indians, upon the Provincial officials, who have shared in plundering them.

Dr. Powell in a recent report, thus speaks of the Punic faith of the Provincial Government : " Even the promises of the joint Reserve Commission, have not so far been carried out, or, acknowledged, and in some instances, indeed, *reserves of land solemnly assigned to them have been alienated and sold.*

"*It is therefore wonderful, to report to you, a peaceful condition among any of the tribes thus treated,* and certainly one's congratulations cannot be attended under such circumstances, with any consciousness of the ordinary fairness or justice. . . .

"Great inconvenience in dealing with Indians arises from the conflicting nature of the relations of the Dominion and Provincial Authorities toward them."

Sir John Macdonald's virtuous indignation, is evidently aroused, by the course pursued by the Provincial Government of British Columbia. In his recently published report, he says :—

"A serious complication has been occasioned owing to the sale *by the Provincial Government* of the reserve of the Sha-ma-us, land after it had been allotted to those Indians" . . . and "The sale *by the Provincial Government* of the meadow lands on this [the En-ke-mip] reservation, has also occasioned great dissatisfaction among these Indians."

The British Columbian authorities, as a matter of course, justify their action, by accusing Sir John Macdonald of like guilt, in arbitrarily selling the reserve above alluded to, though the Indians held it by a sacred title, officially accorded by the state. Thus, the Dominion and Provincial officials, in their recriminations charge each other with bad faith.

It is to be hoped, that, "if the rogues fall out honest men may yet get their dues!"

What a complete contradiction do we find in this situation, and policy, to the policy upheld by that wise, and noble statesman, Earl Dufferin, a man whose soul of honor, renders him invulnerable to corruption or duplicity. Read his words:—

"*The purchase of the Indian title upon liberal terms is recognized as a necessary preliminary to the occupation of a single square yard of native territory.* . . .

"Let me assure you that so long as I administer the government of this country, every Indian subject, no matter what his tribe, what his nation, or what his religion, will find in me a faithful friend and sure protector." . . .

"Even the Indian in his forest, or on his reserve, would marshal forth his picturesque symbols of fidelity, in grateful recognition of a *Government, that never broke a treaty, or falsified its plighted word, to the red man* (great applause) or failed to evince for the ancient children of the soil, a wise, and conscientious solicitude." . . .

THE PLEDGE OF BRITAIN'S WORD.

"The people of Canada and the people of Britain, will not cease to recognize the obligations which have been imposed upon them by the hand of Providence, toward the Indian fellow-subjects, and NEVER SHALL THE WORD, OF BRITAIN ONCE PLEDGED, BE BROKEN, but, from one end of the Dominion to the other every Indian subject, shall be made to feel that he enjoys the rights of a freeman, and that he can with confidence appeal to the British Crown for protection."

In the hands of Earl Dufferin the pledged word of Britain, was sacred and inviolable, it is left to the Government of Sir John Macdonald, and the contemporary Government of British Columbia, to *dishonor that pledge*, and inconsequently betray the trust imposed in them by the people, to guard the welfare of even the weakest, and lowliest of the Queen's subjects. These Britons, make of these British pledges, " ropes of sand," to the dishonor of their country and their Queen.

I would not have my readers infer that I charge the *people* of Great Britain, or the *people* of Canada, with this grievous outrage upon the sacred rights of their loyal fellow-subjects, perpetrated by corrupt Dominion and Provincial officials, who, have dared to prostitute the powers vested in them, by the crown, and the people, to serve their own personal ends.

I believe that the hearts of the English, Scotch, Irish, Welsh and Canadian people, when they read this sad story of wrong, will bleed in sympathy with the poor down-trodden Metlakahtlans, and would rescue them from their unhappy plight, were they not themselves, commensurately tied hand and

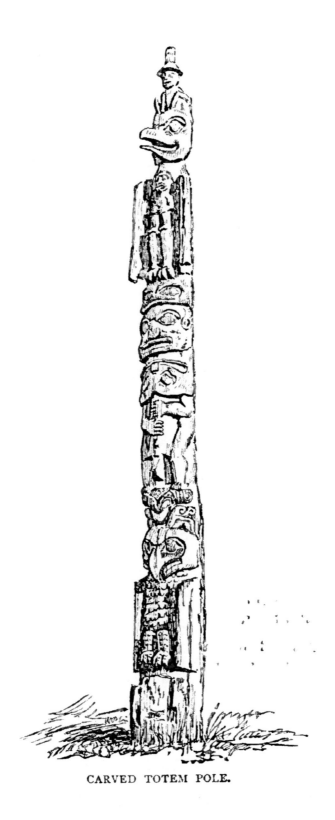

CARVED TOTEM POLE.

foot, by an official system, that renders them as individuals, helpless zeros.

Were the people of Great Britain, free to voice and act their sentiments to-day; without fear, or favor, we should hear no more of Irish and Scotch crofters' grievances, but, rather, right—justice—truth, would prevail throughout all Greater Britain.

I have lived too much in England, and admire too much, the *true type* of Briton, and his proverbial love of fair-play, to believe that, that race, as a race, at heart would defend oppression;—they are eminently a just though long-suffering people, who in their conservatism, will endure wrong to the last degree, before they risk an outburst for redress.

In Mr. Duncan, we have a true sterling type of Englishman—with that full measure of British pluck—heroism—persistence—endurance, that has characterized his greatest countrymen, and has given England her present proud position, among the nations of the earth.

Ignoring all precedents in British and American law, and custom, the Indians of British Columbia, without conquest, treaty, or compensation, are declared to have no rights in the land, which has been occupied for centuries, by them, or their ancestors, this, their land is now claimed to be the property of the Queen, while these," ancient children of the soil" are beggared, and allowed, but the meanest scraps of earth out of the charity, and bounty, of the crown !

The United States of America, have great reason to feel humiliated by the history of their treatment of the Aborigines, but the one great principle, which is also recognized by Great Britain, has at all times prevailed and been maintained. Namely, the Indian has the right of possession which can only be taken from him by conquest, or obtained through treaty, or compensation. It may be, that this has been, but *a form*, and *a mockery*, perhaps, a jug of rum, or a blanket, or a pint of glass beads, in payment for a vast province, but the principle *quid pro quo*— has always been sustained.

To wrest property from a man, because he has not the power to resist, is not a whit better than highway robbery, whether performed by an unscrupulous individual, or by an unscrupulous Government.

Sir John Macdonald has fixed upon himself, but shame, and ignominy; by the cowardly duplicity, which has characterized his treatment of the Metlakahtlans: he has displayed to perfection, that fox-like cunning, and artfulness, which many consider, the proper attributes of a professional politician.

After solemn, and repeated promises to the Metlakahtlans of relief and adjustment, of their grievances; to ignore their prayers, and to barter for his own political gain their land, and their religious liberty to their relentless enemies; has earned him the title of the *Betrayer* of the Poor, the merciless *Oppressor* of the Weak.

CHAPTER X.

SEEKING HOME AND FREEDOM.

TO-DAY we find the Metlakahtlans in sore distress, disheartened, crushed, impoverished, by the combined intrigues, and brutal acts of church and state.

They have been pursued, harassed, and maligned, by a religious society, in the name of Christ. They have been galled beyond endurance with cruel persecution, and, *that too*, maintained with the misapplied pennies, wrung from the duped poor of England, who in tender pity have thus shared their scanty means, with intent to send a ray of light, and blessing, to heathen peoples they imagined still more wretched than themselves.

They have been betrayed, trampled upon, robbed and traduced by the Government, whose sworn duty it is, to protect them as loyal British subjects, in their rights of property, and religious liberty.

The hour has struck.—A climax has come.— These down-trodden people, unable to secure justice, civil or religious liberty in the land of their forefathers; have now resolved, to seek refuge in

Alaska, under the United States Government, whose constitution is founded upon principles of justice, and freedom, to all mankind.

After serious and prolonged deliberations, the Metlakahtlans have decided, that they have reached that limit, beyond which, their endurance, and submission to the servile yoke of oppression, and religious intolerance, would cease to be a virtue. "What an English King has no right to demand an English Subject has a right to refuse—"[*]   "Is not protection as justly due from a king to his people, as obedience from the people to their king?"[†] In their straitened circumstances, they are unable to bear the great expense incumbent upon sending a deputation, to lay their case before her Majesty Queen Victoria, whom they truly believe, would have sympathy with them, and do them justice, could she but know the truth, and depths of their wrongs. Furthermore, they have already wasted much of their substance in sending their deputation, on the vain mission to the Government at Ottawa, and in obtaining legal advice. Their finances are also considerably depleted by the Bishop's shop trick.

Still more serious, however is the hard fact, that at court they would encounter the invincible opposition of the Church party, in the form of that great, wealthy, and influential society, with its

---

[*] John Hampden.   [†] Benjamin Franklin.

vaunted million a year, whose officers have halted at no underhanded means to effect their downfall.

They would likewise meet at Court, the resistance of that powerful, and corrupt Colonial Government of Canada, which in order to cover its own perfidy, and that of the Provincial Government, *coûte que coûte*, would denounce them as lawless, and fight them "*nail and tooth.*"

All who know by experience what a net-work of red tape " doth hedge about " the throne, know how futile, would be a mission from the Metlakahtlans in the face of such overwhelming, and unscrupulous opposition.

How often we have seen the nominal potentates, or emissaries, of the aboriginal inhabitants of various parts of the Queen's domains, like Tawahwai King of the Maories of New Zealand, seeking at the Court of St. James redress for grievous wrong ; only to be feasted, exhibited, placated with empty promises for the morrow, then, to return to their people with the pleasures of a hope never to be realized.

Civilization has shorn the Tsimsheans of their resistant strength and terrors. Once, they were powerful and brave in warfare, and any invasion of their rights was met with valiant disputation. Such is only a memory now. No longer do their dusky warriors, decked and plumed, thirsting for blood and spoils, take to the war-path, to return, if at all, —in triumphant glory to recount their deeds of valor, to youth and maidens who listen with throbbing hearts, and chant, and dance, to the honor of their favorite heroes.

These braves of other days, in yielding to civilization; and in their pursuit of knowledge, have surrendered themselves to the mercy of white men. Shall these helpless people, now be crushed, and robbed, because they are unable to defend their rights? Who does not despise the burly bully, who wrenches the penny from the cripple—why then should we respect a government, which in its power, and majesty, robs, and grinds under foot, its weaker subjects, because they cannot strike back?

But even take the Indian in his savage state, what chance has he, with his bow and arrows, his lance, his scalping-knife, his tomahawk, or, even the musket; against a powerful disciplined army of whites with the modern machinery of warfare?

On what principle of right and equity, can we justify the strong in trampling upon the weak. —Alas, " man's inhumanity to man makes countless millions mourn." And it would seem that the car of civilization has advanced more like that of Jugernaut, than as an ambulance.

I do not approach this subject as a sentimentalist; it was my fate, to be in the midst of Little Crow's great Sioux war in Minnesota, and witness some of the most blood-curdling scenes: when several thousands of the white settlers, men, women, and children were brutally massacred;

among whom were my intimate friends. The fiendish atrocities, of these infuriated savages, have never been surpassed. My hatred for red-skins was then, so intensified by these horrors, that I, in common with many, regarded them as so many reptiles, and their extermination but meet and just. However, on careful study of the cause of that war; and a retrospection of nearly all our Indian wars; I have found the Whites injustice and outrages, upon the Indians the primal cause. Bancroft, well said in speaking of the policy of extermination, in retaliation for some treacherous outrage, or diabolical act of cruelty, perpetrated by the Indians to avenge some invasion of their rights—"judged by this standard has not every nation on earth incurred the death penalty? Human nature is in nowise changed by culture. The European is but a white-washed savage. Civilized venom is no less virulent than savage venom." As a rule, white men in putting the smell of gunpowder into the nostrils of savages, have been actuated by no humane motives.

I have had the privilege of studying the Aborigines in various parts of North, Central, and South America; and my experience has led me to believe, that all have in them the germ of manhood; a germ, that may be developed for good or for evil, according to surrounding conditions.

During the autumn of 1886 while on a hunting trip of several months in the wild forests of Maine and Canada, starting from Kineo, Moose Head

Lake; most of the time far beyond the reach of habitations; I had as my guide Louis Ketchum, a Penobscot Indian; famed, as the most expert hunter and river driver in all that region. Throughout our cruise of something over a thousand miles, in our birch-bark canoes; by the intimacy of constant companionship, I had a rare opportunity of studying his mental traits, his own ideas of life; and of listening, to his analysis of the white men, with whom he had come in intimate contact while serving them as guide: Among these were such men as the Hon. Hannibal Hamlin, Mark Twain and others of renown; and, I venture to believe that no critic could ever penetrate more keenly, or depict more vividly, the true inwardness of these men than did this Indian. Ketchum's knowledge of nature, human, brute and inanimate, I found something amazing; and this, he has acquired solely from observation.

Whatever he did, he did in a masterly manner. He commanded my unbounded admiration, whether by his subtle arts in tracking or decoying game as he led me to the chase; or, by his quick judgment and action when suddenly overtaken, and imperilled, by a squall, far from shore in the great mountain lakes; or, by his expedients and endless resources, in improvising our shelter-camps; or, as with a nerve and muscle of iron he advanced before in his own gracefully modelled canoe, to pilot me through the furious, boiling, bounding rapids,

NATIVE WOOD-CARVING.

anticipating and meeting every surge, trick, and prank, of the treacherous, eddying waters; gliding like a serpent around, or between the threatening ledges and bowlders; alert, but fearless and immobile, while I, though not a novice, and with every desire to be brave, could not resist a degree of trepidation as I followed after, in my frail "*Pocahontas.*"

Ketchum, is a true genius and a hero too; for he has many times courageously risked his life to save his fellows. Honest as the day is long, an untutored man, and yet having a remarkable insight and comprehension of men and things. With his mental capacity and desire for knowledge, had his mind been turned to other pursuits, and had he had the advantages of education, he would I believe have commanded respect in any calling. This Indian is no phenomenon but the prototype, of a vast number of Aborigines of the American Contiennt.

The red man in so far as he demonstrates his capacity, has just as good a right, human and divine, to demand a foothold and rank in the category of humanity, as has the white man; and, especially is this so, when we find him raised in a single generation from the grossest savagery, to a condition in which he rivals the white man in his letters, and in his arts.

It is gratifying to note, that while Canada has so unfortunately taken a backward step in her Indian

policy, the American nation has awakened to the
realization, and recognition of the fact, that the
Aborigines have an equal right to justice and equity
with all mankind. In Canada under the present
administration, there are being enacted such outrages upon the rights, and liberties, of the natives of
the soil, as are a disgrace to any civilized country.
On the other hand, in the United States a better
spirit prevails, and Congress supported by the Government, has during the last session passed laws
which give our Indians, in severalty, every right and
privilege that is enjoyed by white men under the
same conditions.

In this the fiftieth year of the reign of Queen
Victoria, when her loyal and frugal subjects, the
Metlakahtlans would gladly and joyously join in
the jubilee, they are expatriated, and, driven by the
oppression of her unworthy representatives, to seek
in a foreign land, freedom of worship, and homes
that shall be secure to their children, and their children's children.

At the last Christmas day festival, for the first
time in the history of Metlakahtla, no British flag
was raised, and singing "God Save The Queen"
was omitted ; "Hold the Fort" was sung in its
stead. This out of no disrespect, to the good lady,
whom they have been taught to honor, but, because
they have been denied, the rights of loyal subjects,
by those *misrepresentatives* of the crown, who rule
over their country, and *from whom*, they might well

raise their voices in chanting "God Save The Queen, *and her people*."

Unanimously, these people resolved to place themselves beyond the reach of their persecutors, by migrating to Alaska ; the southern boundary of which territory, is only thirty miles distant from Metlakahtla.   To this end, they turned to their staunch benefactor Mr. Duncan, who had ever pledged his constancy, in any consistent and peaceful policy.   They delegated him with full powers to act for them, to visit Washington, and lay their case before the United States Government.   Some of the leading citizens of British Columbia, having watched the course of cruel events, and having vainly joined in protests against the repeated outrages, perpetrated upon the Metlakahtlans, both by the Society, and the State ; and seeing justice denied them by both the Provincial and Dominion Governments, drew up and signed the document—which I publish in my Introduction, heartily indorsing, and commending the Metlakahtlans' cause, to the American people.

Mr. Duncan has been cordially and sympathetically received, and the case of the Metlakahtlans carefully considered by His Excellency President Cleveland, the Secretary of the Interior, the Secretary of the Treasury, the Attorney-General, the Commissioner of Indian Affairs, the Governor of Alaska and the Agent-General for Education, in Alaska.

Every encouragement has been given Mr. Duncan, in this matter, that is consistent with International courtesy.

The following correspondence will explain itself :—

"WASHINGTON, D. C., Feb. 9, 1887.
"THE HONORABLE THE SECRETARY OF THE TREASURY, Washington, D. C.

"SIR : I have the honor to address you on behalf of a community of Tsimshean Indians numbering about 1,000 souls now located at Metlakahtla, British Columbia, near the border of Alaska, and in whose interests, I have been deputed to visit Washington.

"This people for over twenty years, have been struggling their way to civilized life, and their substantial progress has won for them, the admiration of all who have visited their settlement.

"Of late years, however, their prosperity has been cruelly arrested by the untoward action of the Provincial Government in reference to the land question.

"It would seem that British Columbia has assumed that the Indians have no rights in the land, and a land policy has been adopted there, altogether foreign to the edicts, and usage, which have been followed in all other parts of Canada.

"The Indians thus wronged are driven almost to desperation, but rather than proceed to hostilities they have decided to abandon their home and seek, protection under the American flag.

" They are now looking anxiously to this country for sympathy, and for permission to build themselves a village in Alaska.

" The losses involved in such a removal, to such a poor people are very appalling, and, hence the burden of my letter—which is—that if you can by any lawful means, permit them to take into Alaska their belongings free of duty, you will confer a great favor upon a deserving and suffering community.

" I have the honor to be, Sir, yours very respectfully,					W. DUNCAN."

[Indorsed]

" I most earnestly indorse the foregoing request. The removal of these civilized and largely educated Indians into Alaska *will not only add a number of industrial enterprises, but, have a very beneficial effect upon the Natives of that Territory. They will make good industrious citizens whose influence upon the Native tribes of Alaska will go far toward their complete* civilization.

A. P. SWINEFORD,
Governor of Alaska."

[Indorsed]

" I have known Mr. Duncan, and his people for the last ten years.

" Have visited them and inspected their industries upon two different occasions, and consider his settlement the most advanced in civilization of any native people on the Pacific Coast.

"The transfer of these people to the American side of the international boundary line, will be very advantageous to Alaska and the United States.— So much so, that it is the part of wisdom to give them every encouragement.

"As the taking down of their present frame houses, removing them to the American side, and re-erecting them out of the old material, will involve serious pecuniary losses to them, I hope that so far as you have discretionary power in the matter, you will prevent their being troubled with custom dues.

"*A few years ago Congress was ready to vote a large sum of money to encourage a colony of Icelanders to remove to Alaska. Surely the Government can afford to encourage these people who ask for no money help.* Truly yours,

SHELDON JACKSON,
U. S. General Agent of Education, in Alaska."

"Division of Customs,   TREASURY DEPARTMENT,
Form 3.   (H. F. 268.)   OFFICE OF THE SECRETARY,
WASHINGTON, D. C., February 11, 1887.

"MR. W. DUNCAN, care of Bureau of Education, Washington, D. C.

"SIR: You are hereby referred to the collector of Customs at *Sitka, Alaska*, for the Department's decision of this date, on the case mentioned in your letter dated the 9th instant, relative to the free entry

of the effects of certain Indians into that Territory.
A copy of the Department's letter to the Collector
is enclosed herewith.   Respectfully yours,

   (1 enc.)

     (Signed)   C. S. FAIRCHILD,
                             Assistant Secretary."

  "(A. T. 268)   TREASURY DEPARTMENT,
                     OFFICE OF THE SECRETARY,
          WASHINGTON, D. C., Feb. 11, 1887.

"COLLECTOR OF CUSTOMS,

        Sitka, Alaska.

  "SIR: The Department is in receipt of a letter
dated the 9th instant, from Mr. W. Duncan, representing the community of Tsimshean Indians,
numbering about one thousand souls, now located
at Metlakahtla, British Columbia, near the border
of Alaska, in which, stating that the community
proposes at an early day to move in a body into
Alaska, he asks that their belongings, consisting of
their houses, household furniture, hunting and fishing gear, tools of trade, personal effects, etc., etc.,
may be admitted free of duty."

  "Section 2512, of the Revised Statutes, as contained in the act of March 3, 1883, prescribes that
"no duty shall be levied, or collected on the im-
"portation of peltries brought into the Territories
"of the United States by Indians, nor on the
"proper goods and effects, of whatever nature, of
"Indians passing or repassing the boundary line
"aforesaid, 'and the free list also exempts from

" only,' wearing apparel in actual use, and other
" personal effects (not merchandise), professional
" books, implements, instruments, and tools of
" trade occupation, or employment, of persons ar-
" riving in the United States," "and under these
provisions the Department is of opinion that the
request of Mr. Duncan, may be properly granted
with regard to all of the articles belonging to such
Indians, except such as may be found to consist of
merchandise imported and intended as such for
sale.   You will be governed accordingly.   Respectfully yours,
      " (Signed)   C. S. FAIRCHILD,
                            Assistant Secretary."

The Secretary of the Treasury's decision, as will
be observed, facilitates the emigration of the Metlakahtlans to Alaska, by granting them exemption
from custom duties, on their belongings.

The Secretary of the Interior, acting under the
advice of the Attorney-General, decided, that all
lands in Alaska being public domain, it is not competent for the President of the United States of
America, to set apart, any reservation in that territory, and that land in Alaska can only be dealt with
by Congress ;—but, that the Metlakahtlans might
move into Alaska, and settle upon unoccupied land,
reporting the occupancy to the Department.   And,
furthermore said, that when the general land laws,
of the United States are extended to Alaska, "ample

provision will be made to meet the necessities of all law-abiding inhabitants."

The Territorial Committee of the Senate, has for some years, had under consideration the subject of the formation of a Government for Alaska, which shall meet the requirements of the people. Our present Territorial system, it is thought does not exactly meet the needs of the Alaskans, and a modified form, somewhat resembling the Colonial system of Great Britain, has been suggested. Whatever the form adopted, it is sincerely to be hoped, that it will be so wisely ordered, and administered, as to prevent the possibility, of the re-occurrence of such outrages upon life, property, and public decency, as has characterized, the earlier history of Alaska.

It would be a most humiliating culmination of events, if the Metlakahtlans in seeking homes, liberty, and protection ; under the beneficent rule of Uncle Sam ; should find themselves, subject to the whims, and freaks of irresponsible local authorities, who judging by the past, have not always dealt out even-handed justice ; and furthermore, if they should find themselves intruded upon by unprincipled adventurers, such as abound upon that coast. Under such circumstances it would seem a precarious venture for the Metlakahtlans, to tear down their present houses and factories, and re-erect them in Alaska only to find, that they have but escaped from Charybdis to fall into the jaws of Scylla.

As an American Citizen, my own feelings of confidence and reliance, prompt me to believe that the
Metlakahtlan community, with its thrifty industries, in seeking refuge in America, will beyond
peradventure be protected, and fostered, by our
liberty-loving people, when once their cause be
known.

President Cleveland, but expressed the popular
feelings of Americans when he said : *"a farmer
who builds his little house and sets about the improvement of the acres on which he has settled—
when such a man has legally taken possession of
his 160 acres he ought to feel that the Government
is behind him, and that if his rights are ever invaded
the Government will stand by him and see that no
injustice is done."* . . .

*" This is a Government by the people and for the
people, and the people ought to feel always that its
full force will be exercised to protect them from
any unlawful encroachments. I will go even further than that, and say that if by any construction
of the law a seeming injustice is done to the humblest farmer in the furthest corner of the land, then
the law ought to be changed and changed at once.
I am of the people. I believe in the people, and I
stand by them and with them—first, last and all the
time."*

The subject, of land laws, and citizenship will
undoubtedly be dealt with simultaneously, with the
forming of a local government. Senator Dawes

whose " Severalty Bill" promises a new and hope-ful era in the treatment of the Indians of the United States—has been appointed Chairman of a Committee, to visit, and, report upon affairs in Alaska this summer.

Senator Dawes has already shown a keen interest in the welfare of the Metlakahtlans, and regards the establishment of these people in Alaska, as a matter of great importance, to the future progress, of that far-off territory. I learn that Mr. Herbert Welsh whose fruitful efforts in behalf of the Aborigines of America, are so well known, has espoused the cause of the Metlakahtlans, and, contemplates a visit to their village this summer; his report will be looked forward to with interest.

Dr. J. A. Tonner the U. S. Army Surgeon whose good services in reforming the sanitary conditions of the Alaskan Stations, has been so widely recog-nized, writes :—" In going to Alaska our attention was drawn to the superior character, and appearance of the Indians, we saw at Metlakahtla, and I noticed afterward during their visits to Sitka, the apparent influence they exercised over the Koloshes, who bartered their fur for articles manufactured by the Metlakahtlans.

" The Alaskan Indians evinced a disposition to copy the Metlakahtlans, and had much to say about the good white man who had gone to dwell among the savage Tsimsheans, and in a few years made them live like white folks.

"During my stay, of a year and a half in Alaska I was much impressed by the confidence in which Mr. Duncan was held by his people, and the effective work he was doing. I sincerely believe that the proposed transfer of the Metlakahtlans, with their zealous missionary leader, would be one of the greatest benefits that could possibly be conferred upon the Alaskan Indians."

Mr. Wm. H. Dall, in his reports upon his scientific expeditions to the North Pacific, has taken occasion to point out with much emphasis, the folly of superficial, sectarian missionary methods ; but, he has heartily indorsed, Mr. Duncan's work, which he has found imitated with creditable success by some of the American missionaries in Alaska. Mr. Dall, has evinced deep sympathy with the Metlakahtlans in their troubles, and has expressed his belief that the migration of these people, and their leader, would have a powerful influence upon the wild tribes of Alaska. He says, of Mr. Duncan's mission, "it is the only really successful Indian mission on the North West coast, . . . bigotry, and an unchristian spirit, could hardly be pushed further than in the case of the Bishop, who has practically broken up the mission to secure his own supremacy."

Recently, there has been put forward by some individuals, a very short-sighted proposition to turn Alaska into a Penal Colony, to transport the criminals and outcast of the great cities of the United

States to that Territory, to debauch and drag the natives to a still lower state of degradation; there to create a festering pest-pen, and reproduce the horrors of Siberia, and thereby, indelibly smirch the good name of our country.

I cannot believe that the American people, will ever permit the state governments, to so sneakingly shirk their responsibilities, in the care and reformatory measures necessary to protect the public, and provide for their criminals, as this base and cowardly scheme demands.

Nor, do I believe that we shall ever elect an administration so blind, and forsooth so irresponsible, that it will encourage such.

The native Alaskans, however benighted, are our fellow-subjects, and we owe them justice, and protection,—the more helpless, the more they deserve our compassion. It would be an infamous outrage upon the inherent rights of the people of this unorganised state, to foist upon them, because they could not resist us, an eternal pestilence, which would contaminate every fibre of their social fabric. Such a course would contradict the fundamental principles, and, the traditional policy of our Republic,— to secure to all equal rights—to foster the weak—to promote progress. It would debase and crush a struggling Territory; an act, akin to smothering an unborn child, though the quickening is a known fact.

We have heard much of state rights, but what

can be said of a policy which would so defy the
spirit of our constitution, as to heap the criminals of
all the states like vipers, upon the veiled bosom of
a single embryo territory, to inoculate her with
their envenomed fangs.

Every State should guard her own criminals, and
there is no more justice in New York's debouching
her convicts into Alaska, than for turning them
loose upon Connecticut! Or, one city to turn her
small-pox patients loose upon the inhabitants of a
neighboring village! Or, to pour her noisome sew-
age, into the streams from which the neighboring
towns must drink.

The natives of Alaska, in common with the
other natives of the North Pacific, are as a rule intellectually superior to the Aborigines of other
parts of the United States.

Hon. A. P. Swineford, Governor of Alaska, in his
report to the Secretary of the Interior, 1885, says.
They "all are self-sustaining. These people, it
should be understood, are not Indians. Their appearance, habits, language, complexion, and even
their anatomy, mark them as a race wholly different
and distinct from the Indian tribes inhabiting other
portions of the United States. They are far superior intellectually, if not in physical development,
to the Indian of the plains; are industrious, more
or less skilful workers in woods and metals; and
that they are shrewd, sharp traders all who have
had dealings with them will, I think, be willing to

testify. They yield readily to civilizing influences, and can, with much less care than has been bestowed upon native tribes elsewhere, be educated up to the standard of a good and intelligent citizenship. Just in proportion to their educational progress, they should have the rights and privileges conferred, and the duties and penalties of full citizenship imposed, upon them."

Alaska has an area of about 600,000 square miles; produces annually $2,000,000 in furs; $800,000 in minerals; $750,000 in fish and oil; and yields to our government's revenue a *net profit* of over $200,000 above all expenses and appropriations.

The population of Alaska is 35,000 of which one fourth are either civilized, or fairly advanced in civilization, of the latter, one-half are whites, creoles and hyphens.

Add to this population the 1,000 Metlakahtlans, and 1,000 or 2,000 other civilized Tsimsheans, who will undoubtedly follow from Fort Simpson and other neighboring villages, with their annual commerce of upwards of $100,000 and Alaska will gain a vital progressive force, that will materially contribute to the development of her vast latent resources, and speed the day, when she shall take the proud position, of an enlightened, powerful and wealthy state, which shall be an honor to our country.

Missionary and educational measures copied after Mr. Duncan's plan, have already gained a fair footing in Alaska, and are prospering, under the direction of the Rev. Sheldon Jackson, assisted by Mrs. Jno. W. McFarland, Miss Lydia McAvoy, Miss Clara A. Gould, and others.

In educational matters, not only are the savage tribes to be considered, but also 2,000 children of civilized parents.

How unjust, and how unwise, it would be to abort this industrial, educational, and Christianizing work, which is beginning to bear abundant fruit.

Our Government netting above all expenses, and appropriations, a profit of at least two hundred thousand dollars annually, out of Alaska, ought to deal generously with its inhabitants; rather than herd them with criminals, and, I truly believe that justice, and humanity will prevail, and that no such a curse as a Penal Colony, will ever be forced upon our Arctic Province.

With a liberal educational policy, and a well-organized government, Alaska, has every prospect of a bright future. I commend to the calm consideration of political economists, a comparison between the two propositions. Namely, the emigration and fostering, of the vigorous, industrial colony of civilized British Columbians, who will develop and enrich the country; or, the revolting scheme of converting Alaska into a den of criminals, to ruin its future beyond all hope?

The industries of the Metlakahtlans, as I have shown in the second chapter, consist of the usual handicrafts of English and American villages, in addition to their ancient pursuits, of hunting, fishing, gathering berries and clakkass. Being expert voyagers, and renowned for their honesty, and industry, they are much sought for as carriers, to transport in their canoes supplies, up the swift streams to the mines. Several years since, they purchased a small steamer, also added to their industries a co-operative salmon-cannery, from which they have already exported upward of thirty thousand cases; however, owing to the very low price of this staple, the profits, have only yielded fair wages to the people. An amusing incident occurred in connection with the establishment of this industry. Mr. Duncan was introducing a telephone, between his dwelling-house and the cannery. The new invention was regarded with great interest by the Indians. One of whom said incredulously, "this machine *may* speak English, but it *can never* speak Tsimshean!" Great was the amazement, and delight of this man and his fellows; when they found it articulating, the mellow and flowing tones of their own tongue.

These people exhibit great skill, and ingenuity in all their industries, but, especially in woodworking. They are imitative almost to the degree of the Japanese. The officers of one of the first steamers to voyage to this vicinity, relate an incident, illustrative of this trait. The natives were struck with awe, and expressed admiration, at the grandeur and speed of the enormous fire-canoe propelled with invisible power.   They scanned the steamer over in every part with great curiosity, then with significant nods of satisfaction, said, "We will build one like her."   They fashioned out of a large tree, almost a perfect model of the steamer, about thirty feet in length, and painted her black; she had decks, ports, and red paddle-wheels. When finished they launched her amid great flourish and display.   This craft made, it is said, about three knots an hour; the Indians working the paddles and helm out of sight, below deck.

Carpentering, cabinet-work and architecture, are occupations in which they are particularly expert. Their fine church of which I have given a drawing, is built entirely by Natives, with lumber sawn at their own mill.

It has been Mr. Duncan's plan from the first, to keep these people busy, opposed as he is, from principle, to giving charity to those able to help themselves, he has striven to fix in them industrial habits, to make them self-supporting, and to divert their inherent barbaric pride, to a pride of manly independence and self-reliance.   He stimulates them to vie with each other in the pursuit of knowledge, by demonstrating the practical advantages, thereby to be attained

Recently when one of the natives,—whom Mr. Duncan found at Fort Simpson, as an infant in the arms of his savage mother, both having been aban-

DAVID LEASK, SECRETARY OF THE NATIVE COUNCIL OF METLA-
KAHTLA.

doned by the white father who was an employé of
the Hudson's Bay Company—contributed an article
to one of the journals at Victoria, signing himself
" *A Native.*" some of the detractors of Metlakahtla denounced the article as a hoax, and said,
" no Metlakahtlan native, could write such a letter, or be familiar with the famous English authors
this man quotes." Nevertheless the communication
was genuine, and the critics would be still more
astonished to view the library of this man, David
Leask ; so well educated by Mr. Duncan, and now
head school-master, as well as Secretary of the Native Council.

Mr. Duncan's colleague, in the mission, the Rev.
Robert Tomlinson, has successfully devoted some
fifteen years to missionary work, in British Columbia. About three years since, on conscientious
grounds, he resigned his connection with the Church
Missionary Society, to join Mr. Duncan, at Metlakahtla. To do this he has bravely faced the prospects of reduced finances, although, he is married
and has a family dependent upon him.

A devoted Christian medical gentleman, J. D.
Bluett, M.R.C.S., L.R.C.P., having become interested in Mr. Duncan's work from the accounts
given of it by his friends, who had visited the coast ;
volunteered to leave England at his own expense,
to join the mission. For more than two years he
has been at Metlakahtla rendering gratuitously his
professional services to the Indians, both there and

in the surrounding settlements, as well as taking part in the preaching.

Such, then is the stamp of the men who with great self-sacrifice, are now assisting Mr. Duncan, in his missionary work at Metlakahtla.

The village is still governed by the Native Council, and the church is under the direction of native elders. The people are united, in their affection for, and faith in, their leader, and each other. At this moment they seem, "*knit together with heart-break pain*" and are ready to meet unflinchingly, the great sacrifice, necessary to carry out their resolution, to abandon the country of their birth.

. . . "A band of exiles: a raft, as it were, from the ship-
    wrecked
Nation, scattered along the coast, now floating together,
Bound by the bonds of a common belief and a common mis-
    fortune ;"

As I have shown, the United States Government, has opened the way for the Metlakahtlans to enter Alaska ; but, it is of great importance, that with as little delay as possible, after they come under the new jurisdiction, they should have laws to protect them in their lives, and property, courts to admin-ister those laws, and executive officers, to enforce such ; that they may not become "the jilts of capti-ous chances." Legislation is absolutely necessary to secure this end ; and it is proposed by those in sympathy with the movement, to urge Congress to some action during the next session.

For the furtherance of this purpose, I have devoted myself, to the task of collecting the correlative facts, connected with the creation of the Metlakahtla Mission, and with the troubles which now threaten it with destruction. My study of the subject, leads me to believe that the knowledge of these facts, will command for these oppressed people, the warmest sympathy, and support of every liberty-loving citizen of the United States.

At the urgent request of several distinguished supporters, Mr. Duncan, has tarried for a time in the United States, and has spoken before various assemblages of those interested in Indian affairs, in order to acquaint them with the existent facts.*

The late Rev. Henry Ward Beecher, who was ever a champion of the oppressed, extended a very cordial invitation to Mr. Duncan, to speak from his pulpit ; an honor seldom accorded to an outsider be he ever so renowned.

The following is an extract from the *Brooklyn Eagle's* account of Mr. Duncan's address delivered at Plymouth Church.

"BRITISH AMERICAN TRIBES WHO SEEK THE PROTECTION OF THE STARS AND STRIPES. A MISSIONARY'S LIFE-WORK."

" A very interesting and pathetic address, on the condition of the aboriginal tribes of Canada, was

* See in Appendix Mr. Duncan's address delivered before the Indian Commission Conference, Washington, D. C.

delivered yesterday evening at Plymouth Church, by William Duncan, who has for thirty years been engaged in humanizing, Christianizing and civilizing the Indians in Canada. His labors have taken him chiefly among the Tsimshean tribes about Metlakahtla, and of him Lord Dufferin declared that he had *solved the problem of civilizing savages.* Mr. Duncan is a rosy-cheeked, hearty-looking gentleman whose hair is not quite as white as that of Mr. Beecher, who sat on the platform during the address, an interested listener.

"Mr. Beecher introduced the speaker in the following terms: 'I desire to introduce to our Christian brethren Mr. Duncan, who is certainly a missionary, a minister, a priest, a bishop and a ruler by the grace of God, without the imposition of human hands, or any external civil ceremony.' . . .

"'He comes to us well recommended, *not to raise money, but to devise, means of transferring his people to Alaska, so that they may go beyond the reach of ecclesiastical despotism, and avarice, of the men surrounding his* settlement. I think the least the Government can do is to allow someone to settle in Alaska.' "

EXTRACT FROM MR. DUNCAN'S ADDRESS.

"'The Natives of whom I shall speak, are at this present time suffering a cruel wrong. They have adopted civilization, and the white man has taken to the war-path. Ecclesiastical domination, allied with the greed of the white man for land, has combined to crush these poor people. They are the aborigines. They have been cruelly wronged and grievously misrepresented. I have found in my thirty years experience that they are a people who should be fostered. If they had had the chances we have had, they would be an honor to the world. If they were treated sympathetically, they would rise up and be a blessing to the country in which they live.' " . . . . . .

" ' Now these poor people are in trouble—grievous trouble. If they could tell their own story every heart would bleed for them. They are being ground down under ecclesiastical tyranny, and the insatiable greed for land.

" ' If the Native had kept his war-paint on, and his knife in his hand, he would have been recognized by treaties and agreements. Let us devise some means by which these poor people, can be taken to some land where they will be treated as citizens of the country.' "

At the close of Mr. Duncan's address Mr. Beecher arose and put the following questions :—

MR. BEECHER.—Let me ask you what is the plan and purpose that brought you here ?

MR. DUNCAN.—To get our people into Alaska. They want to leave the land of their fathers.

MR. BEECHER.—How far is it from where they are now to Alaska ?

MR. DUNCAN.—The nearest point is thirty miles.

MR. BEECHER.—Are the soil and climate suitable for them.

MR. DUNCAN.—The climate is the same. The land of Alaska is practically the same.

MR. BEECHER.—Do they depend on agriculture now ?

MR. DUNCAN.—No. There is only sufficient summer to ripen vegetables.

MR. BEECHER.—Have they means of transporting themselves and of rebuilding?

MR. DUNCAN.—Well, they have no banking account and little property. The cost of removal will be about $50,000. But it is feared that the government will not permit them to take their houses down because they do not own the land— [on technical English common law—H. S. W.]

MR. BEECHER.—What have you undertaken to do with our Government ?

MR. DUNCAN.—I want a guarantee that they will not be molested.

MR. BEECHER.—Will the Government of the United States make over the land in fee simple ?

MR. DUNCAN.—I have not yet ascertained, Alaska has not been surveyed. . . .

On Mr. Beecher's suggestion, assistant-pastor Halliday moved and General Horatio King seconded, that the pastor, deacons and trustees of Plymouth Church, petition Congress in the name of the assemblage to permit the Tsimsheans to take land in Alaska.

The immense audience among which were many distinguished public men, responded with a hearty and unanimous, " *yea !* "

It seemed exceedingly appropriate that this address, should be delivered from the pulpit where emancipation, and civil, and religious liberty, have been more fearlessly, and powerfully expounded, than from any other pulpit in Christendom.

" Mr. Beecher's creed had one pivotal idea, and that was that Christianity is not a conglomerate of ethics and moral dogma, but a simple and pure and worthy rule for living well and nobly. Believing this, he never hesitated to discuss any public question from the pulpit, and all the great questions of the day, slavery, licentiousness, labor and capital, the lust for power, intemperance, monopolies—all subjects of the hour—were texts for him, and his power was felt in political balances more perhaps than that of all the other clergymen in the land together. He was a St. Jerome, a Xavier and a Demosthenes in one."—New York *World*.

Mr. Beecher evinced a very warm interest in the case of the Metlakahtlans : he said to Mr. Duncan "get your people land in Alaska, and, then we will devise means to help them bear the burden of removal—you don't ask it but they need it."

One of Mr. Beecher's last official acts before the fatal stroke of paralysis prostrated him, was on March 3d to affix his signature to the subjoining Petition.

THE PETITION.

At Plymouth Church on Sunday evening January 16, 1887, Mr. W. Duncan in an hour and a half, gave a résumé of what had been accomplished among the Tsimshean Indians of Metlakahtla British Columbia, during thirty years of Missionary labor.

At the close of his most interesting address our Pastor the Rev. Henry Ward Beecher asked Mr. Duncan, in what practical way, we, as a congregation could aid him in his work. Mr. Duncan replied that he had been deputed by the Indians to visit Washington, D. C., and try to arrange with the Government of the United States of America on their behalf, for a grant of land in Alaska, upon which they may settle.

Mr. Beecher turning to his people, said "you have heard Mr. Duncan's statement, and the object of his visit to this country what is your pleasure?"

The following Resolution was then offered and upon being put to the large congregation assembled, was passed by acclamation.

Whereas,—Mr. Duncan, representing about 1,000 Tsimshean Indians of Metlakahtla has come to this country to obtain from our Government of the United States of America a grant of land in Alaska, on which to settle with his followers and of which they may have a secure tenure;—

Resolved,—that it is the sense of this Congregation in every way desirable for the future welfare of the Indians in question, and the building up of our Alaskan possessions, that so large a body of people, grounded in Christian and Industrial principles, should be welcomed to our soil :—

Resolved,—that the Government at Washington, D. C., be strongly urged to give all possible facilities to enable Mr. Duncan, to secure for this Community of Indians their cherished plans in the establishment of a future home :—

Resolved,—that our Pastor and consistory of this church be requested to forward a copy of the proceedings, and a copy of these Resolutions to the proper authorities at Washington, D. C.

BROOKLYN, N. Y., March 3, 1887.

[Signed]   HENRY WARD BEECHER,
Pastor.

AUGUSTUS STORRS,
President Board Trustees.

L. W. MANCHESTER,
Chairman Board Deacons.

SAMUEL B. HALLIDAY,
Assistant Pastor.

Not only directly, but indirectly, the coercion and turmoil at Metlakahtla has inteferred with the Metlakahtlans industries, causing them losses, and materially lessening their income. The expense of tearing down, transporting, and re-erecting, their buildings, will be very considerable, and while they bravely face this hardship, and will meet it with that heroic spirit, which has ever characterized patriots striking against the grinding heel of tyranny, —or bondsmen making a plunge for liberty,—yet, the hardship will be none the less severe.

The Metlakahtlans though poor, have only asked for homestead-lands, liberty, and justice ; they have not asked the American people, to aid them with money in their dire distress ; for, their benefactor, has so thoroughly imbued them with the spirit of self-reliance, and the dignity, and merit, of personal endeavor, that they look forward to making the desperate struggle, and encountering all the misery and privations necessary to found a new home, by their own sacrifice, and bitter cost, with a grand fortitude that knows no quailing.

In taking this step the Metlakahtlans look to the future ; to use their own metaphor " like the wedge used in splitting the trees, we are making the way for our children : They will be better than we are."

We have seen the quality of the people who are now knocking for admission to our land of historied freedom.

People, such as were the Pilgrim fathers, who knew how, and dared to make sacrifice for liberty of conscience, and freedom of action.

As the resolute Puritan pioneers driven by the tyranny of church and state, under very similar circumstances sought refuge on the Eastern Coast, and fearlessly faced dangers, and hardships, to create a New England, and raise up the bone and sinew of our nation: We may reasonably expect that the Metlakahtlans, who have proved to us, that they are patriots of the true heroic mould, will in facing the rigors of bleak Alaska, build up a New Metla-kahtla which shall surpass that idyllic village which has cradled their enlightenment; and found, on American soil a sturdy race of Alaskan yankees, who shall by means of their own native missionaries, and example of industries, thrift, and morality, radiate a civilization which shall permeate and quicken even the atrocious slave-dealing cannibals, and other heathen tribes—of which there are yet many in Alaska; lifting them to their own level, making them worthy, useful, and responsible citizens; and an active contributive force in the development of that Territory, instead of as at present, an humiliat-ing disgrace to the great American Republic, whose duty it is to rescue them from their benighted state.

In conclusion my countrymen, I appeal to you, as you love liberty, freedom and justice; prove to these people that this is truly the home of the free, and the land of the brave; that our Goddess of Liberty still bears the torch to light the way of pro-gress.

That American hearts beat as one, in full and strong sympathy with down-trodden, and oppressed humanity, whatsoever, the accident of creed, color, or country.

I trust that the perusal of these pages, may awaken in you an interest in these people, and animate you to make their cause, your cause, and that you will heartily support any consistent legislative measures, that may be brought forward, that will secure to them equal land and citizenship rights, with our native-born of like qualifications.

Having studied the circumstances, and condition, of these people very closely, I take it upon myself without apology to appeal, to you, *not in their name*, *but*, in the *name of humanity*, to lend a helping hand and voice, to this band of pilgrims.

In the words of Henry Ward Beecher, " *They don't ask for money, but they need it.*" In the uprightness of their noble surrender, rather than maintain their rights by a bloody warfare, they stand stripped of their patrimony as naked in worldly treasure as the new-born babe! Yearning for an opportunity to demonstrate their unquestionable gratitude, for the chance *to live and let live.*

Find in your generous hearts, a niche in which to place their cause.

I would suggest contributions to a public communal fund, which shall cover their losses, by assisting them to build new, or, re-erect their old public buildings ; and afford each one *an advance* of a small sum, for materials necessary, in erecting habitations suitable to protect them, from the rigors of the frigid North. Such sums to be regarded as loans, and to be ultimately repaid into the public fund, which shall be used only for the common weal.

I feel certain that in America there are many who blessed with wealth, or moderate means, or even though possessed of a bare competency; but enjoying the *priceless boon of an unusurped home*, will regard it a privilege, and a pleasure, to contribute something as a heart-offering, to smooth the thorny path of these afflicted people.

To countercheck the sinister carping, of misanthropes, and those who hastily attribute the motive of some personal benefit, to every initiator of philanthropy; I will here state, that this appeal is made solely of my own accord, without a suggestion from anyone, and is prompted solely, by the keen sympathy excited in my heart, by the wrongs suffered by these innocent people. Moreover, I would say that while I heartily invite contributions, to tide them over this tempestuous moment; under no circumstances, will I personally receive, or in any way, become the repository of such funds as may be offered.

I vouchsafe to suggest that any offerings sent to David Leask the Native Secretary of Metlakahtla, or to Bishop Cridge or Senator W. J. Macdonald, Victoria, British Columbia,* will be certain to reach

---

* I suggest these names, rather than Mr. Duncan's, out of delicacy for Mr. Duncan's feelings, whose mission to this country is other than that of soliciting funds.

the people, and be applied as the contributors may designate.

My countrymen, the fate of the Metlakahtlans rests in your hands. Loyal and peaceful subjects that they are—because they have not the power to resist—robbed, denied justice, their rights bartered away by the present rulers of the land of their fathers,—now driven to seek refuge on our shores— are they to be left homeless, and stranded, in their desolation?

Treated as rebels, because they protest against wrong, must they submit to be down-trodden, and driven to desperation by their heartless oppressors?

Denounced as lawless, because they refuse their necks to the intolerable yoke of tyranny, mercilessly thrust upon them, must they yield,—be co-erced,—terrorized?

Slandered, cruelly persecuted, and torn asunder by a Sectarian Society, under the name of religion, shall they be led to doubt the existence of a brother-hood, of Christianity and humanity?

I sincerely hope that all who read THE STORY OF METLAKAHTLA,—of the bitter wrongs of these people, will give to this appeal an answer which shall have no uncertain ring. Let your sympathy reach them in *this*, the hour of their distress. Let them not be driven to the brink of despair. There are moments, when postponement is calamitous. See to it, that they be allowed to secure homes in a land where their rights shall be defended, where they shall enjoy the blessings of freedom and of peace; where they may work out their own destiny as an independent, and united Christian Community, leading the way for their brethren yet in darkness, and where they may become the true, and loyal-hearted citizens, of the country that fosters them.

SUPPLEMENTAL NOTE.

SINCE the last page of this volume was in type and cast for printing, I have the information, that the authorities are taking steps to prevent by force the Metlakahtlans from taking down and removing their buildings—with the view of checking the proposed exodus. These high-handed measures, are apparently based on a point of *technical law.*—If the Crown claims ownership of the Metlakahtlans' inherited lands, then with equal right, it can claim ownership of the buildings erected thereon. It is to be hoped that this last outrage may not drive the Metlakahtlans "weary with dragging the crosses, too heavy for mortals to bear" to desperate resistance—but if bloodshed follows this catastrophe, the blood be upon the heads of those who alone are responsible.

It is but a fitting *denoument* to the story of beleaguered Metlakahtla.

H. S. W.

APPENDIX.

A PLAN FOR CONDUCTING CHRISTIANIZING AND CIVILIZING MISSIONS ON THE NORTH PACIFIC COAST,
BY MR. WILLIAM DUNCAN, BASED ON HIS OWN EXPERIENCE.

"NEW YORK, March 3d, 1887.
" DEAR MR. WELLCOME :

" In response to your request for me to sketch a plan of Mission work suitable for the North Pacific Coast based on my own experience, I have prepared the enclosed.

" Yours Very Sincerely,
"WILLIAM DUNCAN."

PLAN.

1. Preach the Gospel in the Native tongue :
2. Itinerate among all the tribes of the same tongue :
3. Aim at breaking up the tribal system :
4. Commence a Christian Settlement ·
5. Secure a Reserve of land round the Settlement :

6. Allow all the settlers allotments of land :

7. Encourage handcraft trades in the Settlement :

8. Settlers should not be allowed to alienate land

9 Land on Reserve not utilized to be public domain :

10. Treaties made only with Indians in the Settlement :

11. Government aid restricted to Native towns and employed only on Public works :

12 Intoxicating liquors forbidden in Native Settlement

13. The Missionary to be a Justice of the Peace :

14. A Corps of Native Police organized in Settlement ·

15. A native council elected by ballot to institute and enforce by-laws—Control public moneys and lands, and carry out public works .

16. The Native Church to be unsectarian .

17. Officers of the Church to be elected by the Congregation ·

18. Industries to be introduced and fostered in the Settlement .

19. Every member of the Settlement entitled to serve the public weal some way .

20. Amusements such as athletic games, brass-band, and other forms of music to be introduced and encouraged :

The aforesaid more particularized as follows :—

I. ·Make a breach into the tribal system of the Indians by the preaching of the Gospel. To this end let the Christian Missionary first learn the Native tongue,—then let him itinerate from a temporary centre to all the scattered tribes speaking the same language.

As soon as the Missionary discovers there are some, however few, in the bands who are willing to join him in commencing a Christian settlement, let him at once select a suitable location for a Native town , and then move thither with his followers, and there erect permanent Mission premises—Church and School, but let the work of itineration still go on.

The essentials for a suitable location in such a case would be :—

1. A good beach for canoes :
2. A good harbor for ships :
3. A gentle slope of country extending from the beach :
4. A stream with flow and fall suitable for a saw-mill :
5. Not far from a stream where salmon abound :
6. Being on the line of route of Mail Steamers :
7. Being not less than five miles from every Settlement :

II. Let a tract of land in the locality chosen for a town site be reserved for the Indian settlers, of sufficient size so as to insure :—

1. Enough for agricultural purposes :
2. A preserve for game .
3. A public Park :
4. And securing not less than five miles of land on every side of the Settlement.

Such Reserve should be surveyed at the expense of the Government into allotments as called for by the *Dawes* Bill, granting lands in Severalty to the Indians.

Every adult Indian in Settlement should be allowed an equal allotment of land, whether he use it or not ; and such Indians as cannot utilize the soil, but would rather follow some business or calling in and needful for the native town, should be allowed to rent their allotments to other members of the community.

In no case should an Indian be allowed to alienate his property in the land or rent it to others outside the community to which he belongs.

In case of the death of any land-owner, and there being no heir to take his allotment, not already in possession of an allotment of his own, then such land left without an owner should revert to the public domain of the Settlement, and be controlled by the Native Council.

III. *Treaties* should be made with the *Civilized* Indians

for the relinquishment of all rights to lands outside the Reserve. Such treaties should insure compensation from the Government for lands and ancient privileges which the Indians have been called upon to surrender. The amount of compensation promised should be a reasonable yearly allowance to the Native town or settlement, and the channels for the disbursement of the money granted should be restricted to those, and those only through which the Government are wont to render aid to Settlements of Whites—consisting of grants for Education—sanitary and medical purposes—making roads—and promoting the development of Public works.

Note.—The system of making presents of food and clothing to individual and uncivilized Indians, cannot be too strongly condemned ; its tendency is to sap self-reliance—foster indolence, pauperism and discontent. The Indians while surrounded and fettered by their old tribal associations, do not trace the presents made them to any good feeling on the part of the Whites, but regarding such gifts as a bribe to secure their favor, they remain therefore, both ungrateful and disloyal.

IV For the protection of the Native Settlement, in its pupilage—the Government should make it illegal for any intoxicating liquors to be found in the Settlement, for other than medicinal purposes.

V. Law and order in the new Settlement should be established and maintained by means of the Natives themselves.

The Missionary or School teacher should be granted a Commission as Justice of the Peace, and he should select a number, say from ten to twenty natives, to act as special constables. All that the Corps would require for their services would be a uniform and remuneration when called to special duty. Thus the presence of a Military force, would not be needed except in cases of emergency as in white settlements

VI. For the good Government of the Settlement a native

Council should be organized and trained in its duties, by the Missionary, for the management of local affairs.

The Council should have at first, partial, and ultimately, full control of public works—and the public moneys of the town,—and be empowered to look after sanitary affairs, and the public morals.

The Election of the Council should be by ballot, and every member of it voted for by at least nine-tenths of the voters.

The number of Councilmen should be regulated by the size of the Settlement—in the proportion to one councillor for every ten families.

Native Chiefs should have to stand their chances of election into the Council like others, and thus tribal fetters detrimental to the progress of the Indians, would be removed and the best men for governing would come to the front.

VII. For the stability and growth of Christianity, Missionaries should not display their denominational proclivities. All should work together in brotherly unity for the planting of the Gospel in its primitive simplicity, avoiding every unessential ceremony and most of all, every priestly assumption. As soon as a congregation gives evidence of having an intelligent appreciation of the Gospel, and soundness in the faith—let it be called upon to elect its elders, and officers to assist in the Church work. Elders should be elected yearly by ballot.

VIII. Let Industries be established and fostered as fast, and as much as possible, but no coercive measures should be taken to enforce the adoption of civilized modes of living. Let the people be educated up to every step, before it is taken.

IX. Let it be a rule in the Settlement that every member of it should be identified in some way or other, with the public weal, by rendering his assistance to promote it. A fire brigade would enlist a good many.

X. Amusements in the way of music—and recreations should by all means be encouraged in the Settlement.

MR. DUNCAN'S ADDRESS BEFORE THE BOARD OF
INDIAN COMMISSIONERS, AND THE CONFER-
ENCE OF MISSIONARY BOARDS, AND INDIAN
RIGHTS ASSOCIATIONS.

By invitation of the President Mr. Duncan delivered the following address before the Board of
Indian Commissioners and the Conference of Missionary Boards, and Indian Rights Associations at
the annual meeting held at Washington, D. C.,
January 6, 1887—

Mr. Duncan's address :—

Mr. President and ladies and gentlemen : I feel it to be a
very great honor that I am permitted to be present with you
this morning. I have not met such a body as this before
during the whole of my life ; a body where all who sympathize with the Indian are admitted and invited to participate. I have listened with very great interest to all that has
been said, and am ready to indorse especially a good deal
of what has been said in reference to the capabilities of the
Indian to be made a good, honest, and upright Christian
man. It has often been said that it was impossible to improve the Indian ; we have lived to prove that utterly false.
For thirty years I have devoted my life to the Indians, and
I have lived to see in this present generation men drawn out
from the very lowest and the most degraded, barbarous savages to be men that I am proud of.

I may give briefly, in a few moments, a statement which

will explain to you where I have been living. About thirty
years ago I left England to come over to this country; I
had to go around South America, for there were no railroads
across the country in those days. I went to a place where
it was supposed the largest numbers of Indians were living
in one locality, that is, at Fort Simpson, in British Columbia. There were two thousand three hundred Indians located there; they were not the kind of Indians you have in
these Territories; they were not moving about from place
to place, but they had a large village; I counted two hundred and forty large houses. They were in the most degraded condition; so degraded that it would be simply impossible for me to tell you in detail the abominable sights I
saw. They had gotten down to cannibalism, for I have seen
them there acting under the influences of their medicine
men, committing the most horrible outrages upon human
bodies. I found them in a most savage condition, so savage
it was not safe for a white man to move among them. On
my way out the few whites that were established in a fort at
Victoria, about 500 or 600 miles from the place to which I
was destined; endeavored, with all their power, to keep me
away from these people. They said they would be certain
to hear of my death. I begged that I might be permitted to
live in a stockade that had been erected by some white men
up there for trade; I begged to live there until I could
speak the Indian language. I was given that privilege, and
for eight months I did nothing but study the language, for I
did not believe in mutilating the Gospel by going and talking to them in broken English, or in Chinook jargon, as I
wanted to give it to them in their native language. I therefore for eight months did little, or nothing but to keep myself close in the stockade with an Indian, who did not know
English. By the acting of words I got a good deal of his
language from him, and in eight months I was able to
preach. At that time I went out to the various camps. Al-

though they were living in one locality, I found they were divided into nine different tribes or bands, under their old chiefs.

The Indians themselves ridiculed the idea of their ever accepting the white man's teaching. They have their own stereotyped notions about God, as they have about every-thing else. The white man is another being altogether to them.

I simply kept straight on teaching day by day, and al-though I was attacked on various occasions, and my life was in jeopardy over and over again, yet by God's help I was able to persevere. At first I did not attack these people in their customs; I did not ridicule them or speak against them wantonly. I went on simply teaching them—giving them light I saw they wanted light, and as the light began to dawn, those works of darkness began to disappear, and in a very few years their heathenish customs simply dwindled away My great point was to get an influence over them; to isolate as soon as possible the little germ of Christian truth which had made its way into their minds—to get it away from heathen influence. Therefore, for the first five years I worked there, it was with the view of getting a party to begin a new life—a new era in their history. After five years' efforts I succeeded in getting 50 under my influence, and these 50 left with me. We started a new little colony 17 miles away from the heathen camp, and that 50 has grown into a 1,000. It finally became so strong, so loyal, and so thoroughly civilized, that its power has extended all over the country around, upon all sides of us, even to Alas-ka The Indians have become anxious for teachers. There is no longer any barrier; it has disappeared, and now they see just as other men see; it is to their advantage and to their comfort, and happiness, to know God, and to live in a civilized and Christian way.

I will just mention two or three points, which I believe essential for the advancement of the Indian. It is a sad thing that almost every department necessary for the advancement of men everywhere, in every part of the world, has been well studied except the Indian question ; it has never been thoroughly and consistently studied. There have been more mistakes on the part of the white man, a great deal than on the part of the Indian. In my opinion the giving away of presents to the Indian, has had the effect of pauperizing them ; bribing them to keep quiet, terrorizing them ; in fact every measure which has kept them back has been a mistake. Trust the Indian! I can indorse fully what I have heard Captain Pratt say in regard to trusting the Indian. The way I acted when I got this little colony was simply to trust them as men we had raised up, who had become capable and industrious. Those men are now able to compete with the white men in their various industries, and we have now a ship taking away from our little province 8,300 cases of canned fish, all done by the Indians. [Applause.] We manage a saw-mill, and run a little steamer, all done by the Indians. The people said *I was mad* because I was trusting these Indians, but I had not been deceived by them. I saw from the first that the only way of advancing them was to trust them. I have had instances of men doing wrong, yet I may say I have had fewer such instances among the Indians, than among the same number of white men. I believe they are capable of all the brain power, of all the conscientiousness, and of all the ability necessary to make splendid men of themselves, and it is a disgrace to our nation, a disgrace to our civilization, that we have Indians now at the present time in the state they are. [Several voices : Amen! That is so! Applause.]

One of the most embarrassing questions that was ever put to me by an Indian, was one that was put when I first went there. It was this : " What do you mean by 1858 ? " I had to tell him that 1858 represented the number of years that we had the Gospel of God in the world. He said, "Why didn't you tell us of this before? why were not our forefathers told this?" I looked upon that as a poser. He said to me, "Have you got the word of God?" That, in the English language, would be equivalent to saying, "Have you got a letter from God?" I said, "Yes, I have God's letter." That would really be the idea that would reach the Indian He said, "I want to see it." I then got my Bible. Remember, this was my first introduction. I wanted them to understand that I had not brought a message from the white man in England, or anywhere else, but a message from the KING of KINGS, the GOD of HEAVEN They wanted to see that It was rumored all over the camp that I had a message from God. The man came into the house and I showed him the Bible. He put his finger very cautiously upon it and said, "Is that the Word?" "Yes," I said, "it is." "The Word from God?" I said, "It is." He said, "Has he sent it to us?" I said, "He has, just as much as he has to me." "Are you going to tell the Indians that?" I said, "I am." He said, "Good, that is very good."

Now, you see, if I had gone out there in the name of a single party; if I had gone and told them I had come from the queen, or from a nation, immediately I would have created in that man's mind a sort of antagonism; but as soon as I told him I had a message from God, who made him, he instantly began to pause and think, and wanted to know about that message. When I was able to tell those Indians in their own language the Word of God, it just had the same effect upon them, that it has upon the white people, and their congregations are as earnest, as conscientious, and as indefatigable in their worship of God, as any congregation of white men The influence of this work has spread all over the country.

I will just give you a brief idea of how I was deceived, on

that point, in a very heathen tribe. They had heard that I was coming, and the chief, in order to show his great delight at my arrival, put up what they call a large cap. Their cap was an umbrella. They had no idea of preventing rain from falling on their heads by its use, but looked upon it simply as a web-footed cap, and so they used it on state occasions. As soon as I landed I saw the man with the umbrella, and saw the excitement. He sent a message to this effect : "I would like you to come into my house, and I shall send my messenger to tell you so." I immediately encamped upon the bank of the river. By and by, I was told that all things were ready and prepared to receive me. I said to my little crew—for in those days I took only boys with me, being afraid to take men, as they might kill me for the purpose of getting my clothes—I said, "What are they going to do when I go into the house?" "Dance." "Tell them I did not come here to see dancing, and I cannot go therefore." They told the messenger, to tell the chief that I objected to seeing them dance, that I had come with a solemn message to them. The chief replied, "Tell the white chief he must come ; if he doesn't come to me I won't go to hear his word ; but if he will come I will go and hear him." That changed the matter altogether. I had a little consultation with my boys, and they said, "You had better go ; if you do not go the chief will not come to hear what you have to say." I walked up to his house, I confess, in a very grum kind of a spirit. I did not like to attend a dance. The idea of a missionary going in to see a dance! [Laughter.] But I saw that I had to do it ; public opinion was in my favor. [Laughter.] I was very glad afterward that I did go. When I entered the house there was a person there ready to point out a seat for me. There was a bear-skin spread over a box for me to sit on. The chief had all of his men placed around in different portions of the house, which was a very large one. I observed that he had gotten a large sail and used it for a curtain in part of the room. Very soon I saw two men step out. One had a rod in his hand beating the floor. They had a kind of theatrical performance. The old man, after stamping his foot and putting his rod down very firmly, said, in his own language, of course, "The heavens are changing." The other man was there to respond, "Yes, so it seems ; the heavens are changing." A few little remarks of this sort were made, and then the sail was drawn aside and out dashed the chief, dressed in most magnificent costume, his head being completely covered with feathers and other ornaments. He had his rifle in his hand. He shook it and then pointed it in my face ; walked up a little way to me and then put up his hands with his rifle in it , he looked through the hole in the centre of the roof where the smoke came out, and immediately began a beautiful prayer. I was astonished. This was no dance. If I could only give you his prayer in his own beautiful and eloquent language, you would be astonished also. I can only give you the substance of it. It was something like this : "Great Father ! Great Father of Heaven ! Thou hast sent Thy Word ! Thy letter has reached this place. We, Thy children here, are wanting it. Thy servant has come here with it. Help him to teach us and we will listen Thanks to Thee, Great Father, for sending Thy word to us."

That is just the outline. It was uttered in a most pathetic, eloquent, and solemn manner.

Having said this little prayer, he looked at me, thanked me for coming. Then he began to dance, and the Indians began a chant, clapping their hands. It was an extemporaneous song, and I listened to it with a great deal of pleasure. There was a man among them who made a hymn, just as they wanted it, and when they wanted it. The tune was a sad one in this instance. It was a chant ; the words were all extemporized by this man. I found that the song was all about God having sent his servant and his messenger to teach the Indians. They clapped their hands and sung with the greatest joy. It was a grand reception.

The Indian is all that ; but as soon as he begins to see that he is treated with a sort of dread, or fear, or suspicion, or you try to terrorize him, or drive down his throat what you believe, and what he does not believe, he then stands aloof from you. He wants to be treated as a brother. He wants to be treated as a man. The Indian has all in him that is necessary to make him a President of the United States, and it may be that some day you will have a man of Indian blood the President of this great nation. [Applause.] They have all the qualities necessary to make men of themselves. They are men who, when they understand it, can preach the Gospel in a most eloquent and effective way; they are men who can appreciate and receive it just as much as you and I.

Of course they have their characteristics. I will just allude to one point in regard to which I am reminded here. I see representatives of various denominations, and various Christian bodies all united, gathered here to tell of the efforts they are making in the one great work I say God speed those organizations and denominations. God speed their work. But let me say that when you go to talk to the Indians, bury all church creeds and doctrines, and give them the Gospel pure and simple. Take him that, and he will bless you, and he will grow up to be an honor to the country.

Here comes in the great difficulty, that we have, in uniting in our efforts on behalf of the Indians. Here is where we have often injured the great work, by jealousy, rivalry, and sectarianism. Let us go simply in the name of Christ. Simply take him the Gospel Let the Gospel itself develop the Indian, and then you will see a real, true, and substantial, Christian man.

Now, with regard to his physical and temporal affairs. The trouble is, we leave the Indian down in the mud. We do not believe in a missionary being only a teacher of religion, as such. A missionary, should be a man who will look at the Indian as a whole ; take him body and soul, and try to lift him up. My endeavors have been to make them self-supporting. We have no Government aid. I wish I had time to tell you about the present policy of the Government under which we live,* but I cannot tell you all I want to say about it, as it would take too long. I will say this, however, that they do not believe in helping the Indians. They believe in paying the Indians to keep quiet. If he has his war paint on, they will pay him money to keep him quiet, but they have given evidence that they do not care for the Indian if he is an improved, civilized Indian. Which is certainly a great mistake.

What we want is to lift, or assist these Indians, as soon as possible by these religious associations so as to make them independent of the Government. The Government has no soul, no heart , a Christian has a heart.

Now, Christian men and Christian ladies, come forward and help the Indian ; get him out of this difficulty with the Government, and make him a man, and then he will be treated as other men are by the Government.

I would say, therefore, by all means take and teach the Indian how to support himself. . . .

In the first instance, when I began in this little place, I had no house. I lived in one of the little Indian bark sheds, by and by we began to build, and little by little help came to us.

I very soon saw these Indians were desirous of learning all kinds of work. I put up a little saw-mill, and when the Indians found out I was going to make water saw wood, they first of all did not believe it. . . .

---

* The Canadian Government.

Then we began to make soap. I knew it was necessary to teach the Indians to be cleanly. . . . After that we had cleanly Indians.

Then I erected a blacksmith's shop, and a cooper shop, and a sash shop, and planing arrangements. Afterwards I started weaving, as I wanted to get the Indians to making their own coarse clothing. They have now learned to spin, and have already produced some shawls. They are not very pretty ; I do not suppose they would be wanted here, but they are very useful to the Indians. But the greatest industry of all is the cannery. I said to myself, " Why, see these poor aborigines of the country ; robbed out of everything," and so I started that business. Altogether, since we began, we have put up over 30,000 cases of salmon, and their salmon has commanded as good a price in the market as any salmon does.

I say, let us give them all the industries that we can. I have seen enough to convince me that the Indian problem is solved, so far as the Indian is concerned, but it is not solved so far as the white man is concerned. This is because of our ignorance. Therefore, whenever a man speaks to me about the difficulties of civilizing the Indian, I always tell him that the difficulties are on the side of the white man ; that the white man is pig-headed, stupid, and doesn't know anything about the Indians at all. · Every man would have a different impression of the Indian, if he had lived amongst them as I have done. I am happy to say that I am proud of the Indians. I have seen the Indian dying, and dying with the same hopes that cheer us. They hold to the same faith, and grasp the teachings of the Saviour, as eagerly as do the white men. In dying they die with the blessed hope of meeting their Saviour above.

Ladies and gentlemen, let us do what we can for these people ; do not let them be crushed out ; do not let them die, as it were, with the curse upon the white man, but let us remove this curse ; remove these wrongs and lift the people up, and God will bless the nation and the people who do it

At a subsequent session of this assembly, Mr. Duncan participating in the discussion on the subject of Indian land and citizenship rights, made the following remarks :

MR. DUNCAN.—I am in sympathy with treating the Indians as men, and in keeping them as Indian communities. I do not believe in their being scattered among the white men, because they are weak and they will go to the wall. They are not in a position at present to cope with the white man. First bring them up to manhood ; teach them how to maintain themselves, and then send them out into the world. They should, in their present condition, be treated as children are treated by parents until they reach manhood. In British Columbia, I found in the 50 men I had, that there was a little germ of life ; they had gotten the seed of life in them. There was an aspiration after a better life ; they had gotten to know the God who could help them, and to look up to Him. We started, and we grew. Gradually we asserted our position by accumulating all the appliances of civilization. We had law. I organized a native council. This native council managed its business as well as the council in Washington could. I organized a native police force. In every way they managed their own little affairs.

Therefore, I say, if you want to develop the Indians you must keep them in communities ; don't divide them upon different portions of land, and scatter them away from civilization. Becoming thus isolated, they will feel themselves cut off from the world, and that will not tend to develop them. You cannot make all of them farmers any more than you can make all white men farmers. Have a community, and some of them will become blacksmiths; some farmers, some tinsmiths, some shoemakers, and others will follow other of the different trades.

I will state that our Government has declared that these Indians have no rights in the land, except such as may be accorded them by the charity of the Crown of England. They, therefore, are allowed to use the land on which their forefathers lived, and on which they were born, *by suffer-ence.* In view of this condition of affairs they are border-ing on a state of desperation, and that has led me to come here and see if I cannot get permission to have them transfer themselves to the Territory of Alaska. There seems to be no difficulty with the Indians, it is all with the white man. The insatiable greed of the white man, leads him to desire to obtain all that the Indian has, and if he cannot get it without law, he will have a law enacted which will enable him to get it. That is the condition of things in British Columbia, where there are about the same number of white men in the province as there are Indians. This is a fact. The British Columbia Government represents about 30,000 white people, and there are 30,000 Indians in that same province. I do not know how many millions of acres there are in British Columbia, but I know this, that while there are 30,000 white people and 30,000 Indians, the Indians were to have just 2 acres a head—that is, 60,000 acres in all —of forest, lake, and bog, while the white man was to have the balance And yet, notwithstanding this, the Indians' are told that even 2 acres do not belong to them; that it has been given to them out of the bounty, and the charity, of the Crown of England. That is what has led the Indians to say, "After all we have been told by good and great men among the missionaries; after we have been told that we are on the right track when we accept the religion of the Bible, and follow the steps of the white man; all at once we are brought face to face with injustice, wrong, cruel

wrong ; and when we ask if we may have the same privileges as white men, when we adopt their laws, we are told
we cannot have them."

When the Indian has developed in the manner he has, in
the little colony of which I have spoken, what a shame it is
to say that now the Government, the Government of the
people, is the difficulty, is that which will not only hinder
further progress, but which will destroy all that has been attained up to this time. We are now endeavoring to get
these people into a Territory where they, perhaps, will not
be disturbed in their comfort and future happiness. I will
simply say this, that it seems to depend entirely upon the
success of my visit here whether the result shall be war
or peace ; whether these Indians will go back to their barbarism, or whether they will join those inclined to war.
Whether these poor people will be dragged down again to
shed man's blood, rests upon the proper determination of
the question, as to whether the insatiable greed of the white
man, to possess all that the Indian holds, shall be allowed
to prevail or not.

MR TIBBLES.—Wouldn't this whole difficulty be settled
if these men were put on legal status exactly the same as
white men are ?

MR. DUNCAN.—Yes, that is what we want.

MR. WILLARD.—Do you want anything more in order to
insure complete success, than, for the Indians to have title
to their land?

MR DUNCAN.—All the Indians want is this, to feel a
secure tenure of the land on which they live ; to feel secure
in the buildings that they erect, and that the industries
they establish may continue to be theirs. We have been
earnestly struggling for many years ; by the most persever-
ing efforts I have succeeded in establishing branches of industry among these Indians, which have enabled them to
support themselves, and yet, they have not the merest

shadow of a tenure to their lands, or to their industries, for that matter. Let me state an instance in point. The premier of Canada, Sir John Macdonald, went this last summer into British Columbia and sold an Indian reservation there for $60,000, without even consulting the Indians who lived upon it; nor did he even consult his colleagues in the Government, but simply, as an arbitrary measure, took the matter into his own hands and sold the land to a private citizen for $60,000, that sum being about a quarter of its value!

MR. TIBBLES.—Is there any possible way to secure this tenure, that you speak of, to the Indians except by placing them on the same equality before the law as the white men, for you cannot whip Great Britain?

MR. DUNCAN.—We cannot get those rights; that is what we want. The Indian simply wants the same privileges, the same laws, the same immunities as the white man, and he will pay the taxes the same as the white man.

CAPT. PRATT.—The picture that Mr. Duncan has drawn is a very beautiful one; he certainly is engaged in a grand work, and has accomplished wonders, but I would like to ask him what would become of that community to-day, if the head were taken away?

MR. DUNCAN.—I am very happy to answer that. Had I preached William Duncan it would have been so, but I preached Christ, and in the strength of that Gospel, that has done so much for the white man, I can safely leave the Indians there. I assure you that we have at the present in that community, as substantial and Christian men and women, as are to be found among any community of white people. They are now in a position to be left to attend to their own affairs, without any assistance from me.

CAPT. PRATT.—I would like to know how Mr. Duncan reconciles what he has been telling us, in answer to my question with what he said a little while ago, that upon the success of his mission here depended whether they would have war out there or not. I cannot see the consistency of these two statements. He is here to do something to prevent war, and yet if he is taken away everything will go on all right.

MR. DUNCAN.—I will tell you that for five years this community has been put into a very difficult position. It has been persecuted, and their progress has been impeded, in fact almost stopped. Last year three of them were deputed by the community to visit Ottawa with me. We went there. These poor people supported the families of these three men who went away while they were absent. We spent three months at Ottawa. Promises were made by the Government, that so and so, should be done. All these Indians asked for was for justice. They wanted the survey that had just been made adjusted. I stated at Ottawa that these people were not like other Indians, receiving subsidies from the Government ; that they had to fight their own way, and that all they wanted was to have their surveys properly adjusted. The officials promised certain things These promises were simply shelved and nothing done. At last the Indians were driven to a sort of feeling of desperation, and about two months ago, while I was away at Victoria, a ship-of-war went up there and arrested eight of them. And for doing what ? Nothing more than any white man would have done if placed in a similar position These three Indians that went as a deputation to Ottawa last year represented to the Government that the survey commission had been up there, and without consulting them had made certain lines in reference to their reserve, which lines were found to be, when the Indians returned and had thoroughly looked into the matter, very incorrect and injurious to them. Therefore, they wished the reserve commissioner to return, and they would show him where his mistakes had been made. We expected him to come, instead of which, last autumn, a party of surveyors arrived. The Indians naturally protested. They said, " We have represented the matter to the premier ; here is his letter, read it, in which he promises this, that, and the other shall be done, and yet nothing has been done. Therefore we ask you not to make this survey, as it is not right " The surveyor wrote a report to Victoria that he was obstructed, and a man-of-war was sent, and eight of these men were put in prison. These eight men are suffering for what eight hundred would have done— endeavoring to stop the reserve being surveyed on wrong lines ; lines represented to be wrong to, and acknowledged to be wrong by, the head of Indian affairs. Therefore it is that these Indians want, if possible, permission to go over to the border of Alaska, where they may have the benefit of the laws of your country.

Now, as a direct answer to Capt. Pratt's question, the Indians have intimated to me that if they are not allowed to go to Alaska, and have the privilege of settling there, and be-coming free men, and citizens of that country, they will leave the place where they are and join the interior Indians, where they feel they have a position of strength, and where they will be able to cope with the white man, with the rob-ber, with the man who does them an injustice. I was told by my Indians that the other tribes of Indians, that were still uncivilized, were urging my people to join in a defensive war. I am still hoping that we shall be able to bridge over the dif-ficulty, and let these poor people know that there is still in our Christianity that which they can grasp ; something that is tangible ; something that is not merely a theory of relig-ion, which will not leave them to fight all their battles by themselves, but something that will reach out to them a helping hand, and enable them to remain as they are now, a happy and self-supporting people.

Suppose I should have to go back to these Indians and say, "There is no room in America ; the white man has turned his back upon you, as Canada has." What will be the effect ? What will these people then do ? Are they to be left to live upon lands on which they feel they are allowed merely by sufferance of the Crown of England? I say no man living could exist under such circumstances, and be content and happy. What they will have to do if they cannot go to Alaska, will be to go up the river and join these other Indians. Whether that will result in war or not I cannot tell.

THE PRESIDENT, HON. CLINTON B. FISK.—When Lord Dufferin made that wonderful speech at Victoria, after referring to the Indians of British Columbia, he said, in that wonderful appeal to the people, "You must do for these Indians as you would do for yourselves. There will be no peace for you until they become citizens of the Crown and British subjects, and have their own homes." I had a conversation with him in New York, and I have never heard a man voice my sentiment better than he did.

PRESIDENT GATES.—Mr. Duncan has, in very forcible and eloquent language, made known to us to-day the great success that he has achieved among the Indians of British Columbia He has shown us what can be accomplished where you have a good and earnest man, working in behalf of his brethren ; preaching Christ ; instilling Christian principles, and at the same time enforcing such with good sense , making practical his teachings : looking after the wants of the men ; supplying them with saw-mills, and with other means of providing for their necessities.

MR. DUNCAN'S REFUTATION OF SOME OF THE
  FALSEHOODS ORIGINATED BY BISHOP RID-
  LEY AND PUBLICLY STATED BY THE DEPU-
  TATION.

BISHOP RIDLEY is the author of the following
statement, and in substance it was repeated in
public assembly at Metlakahtla by the Society's
Deputation in Mr. Duncan's absence.*

The Charge.—" I [Bishop Ridley] requested him [Mr.
" Duncan] to hand over to me all the books, and all the
" property of the Society. This he refused to do, but
" afterward handed over some of the accounts to Mr. Col-
" lison. . . . The store and its stock was believed by
" the Church Missionary Society to be its property before
" the destruction began. . . . We have been told that
" the Public works were stopped by the rupture, and I beg
" to add that the funds from the Church Missionary So-
" ciety, and not his personal credit enabled him to carry
" on the public works previously. For instance here is an
" entry in the Church Missionary Society's periodical for
" September, 1870 (*The Record*) ' Metlakahtla Fund, A
" Friend, £25.' Such entries are very common in the So-
" ciety's accounts. If the profits of the store built up the
" Public Works at Metlakahtla—I should like to know what
" use he made of such contributions? If he is so ready to
" lay before the Commissioner an account of such moneys,

* See page 254.

" why did he cut out those twelve pages from the Society's
"Ledger which detailed such account? The Society will
" be glad to receive an account from Mr. Duncan of the
"expenditure of the large sums so received. They asked
" through me in vain."

Here then it is seen the Bishop charges me with having
refused to render up to the Society certain property stock-in-
trade and accounts, also with having cut twelve pages out of
the Society's Ledger which contained the record of money
received by me from the Society, and the expenditure of
which money the Society has sought in vain to obtain.

I will first meet these charges in few words and then enter
into details and explanation.

Immediately after receiving the letter disconnecting me
from the Society, I ceased to exercise any control over the
property of the Society, and within a day or so I left the
mission premises. The persons I left in the Mission House
were Mr. Collison and family. The Bishop had gone away
The Society had no stock-in-trade at Metlakahtla or ever
had—for me to hand over. The Society's accounts I handed
over to the agent Mr Collison appointed to keep them.

Whoever told the Bishop, that the Public works at Metlakahtla, were stopped by the rupture made a mistake. The
fact is the Public works have been largely increased since
the rupture which was certainly not " due to Mr. Duncan's
connection with the Society."

The Book which the Bishop says I cut, was not a Ledger,
but contained only *copies* of the yearly accounts ; both the
originals having been sent to the Society which accounts,
originals, and copies, were complete in every particular when
I handed them over.

Now for details and explanation—

1. I have to state that until the advent of Bishop Ridley
all the money drawn on account of the North Pacific Mission from the Society, for over twenty years passed through

my hands, and every penny was accounted for by me to the Financial Secretary yearly.

2. In not one instance, to my knowledge during all that time was I ever notified of any discrepancy, or omission, till the last year, when the Financial Secretary wrote to ask me for an explanation on two items. One item was, that a draft for £500 had been presented to the Society for payment, which draft did not appear among those accounted for in my yearly statement.

This omission was explained by the fact that Bishop Ridley, had drawn the draft, but had failed to advise the Society, or render to them, or myself any account of it, or for it.

The other item for explanation, was that the total sum of general expenses of the Masset Mission Station, as it appeared on my statement, did not agree with the amount rendered direct to the Society by Mr. Collison—the missionary at Masset. This discrepancy was explained by Mr. Collison himself to the Financial Secretary—showing the account as sent through me was the correct one.

3. That the accounts in the Society's hands will testify how careful I have been over disbursing the Society's funds, and that, year by year, as I was able, I sought to lighten the general expenses of the mission, by contributions from my own salary, and from money paid me for services rendered to the government, and also from profits arising from our village industries.

4. I was ever careful to guard against using the Society's funds for any object, however good, outside the limits allowed generally to all missions.

The mission-house, and premises and school-house were within those limits and they are the only buildings erected at Metlakahtla by the Society's money—*though not exclusively* by *their money ;* and, these buildings I resigned the use of immediately I was disconnected from the Society.

Not even the new and costly church, much less the work-shops at Metlakahtla ever cost the Society a penny, that I am aware of, and as for the Society having any stock-in-trade, or machinery at Metlakahtla, the claim is simply absurd. For how could a Society be owners of a property they never acquired or possessed—or ever erected—maintained, ordered or controlled? Stranger still, if the Society knew they had a trade at Metlakahtla, for which they were responsible, and from which profits were accruing, that they should have allowed it to go on for so many years, and never once, remembering to call their agent, to render an account of it, till, after they had dismissed him!

As I have before said—the claim is simply absurd ; and I must add, that not one of the Society's officers, whose business it was to put it forward, had it existed, ever once breathed it to me. And I have reason to believe that even Bishop Ridley—whose business it was not—never dreamed of such a claim, till after the rupture ; and until he needed to look for stones to throw at me.

All that can be said in truth is, that I was a missionary, or teacher under the auspices of the Society, and while I was doing the work of a teacher, as enjoined by the Society I added other labors to my lot, with the *sanction and approval of the Society*, but not by their orders, or instruction, nor at their cost, or risk, or for their benefit, but at my own cost, and risk, and for the sole benefit of my poor people.

The Bishop no doubt assumes, that because a few friends made use of the Society's clerks, to transmit their subscriptions to me, that therefore, all that I erected by that money, and money from any other source, belonged to the Society. As well might it be said, that the Lord Mayor of London, owns a hospital in Spain, because some subscribers to that institution influenced by him, sent their subscriptions to it through him.

5. I will now state from what sources the money came,

which I have used for secular purposes, and church-building at Metlakahtla.

The starting of a fund was in 1863, about a year after I commenced the Settlement. All the money I had to begin with, was my own private means, augmented by a few loans from Indians, and a small grant from the government, to help me in purchasing a schooner. The loan was all paid back to the Indians in due time, and also the proportion of the government grant was returned, (though not asked for) when the schooner was sold.

Seven years later (1870) I visited England, and many friends anxious to assist my work, insisted upon my taking their subscriptions personally, and not as was usual through the Society's funds.

After I returned to Metlakahtla (1871) many subscriptions were sent me, from time to time. Some through the agency of the Society, and others by channels, and from persons, not at all connected with the Society.

The Indians at, and around Metlakahtla, also subscribed liberally toward the erection of their new church.

All these subscriptions I carefully recorded, and I have the records for inspection, and the total amount received by me from *all quarters* is Five Thousand eight hundred and seventy-seven dollars and ninety-one cents ($5,877.91), very nearly about £1,200.

I may here mention, that those subscriptions which were sent to me through the agency of the Society, were always accompanied with a paper from the Society's office, containing the names of the Subscribers, and the amounts.

One of these papers dated Church Missionary House March 24, 1873, is I am glad to say, still in my possession and is headed "*Amounts received for the private account of Mr. William Duncan*" and this was the usual heading of every such paper.

Under these circumstances, therefore, I cannot see that I

was called upon to render any account of my Secular fund, to the Society, as they only stood in the position of Agents, or Bankers, in such case ; and I must add that *I have never been called upon by the Society, to render to them any account of such fund, or the disbursement thereof.*

I am at a loss now to reconcile the Society's silence to me personally, or directly for upward of twenty years, with the statement of the Bishop that through him they have sought for an account from me, but have sought in vain.   Would it not, I ask have been more reasonable, and proper for the Society, to have written to me for the account they sought, rather than that I should first hear of their request through a Bishop, and a stranger to those accounts !

The only persons to whom I feel accountable in regard to the subscriptions, are the subscribers themselves , and the question to settle for their satisfaction,—is—have I spent or used the money intrusted to me, as they intended I should ? In answer to that question, I will here give a brief summary of outlay from the secular fund.

1	New Church total cost........	$12,572 65
2	Current expenses of Church for 1874 to 1881 ..	387 58
3	Assistance rendered to Indians building their New Houses and sums spent for their help	7,238 93
4	Establishing Industries at Village and buildings for the same	11,426 10
5	For Village Improvements and Public roads, houses and wharves......	3,040 76
	Total	$34,666 02

To the above, should be added a large sum which I have given to the Society during the years I have been at Metlakahtla, and which their own books will verify.   The total amount cannot be less than three thousand dollars, ($3,000.-oo) thus showing that I have spent over six times the amount I have received in aid, from every quarter.   Even the Metlakahtlan Church alone cost me more than double the amount of all subscriptions sent me ; and yet, the Bishop asks what has become of all the money I have received.

Now it may be asked how has all this money been realized ? I answer—It has come to us from God's blessing on our labors, and in lawful business transactions. It must be understood too, that I have not hoarded any of my salary, or fees paid me for services rendered to the Government, but I have thrown all I had into the work.

Let me now explain about the cutting out the pages of the so-called Society's ledger, which the Bishop makes so much talk about, and most assuredly lost no opportunity of using against me.

I have already said the book referred to is not a ledger at all, but contains only copies of yearly cash statements sent to the Society the originals having been transmitted to the Society yearly.

The book is a large one, and it would have taken a vast number of years to fill it, if it was kept for its original purpose alone : so for economy's sake, I made use of it to *record the names of subscribers to my secular fund.* Hence I counted off many blank pages, sufficient to hold copies of yearly accounts, to the Society for many years to come, and then, commenced to enter the subscriptions sent to me on *my private* account.

After I was disconnected from the Society—I had of course to hand over this book, and to save the labor of copying, I carefully cut out the seven leaves which my secular fund account occupied. I did this with the full knowledge of the Society's Agent, and without any protest, being made on his part. *The accounts of the Society I never touched* and, if I had, it would have mattered nothing, as the original accounts were already in the hands of the Society in London. Nor did I, in any way materially injure the book for the purpose to which it is applied.

I will now explain why I have carried on the secular work

at all. The Bishop fears not to make random statements
for the public to hear about the losses, which he would have
people to believe the Society have sustained, in destruction
of buildings at Metlakahtla.

I commenced then, the secular work at Metlakahtla, in
the first place, as a necessity, and as a protection from unjust, and iniquitous traders ; and I have carried it on from
year to year, and extended it because I could find no one
else, to take it up on my lines, which are to render it an aux-
iliary, to the furtherance and maintenance, of the spiritual
and educational work, at the settlement.

My experience has led me to recognize the necessity for a
missionary being everything to the poor people, for whom he
labors in the Gospel, and if he would have his work prosper,
he must aim at doing good to the bodies, as well as the souls,
of his people,—and concerning himself with whatever con-
cerns them.   More particularly does this apply to missionaries among the North American Indians, who are a race of
people without the means of appliances necessary, for advancement in civilized life, and whose labors in hunting
are but barely sufficient to supply their daily needs. Here
I would ask, how can such a people as this, if they become
Christians, be expected ever to maintain their own churches,
and schools, unless fresh industries are introduced among
them, and markets opened to them, for what they can be
taught to produce?

In corroboration of my views on this subject, I may refer
to the state of the Indians in the territory of North America,
where the Hudson's Bay Company hold sway—and among
whom the Gospel has been preached for many years. I
believe it will be found, as the missionaries report, that
most of these Indians are as poor now, as they were reported
to have been fifty years ago, and hence, no nearer being able
to support Christian teachers, or school-masters for themselves, now, than they were then.   This in my opinion should

not have been the case, and if missionaries had followed more nearly the footsteps of their Master, instead of minding the conventionalities of churches at home, or fearing what the world would say,—it would not have been the case.

Such being my convictions, I have labored, though with small means to open up industries, and trade at Metlakahtla : —My aim and object being to establish, and secure to the natives an industrial plant, sufficient to sustain all the mission expenses, and after my death, to render the church and school of Metlakahtla independent of foreign aid.

How nearly I had arrived at the goal of my hopes, may be conjectured, when I offered to the Society (at the conference) to take the risk of finding the finances necessary for the mission, if the church might have its independence.

It is to be regretted the Society did not accede to my proposal, especially so, as it would seem, from a circular they sent me in 1877, I was but advancing on the lines they desired their missionaries to work. The words in the circular were,—" What the committee wish to see in these converts, is not submissiveness to the Church of England, but a desire for and ultimately the attachment to an independent church of their own."

It is sadder still to tell that the Society, not only disallowed my proposal, but have allowed their Agents to do their utmost in compassing the destruction of our temporal affairs, and all for the mean purpose, of starving me out of Metlakahtla.

It was the Bishop's constant assertion of the claims of the Society to the building erected by our secular fund, that led us to seek and obtain legal advice, on the subject, and it was in obedience to this advice, that the Indians took down, some buildings which happened to be in proximity to the mission premises.

The loss of the buildings, was a blow to the temporal

progress of the village, but not any loss to the Society, for the buildings had cost them nothing.

I ought to mention, that while the Indians were taking down and removing the village store—the Bishop read the Riot Act, and wrote an alarming report to the Government, that a riot had taken place at Metlakahtla. A ship-of-war with two magistrates on board promptly arrived to quell the supposed riot, but on investigation they found that there had been no riot at Metlakahtla, excepting in the Bishop's heart and brain.

I must in connection with this matter, further quote the Bishop's words before the Commissioners He said :—" The property that was destroyed is reckoned to be worth seven thousand dollars "

Now I would like to ask if the Indians destroyed seven thousand dollars, worth of property belonging to the Society, why, were they not punished for their acts, and why did the magistrates acquit the Indians without even calling a witness against them?   There is but one answer, viz. the charge was not true.

W. DUNCAN.

TOMLINSON'S REFUTATION.

METLAKAHTLA AND THE C. M. S.

BEING A DEFENCE OF THE POSITION TAKEN BY THE NATIVE CHRISTIANS AND THEIR TEACHERS, AND AN ANSWER TO THE FALSE CHARGES BROUGHT AGAINST THEM

EVER since the rise of the unhappy dissensions between the C. M. S. and the native Christians, we, though urged by our friends to come forward, have hitherto held back, and thus the C. M. S. have made their statements without contradiction, and many of their friends and supporters no doubt think that we have kept silent because we were unable to refute these statements. Such however is not the case; we had good reasons for remaining silent up to the present.

Our respect for the Society with which we had been so long connected, our unwillingness to believe that the Society were aware of what their agents here were doing, or that they would sanction their actions, our hope that the Society would have their eyes opened to the true state of affairs, but above all, the fact that it was no plan or wish of ours to oppose the Society by setting up an opposition mission or church, but simply to endeavor to assist these native converts to establish and maintain what they wished and had asked for, an independent native church. Now, however, the case is altered, two deputies sent by the C. M. S. have visited Metlakahtla, and extracts from their report have been published by the Society, and the Committee have expressed their determination to continue the line of action adopted by Bishop Ridley. We feel that to remain longer silent would be to permit the gravest misstatements to pass for truth.

Mr Duncan will soon publish a separate pamphlet giving an account of the troubles caused at Metlakahtla by the agent of the C. M. S.

WILLIAM DUNCAN.
ROBERT TOMLINSON.

A REPLY TO THE ARTICLE ON METLAKAHTLA IN THE "CHURCH MISSIONARY INTELLIGENCER" OF SEPTEMBER, 1885.

In their preface to this Article the C. M. S. ask their readers to refer to the account of the Government Commission at Metlakahtla which appears in the *Intelligencer* of May, 1885. Anyone who does so will find there, p. 240, as follows. "Almost up to the time of the separation there was no reason to suppose that the Mission was other than a distinctively Church of England one," and if he will then turn to their present Article at p. 663, he will read. "It had long been known to the Committee that the Mission which had been so favorably begun was not being carried on according to the principles which they upheld, or in a way which they could approve." Here is an evident contradiction. Does not this show what straits the Society are put to in their effort to exonerate themselves, and at the same time condemn Mr. Duncan?

They clearly see that to be found supporting the line of action which Bishop Ridley initiated, and opposing what they had so long supported and approved, requires an explanation.

They refuse to admit to themselves or their supporters what is undoubtedly the true reason, viz, that with changing years *they* have changed, and that where once they were satisfied with a union in spirit and doctrine with their converts, they now demand uniformity in ritual and practice.

They cannot deny that they approved of and praised the work as carried on at Metlakahtla, but they are unwilling to adopt the straightforward course and acknowledge that their views have changed, and so it is that in casting about for some plausible excuse, they find themselves aground on one of the many quicksands which ever beset those who desert the path of rectitude.

And now we would ask, whom did the C. M. S. Deputies come to Metlakahtla to see? Not Mr. Duncan, for he was in England, and did not reach Metlakahtla until all their interviews with the native Christians were finished. Then why in their report are they chiefly concerned with censuring him? Let anyone who has read the C. M. S. publications since the founding of Metlakahtla collect a few of the many notices of that Mission wherein Mr. Duncan is spoken of in terms of affection, praise and admiration by the Society and its friends, and then try to realize that this is the Mr. Duncan referred to in the Deputies' report where he is said to be undoing his former great work, deliberately disobeying his Lord; inciting the Indians to riot and lawless acts, that it was he who from pride and jealousy " drove all the ordained Ministers from Metlakahtla " and demanded that it should be a lay Mission, claimed all the C. M. S. funds that passed through his hands as his own, denied that he was assisted by, or connected with, the C. M. S. at any time; persecuted the few faithful who still adhered to the C. M. S., and demanded thirty dollars from each of them; and lastly, that, " it was his unconciliatory temper that thwarted every effort the Deputies could devise for the creation of harmonious action between the two sections."

History repeats itself, but who would have thought that after the lapse of so many years the conduct of the people of Lystra toward Paul and Barnabas would be repeated by the C. M. S. with the difference, that while the one used stones, the C. M. S. used the deadlier weapon of the pen.

The Deputies say they " made every exertion to ascertain the exact state of public opinion at Metlakahtla." They addressed the Indians and received their replies in writing. The wording of the English of these replies is by Mr Tomlinson, but he studiously avoided introducing anything except what had been decided upon by the Indians assembled in meeting. This course, suggested by the people themselves, was deemed the wisest, as it enabled the Deputies to arrive at what the Indians wished to say, in the easiest way. The Deputies were on the spot and were assisted by an adherent of the C.M.S., as interpreter, whom they had chosen with the special object of preventing their being imposed upon

If the Deputies had any doubt that these letters accurately expressed what the Indians said, why did they not raise the question when at Metlakahtla? They never expressed the least doubt to the people while here. Moreover when addressing the Indians, they spoke of their letters as " your words," " your letters," *but now, unwilling or unable to meet these words of truth and soberness, they presume to doubt that they emanated from the Indians.* Is not such an imputation unworthy of the men themselves, and the great Society which has indorsed it ?

No fair-minded person can read the extracts from the Deputies' report and compare them with the Indians' letters and not be struck with the absence of any attempt on the part of the Deputies or the Society, to meet the Indians on their own ground. Abuse of Mr. Duncan, interspersed with remarks derogatory to Mr. Tomlinson, the conduct of the Mission work, and the people's condition is not an answer, it is only a repetition of the old story : " No case, abuse the opposing counsel."

While we felt so sure of the justice of the Indians' cause, that no stand could be maintained against it without deserting 'he platform of truth and Christian principle, we did not anticipate that the C. M. S. would be found relying upon misstatements and untruths to aid them in opposing a large body of native Christians, struggling to maintain Christian law and order in their settlement ; and whose whole creed and practice is based upon the written Word of God. These are hard words, and I would to God they were not true ; but how can we think otherwise when we read the following statements which we know to be one and all simply untrue?

First, at p. 655. " When the Mission was, in its infancy, removed from Fort Simpson to Metlakahtla, the chief, at whose suggestion the change was made, gave the Society the piece of land on which his own house was built, and the principal Mission-buildings were erected on it."

Second, at p. 667. " Mr. Duncan represented all the funds that passed through his hands as his personal property, and the Society was practically ignored. In fact there is clear evidence that on one occasion he distinctly told the Indians that the Society had never sent him, or supported him, or gave him anything."

Third, at p. 669. " He (Mr. Duncan) ultimately drove them (the ordained Missionaries) away one after another."

Fourth, at p. 669. " His last demand was that Metlakahtla should be carried on purely as a lay Mission."

Fifth, at p. 672. " If they were allowed to purchase at all, it was at the risk of insults and annoyance. It was therefore imperative that another store should be established for the benefit of these Indians, otherwise they would have to suffer the worst penalties of the petty boycotting system."

Sixth, at p. 673. " Another extraordinary regulation was that a demand was made on each person who adhered to the Society for the payment of thirty dollars, which sum, it was alleged, had been given by Mr. Duncan, from his own money, to nearly every householder as an assistance in building his house."

All these were learned from hearsay, and in no instance

could the deputies have made any bona fide attempt to verify them and yet they are set down as absolute facts by these very men who say, p. 666. " We were careful to set aside mere hearsay and surmises and to learn the facts on full and reliable evidence."

Let us now consider these statements seriatim.

First. If the Deputies had inquired of some of those who accompanied Mr. Duncan when he first settled at Metlakahtla (and several of them were among those who met the Deputies), they would have learned the true state of the case and seen how groundless their statement was.

Second. The Deputies say they read this statement. Where did they read it? and why did they not produce this "clear evidence?" Why did they not ask the Indians if any such representation had ever been made by Mr. Duncan?

Third. They need only to have examined the documents in the Society's possession and they would have known that Mr Duncan was not responsible for any of those leaving Metlakahtla. The Rev. F. B. Gribbell left on account of his wife's health, the Rev. R. A. Doolan was unwillingly compelled to return on account of death in his family at home, and the Rev A. J. Hall was moved to Fort Rupert on the advice of Bishop Bompas. There were only these three ordained Missionaries sent to Metlakahtla who left it before the separation.

Fourth. The demand that Metlakahtla be made a lay Mission was made at a conference held at Metlakahtla in August, 1881, by the Revs. Hall and Collison, without consulting Mr. Duncan or obtaining his consent, as can be learned from the minutes in the possession of the Society.

Fifth. It was only necessary to ask for the names of those thus treated to clear up this wilful misstatement.

Sixth. No such demand was made by Mr. Duncan from any of the Society's adherents for the repayment of the thirty dollars he had given to assist them in building their homes, here again it was only necessary to ask for the name of the one who it is said paid that amount and this statement would have appeared in its true light as utterly untrue.

Intense indeed was the feeling of painful surprise in the minds of these simple-minded Christians at the *utter disregard for truth* into which the Deputies and the Society have permitted themselves to be led. But it is not alone by the untruths above referred to that the *animus* of the Deputies and the Society against the native Christians and their teachers at Metlakahtla is shown. The very way in which they give expression to the praise which a fear of contradicting members and friends of the Society who have at various times visited Metlakahtla has wrung from them together with a *succession of misstatements* and *half-statements all clearly show this.* For example, in the opening paragraph of Mr. Morris' statement he would have us believe that it was only years ago, at the beginning of his labors, that Mr. Duncan displayed any missionary devotion, etc., whereas up to the very time of the separation the progress of the work was receiving the very warmest praise, not only from the society but also from those in authority. Even Bishop Ridley on his arrival sent home a letter expressing his approbation, and Admiral Prevost, a vice-president, who had twice visited Metlakahtla, shortly before the separation addressed numerous meetings in England on his return on behalf of the C. M. S., and on each occasion spoke in praise of Metlakahtla.

The Statement that Mr. Duncan visited England last year on his *private* business is one of those *half-statements* which has adroitly been turned to make a point against him. His visit to England was made for the sake of these people and with the hope of aiding in the settlement of these unhappy troubles, but because while in England he transacted some private business, if such a term can be applied to a business which so intimately affects the temporal welfare of these

people, it is asserted he went for that purpose. Again the
Deputies speaking of the case of Ada Stanley say, " he (Mr.
Duncan) alleged that the shawl which was taken from Ada
Stanley in default of payment was voluntarily given, but in
point of fact it was given to avoid imprisonment," the fact
being that the village rule which she violated does not in-
clude imprisonment in case of non-payment of fines ; and
further they go on to say that the two men sent to prison in
this case by the Stipendiary Magistrates were only set free
on technical grounds, implying that they were really guilty,
but only escaped through some flaw in the proceedings,
whereas had they inquired of anyone present in Court when
the Judge signed his order for their release, they would have
learned that they had not violated the law, and further that
the village has power to make rules and impose fines so
long as they do not use compulsion.

The above are only a few out of a number of statements
of a similar class, but a perusal of the correspondence and
Mr. Duncan's statement, will bring to mind and refute many
more.   In no one instance, perhaps, does the bitter animosity of the Deputies and the Society, show itself more clearly
than when they came to speak of the Lord's Supper. This
is a subject of the deepest interest to every friend and sup-
porter of the C. M. S., and without doubt the Deputies and
the Society owed it to these friends, to give them a clear
account of the reasons which those Christian Indians gave,
for not yet having this rite established among them. The
Deputies never so much as mentioned that they had brought
this matter before the people and yet they had given the
Deputies a clear exposition of their views on it ; but they
deliberately charge Mr. Duncan with withholding the rite,
and this too, in contradiction to the Indians' plain statement.
Could their bitterest enemy have acted more unfairly ? And
here, it can scarcely escape the notice of even an ordinary reader of the C. M. S. account, *how unwilling the So-*

ciety has shown itself to publish the Indians' words. From the beginning of this trouble, it has been characteristic of all the notices in the Society's publications bearing on the subject, that *they have abstained from publishing any one of the many communications they have received both from these people and their teachers. If only some independent Christian minds could gain access to the correspondence from both sides, how astonished they would be at the real state of the case ; and how grieved that the Society has so persistently misrepresented it!*

Mr. Blackett, in speaking of the religious teaching among these people, after admitting that the attendance at public worship was all that could be desired, reproduces the sneer uttered against the Apostles of old, " Whence have these men learning" because he found native teachers whose knowledge of English he considered limited, teaching " with only an English Bible in their hand," they were teaching word by word, only brief texts. He does not even urge that there was any error in the teaching, but simply because these native teachers were following the old Scripture rule of " line upon line, precept upon precept, here a *little* and there a *little*," he would cast them aside and replace them with European priests, who with their ignorance of the language, idiom, and habits of thought of these people could not give them even this little accurately.

The Deputies say further, p. 668, " we heard of no gatherings for prayer or for mutual edification, and there are no signs of missionary zeal among them ; nor any attempt to make known the Gospel to their heathen fellow-countrymen." We can thank God that this is *only true as far as the Deputies are concerned*, such meetings are regularly held, and there was no cessation during the Deputies' stay.

Teachers have been sent out at various times from among these people to the surrounding tribes, and at that very time a subscription was being raised to meet the expenses of two of their number to be sent out in the autumn when the people are at their villages ; the Deputies made no inquiry, and as there was no bell-ringing or noise about all this, of course they heard nothing.

We leave it to our readers to imagine what was the spirit which must have actuated the Deputies, when throughout their report they refuse to recognize the position these Indians have assumed as members of an Independent Native Church, and persistently speak of them as Mr. Duncan's Indians, as if Mr. Duncan had set himself up to be the head of a new sect or church. If such had been his intention he would have acted very differently from the way he has done. His desire is best expressed in the words of Gideon, " I will not rule over you, but the Lord shall rule over you," and the attempt of the Society to fasten upon these people a denominational title opposed to the very principles upon which they had formed themselves into a Christian community, is only an exhibition of their vexation at being detected in an attempt to hinder this really laudable effort.

The Deputies are strong in their denunciation of Mr. Duncan for upholding the Indian title to the land ; Mr. Duncan is not by any means the first, or the greatest advocate, for the recognition of this title, as will be seen from the following extract from a speech of Lord Dufferin when Governor-General of Canada, delivered at Victoria in 1876, " Now, we must all admit that the condition of the Indian question in British Columbia, is not satisfactory. Most unfortunately, as I think, there has been initial error ever since Sir James Douglas quitted office, in the Government of British Columbia neglecting to recognize what is known as the Indian title. In Canada this has always been done : no Government, whether provincial or central, has failed to acknowledge that the original title to the land existed in the Indian tribes and communities that hunted or wandered over them. Before we touch an acre we make a treaty with the chiefs representing the lands we are dealing with, and having agreed upon and paid the stipulated price, oftentimes arrived at after a great deal of haggling and difficulty, we enter into possession, but not until then do we consider that we are entitled to deal with an acre."

And again further on, " Now I confess I consider that our Indian fellow-subjects are entitled to exactly the same civil rights, under the laws, as are possessed by the white population, and that if an Indian can prove a prescriptive right of way to a fishing station, or a right of way of any other kind, that that right should no more be ignored than if it was the case of a white man. I am well aware that amongst the coast Indians the land question does not present the same characteristics as in other parts of Canada, or as it does in the grass countries of the interior of the Province, but I have also been able to understand that in these latter districts it may be even more necessary to deal justly and liberally with the Indian in regard to his land rights even than on the Prairies of the North West. "

Lord Dufferin's views on the Indian land question as set forth in the foregoing extracts are fully confirmed by legal opinion obtained both from Dominion and Provincial lawyers.

The Society in speaking of their adherents at p. 664, say, " They are 100 in number and have hitherto been supposed to be one-tenth of the entire community, this estimate does not appear to be quite as accurate as we are now informed [hearsay again] That the *total number does not exceed* 600 instead of being 1,000 as previously reported. " The population of Metlakahtla according to an enumeration which has just been made is as follows ; adherents of the Society (including boarders in the Mission House, although some of these do not properly belong to Metlakahtla) 94, members of the Native Church 854, total 948. From this it will be seen how inaccurate the information is on which the Society rely and how ready they have been to accept whatever seemed to favor themselves or disparage these people, *ex hoc uno disce omnes.* . . .

Following is an extract expressing the "deliberate opinion" of the Deputies on the same subject. "After our residence among the Indians, and our informal and unrestricted intercourse with those attached to the Society, we have no hesitation in expressing the opinion that the work done among the latter, is sound and very encouraging. There is a marked contrast between those attached to the Society, and the majority. The general appearance and straightforward bearing of the former impressed us favorably, while on the other hand, we brought to the notice of Mr. Tomlinson, that the course pursued in respect to the majority, was demoralizing to their own agents." It is not our object in this reply to show how groundless are the praises here bestowed on the C. M. S. agents and adherents; but we quote a speech from one of their number, a communicant, and one of their leading members. Samuel Pelham's speech in a meeting with Metlakahtla Christians October 12, 1886. It was at his own request that this meeting was held, and his words as afterwards written out are as follows :—

" MY BRETHREN:—Ever since we were separated I did not sleep well nor feel happy because I left you. I missed the true Christians who used to help in God's work. I often said to myself where is the old path, the path of Christian union. Above all I miss your presence in reading and talking of God's words. I say this because not one of those of our party care for things that I used to taste with you, that is talking and thinking of heavenly things or considering God's word. Whenever I ask any of our party of these things they do not know. I speak concerning our party—

Who shall I ask of them? Will Donald give an answer if I ask him of God's word? I tell you not one of them ever thinks of such things except Matthew—sometimes he and I have a little talk about God's word. I speak to you now because I know you have no bad feelings to me, I know all of you, and I want that love that I missed so long to be restored to me again, and to join with you in the good work as before, and no more to put on the " devil face " when we meet each other. It is not only myself I am speaking about, but the rest of my family who are still with the party we belong to, that all of us may again feel that happiness that we have tasted when we first came here. I know that many of you are striving for the same good work and considering God's words, but on our side none of them ever do such things. I feel this feeling working in me for quite a time, and I cannot refrain from telling you what God has put in my heart to tell you. "

Such are his words, yet he still continues with his party, so it is not for us to comment upon them. Before we conclude we cannot help referring to a matter which has been so presented to their readers by the Society as possibly to mislead them, I refer to the position assumed by the Society as the defenders of religious liberty at Metlakahtla. Now how will such an assumption be borne out by the facts? Years ago a small body of Native converts under the direction of an European Missionary drew up certain rules, and agreed that both themselves and any who might join them should obey these rules.

To avoid interfering with others or being interfered with themselves, they chose a site for a settlement, and the condition of becoming a settler on this site was a promise to obey these rules or leave. The C. M. S. knew that these rules had been made and showed their approval of them by indorsing what their Missionary had done. For years these rules were carried out in practice and drew nothing but praise from the Society, although during that time several to whom these rules were irksome had to leave the settlement. The blessing of God rested on these rules and the settlement increased and prospered. These are the same rules which the people are contending for now, and yet the Society which for so many years approved of them and applauded the Indians for maintaining them, are now their bitterest opponent. Now why is this?

Neither the principles on which these rules are founded nor the rules themselves have changed, then why the opposition from the C. M. S.? Because the Society has changed.

A few years ago, as the extracts from the Annual letters show, the single aim of the Society was the glory of God and they would have rejoiced that a body of Christians such as those at Metlakahtla had the courage to form themselves into a Native Church bearing their own burdens Now, however, the aim of the Society is twofold, and no advancement in Christianity by their Converts will satisfy them unless at the same time there be a corresponding attachment to the rites and ceremonial of the Church of England.

Had Mr. Duncan been as anxious for the establishment of the Church of England among these people as he has been for simple Gospel Christianity we would still be hearing his praises sounded by the C. M. S. These Christians are only anxious to be allowed to continue in the enjoyment of the privilege of union which they believed they had secured by founding their village in the way they did. How far the C. M. S., by opposing them in this lawful and laudable demand, appear as the defenders of religious liberty, we leave to our readers to decide.

In conclusion we would remark that this attempt of the C. M. S. to put a stumbling-block in the way of young disciples endeavoring to form themselves into a Christian community with rules and ceremonials based on the simple word of God and suited to their particular needs, must from its very nature be displeasing to God and we need not wonder, should the Society persist in such a narrow-minded course, if God withdraw his favor and blessing from them.

Again and again the Society deplore the failure of this Mission, "how sadly," say they, "has the success of the early days been clouded over." How clouded over? Have the converts relapsed into heathenism? Have they cast aside the simple Gospel and adopted some strange form of belief? Thank God, no. They still cling to their simple faith. They would guide their lives by the light of God's own word, and obey their Lord's every command; yes, His *every* command, for it is not from ignorance, or a spirit of disobedience, but as they themselves plainly tell us from a feeling of reverence and because they realize the true object for which it was instituted, that they have postponed the introduction of the blessed rite of the Lord's Supper among them. Threatened and harassed as they have been with the whole influence of Church and State against them it is a triumph for the Gospel that they have continued united and firm in seeking by lawful means to maintain their right both as Christians and loyal British subjects, and that is what the Society is weeping over instead of rejoicing that these converts, many of whom only a few years ago were sunk in the depths of heathenism, have organized themselves into a Native Christian Church. "How the gold has become dim and the most fine gold *changed!*"

ROBERT TOMLINSON.

POSTSCRIPT.

METLAKAHTLA, Jan. 31st, 1887.

Since writing the above, the printing of which has been unexpectedly delayed, my attention has been called to a paragraph in the C. M. S. *Intelligencer* for Dec. 1886, which sadly *illustrates and accentuates the leading characteristics of previous notices viz.: ignorance, innuendos and untruthfulness.*

Notwithstanding the frequent communications which the C. M. S. Committee acknowledge to have received from their agents here, and the visit of Deputies last spring they are still so ignorant of this land question and its bearing as to say " The Provincial Government arranged to survey the land as a token of their control over it, and to appoint an Indian agent." It was the Dominion and not the Provincial Government who did this.

The point would hardly be worth referring to were it not that the C. M. S. so confidently asserts their thorough acquaintance with the case in all its bearings. The force of the charge against Mr. Duncan of sanctioning lawless proceedings, accompanied as it is with the insinuation that he instigated them, must necessarily depend on what action was taken. The Indians put up a house on the two acres, and they stopped a surveyor

The Indians claim the two acres which are situated in the middle of their village as their property, and they also claim that these two acres were unjustly taken from them by the Provincial Government. Legal opinion went to confirm their claims but the Government refused to surrender the land and it was that the matter might be tested in the courts that the house was quickly and quietly erected on the land.

No interference was made with the Bishop's domestic arrangements. This was a perfectly legal and proper proceeding on the part of the Indians and carried out in such an orderly way that even our adversaries could not associate it with disorder or riot.

In preventing the surveyor sent by the Dominion Government, the Indians were simply asserting their just and equitable right to be dealt with on the same principle and in the same way as *all* other Indians in *every* other Province of the

Dominion. They are not asking to be permitted to prevent the settling up of the country, but that those privileges and rights which they have enjoyed for ages, and from which they derive much of their living, should be secured to them, or where this is impossible, that they should be remunerated for their loss.

That in stopping the surveyor they unwittingly violated a provincial statute is true, but it is also true that as soon as they knew of the statute they immediately pleaded guilty to the violation, expressed their regret, and bore their punishment without a murmur, and thereby gave proof of that law-abiding and Christian true spirit which has actuated them from the first.

As regards that portion of the paragraph which refers to the landing of Bishop Ridley, had it appeared in an ordinary newspaper it might well be treated as a huge joke, but appearing where it does it affords a most melancholy example of the length to which the agents of the Society, emboldened by our long forbearance and silence, are prepared to go in their endeavor to blind Christians at home and to bolster up the indefensible position of the Society at Metlakahtla.

That the building was occupied by armed men—that there was the smallest idea of preventing the Bishop's landing—or the least show of resistance, or any ground for apprehension on the part of Bishop Ridley, . . . or that crowds of Indians awaited him, or that they were cowed by and fell back from his armed adherents, is all simply untrue. Can anything be more lamentably shocking than that, in giving a simple account, those who were eye-witnesses and supposed to be above equivocation, much more falsehood, should fall so low?

Two questions naturally suggest themselves in connection with this incident. The first is, whether the Bishop, by sanctioning, if not directly approving, of the conduct of the

C. M. S. adherents at Metlakahtla, men and *women* coming
armed to protect him and this be it remembered *against
those who had not even threatened him much less displayed
arms*, whether, I say bearing this in mind, the saying " that
Missionary work which once was carried on by a Henry
Martyn is now carried on by a Martini Henry," has not
passed from a sceptic's sneer to an actual fact ?

The second and more serious question is, *if the notices of
these missions which have appeared in the Society's publications are so much at variance with the facts they are supposed to relate what credence can be given to the accounts of
the work carried on at other missions of the Society?* Has
not the time come when the Christian public should demand
an opportunity of judging of these facts other than from the
garbled accounts of prejudiced secretaries ?

ROBERT TOMLINSON.

THE METLAKAHTLANS APPEAL TO THE COMMANDER OF THE CORMORANT FOR PROTECTION.

I beg to call special attention, to this appeal from
the people of Metlakahtla.—H. S. W.

THE INDIANS' GRIEVANCES.

From the *Daily Colonist*, Victoria, B C , November 17, 1886

THE following petition from the people of Metlakahtla
and Fort Simpson was presented to the captain of H. M. S.
Cormorant on her arrival at Metlakahtla :

SIR · An attempt has been made on behalf of the Dominion and Provincial Governments to take from us by force
part of our patrimony and the inheritance which we received
from our fathers. We have reason to believe that this attempt will be renewed, and therefore we ask your assistance.
We firmly believe that these lands are ours and that those

that would take them are acting illegally. The reasons why we believe this are: That we inherited them; that no surrender of these lands has been made by us to either government, nor has either government made any treaty with us about these lands. Lord Dufferin, when Governor-General of Canada, told us that in every other province of Canada the Indian title had always been acknowledged, and that no government, either provincial or central, had ever claimed a right to deal with an acre until a treaty had been made. We sought for legal advice in the matter from an eminent lawyer in the province. His written opinion, backed by a further legal opinion previously obtained in Canada, bears us out in our claims. We have asked both governments to have the matter settled in the law courts, and that we are willing to abide by that decision. Instead of doing this they try to frighten us and to force us to give up our rights. Under these circumstances we appeal to you, as captain of one of H. M. ships of war, to protect us and our property. Though Indians, we are and have been for years loyal subjects of Her Majesty. We have no wish to oppose the law or the authorities. We are only anxious to prevent our possessions from being taken from us, and we know that it is to protect the interests of all, even the poorest of Her Majesty's subjects, that ships of war and soldiers are maintained.

(Signed)

PAUL LEGAIC,
ALFRED DUDOWARD,
MATTHIAS HALDANE,
DANIEL AURIOL,
ALBERT SHAKES,

For the people of Metlakahtla and Fort Simpson.

SERIOUS LOSS TO THE PROVINCE.
EDITORIAL FROM THE DAILY COLONIST.

From the *Daily Colonist* Victoria B. C.

THE INDIAN TROUBLES.—We are informed by the Rev. William Duncan that he is deputed by the Tsimshean Indians to proceed to Washington and interview President Cleveland, and his Cabinet with a view to removing the entire nation to Alaska, just beyond the border. If his mission meets with success the Indians will remove, "bag and baggage," to the land of "the midnight sun," and luxuriate in Uncle Sam's territory. Mr. Duncan goes east to-morrow morning, and hopes to make the necessary arrangements. The loss would be a serious one to the province.—*Editorial.*

CORRESPONDENCE ON THE CHURCH AND STATE COERCION, AND THE INDIAN LAND RIGHTS.

THE following animated correspondence, appeared in the British Columbian journals, during the past several months, and will be perused with interest by those who desire to more fully acquaint themselves, with the details of this story of grievous wrong.

The letters from the defenders of the wrong-doers, seem almost to answer themselves by their obvious, wilful distortion of known facts, and the iniquity of their propositions.

The correspondence is printed in order of the date of publication, beginning with the letter of Bishop Cridge, the earliest resident (living) clergyman on the Canadian Pacific coast—and a man who has enjoyed rare opportunities for acquiring a thorough knowledge of this whole question from its very incipiency.   H. S. W.

THE METLAKAHTLANS.

From the *Daily Colonist*, Victoria, B. C., October 28, 1886.

TO THE EDITOR . The intended despatch of another war-vessel against the Metlakahtlans leads me to solicit a space in your columns for a few words in the interests of justice and peace. My familiar acquaintance with the affairs of that settlement from the beginning, and my firm conviction of the peaceful character and loyal intentions of its inhabitants, induce me to use my humble efforts to move the government from their design. To those who have impartially watched the course of events it will be apparent that the Metlakah-tlans have been guilty of no illegal acts, nor hostile demonstrations, in the steps they have taken to establish their rights to their ancient inheritance. They have in a peaceful way done no more than what is common in disputes about land to bring the question to a legal issue. The issue is twofold, first with the government, and secondly with the Church Missionary Society, an ecclesiastical sect (for in this province it is simply a sect) whose services they have dispensed with.

The issue with the government is vital, being nothing less than denial of their title to the land. The Metlakahtlans, resting on the principles of natural justice held all the world over, claim that they have a communal title to the land held by their forefathers from time immemorial, and that no power has, through conquest, acquired the right of giving it away. This view of the case has been enunciated by the most competent legal authorities, and was endorsed by the Viceroy of the Dominion, the nearest approach to the pledge of majesty that could be made. The Metlakahtlans claim a right to the land, not through favor of any reserve made by government, but because it is their patrimony.

The governments deny this but the Indians know it; and, therefore, they have regarded the act of the government in surveying the reserve, not as a friendly proceeding in their interest as wards of the crown, but as a preliminary step to depriving them of all right and title in the land, if needs be by force of arms. They therefore looked upon the surveyor in the light of a trespasser, and in pulling up his stakes they intended no rebellion, but employed their only or best means of bringing the contention to a legal issue.

To this end they have also subscribed a sum of money to meet the expenses of the action, and this they conceive to be the highest pledge they could afford of their loyal and peaceful intentions.

The contention with the ecclesiastical body referred to is somewhat different.

The "Society" who were permitted to occupy the site of the mission house solely on account of services rendered to the inhabitants, now that those services are no longer required, still hold possession, apparently claiming ownership or at least the right of perpetual occupancy. The Metlakahtlans, therefore, have taken, without violence or riot, the step of erecting a building on the land in question with the sole view of bringing this contention also to a legal issue. Should the Society take the legal, peaceful means of redress open to them through a civil action the Metlakahtlans are prepared to abide by the ultimate decision of the law, whatever that may be. But as long as the governments seek to coerce the Metlakahtlans into submission by the sword it is hardly to be expected that the Society will be anxious to redress themselves.

This brings me to speak of the rights of the Indians as subjects. The state of pupilage in which they are means only restraint in certain social and civil respects, but does not affect their immunities in respect of *life, liberty, and property*, none of which, any more than those of white people, may be infringed upon except by due process of law. If I am correctly informed on this matter, the house of an Indian is as sacred as that of a white man, and not even the government can make forcible entry. If it be alleged that he has no title he can only be ejected by process of law. If this be so, then the forcible measures taken, or to be taken against the Indians, are surely illegal. And certainly no less contrary to sound policy. The consequences of resorting to a policy of war may be very grave. The Metlakahtlans certainly will not resist her majesty's forces. But the tribes far and near are watching the case with intense anxiety, as that on which their own rights depend. They will regard forcible seizure at Metlakahtla as the forerunner of what will happen to themselves, and there are not wanting signs to show that in such a case they will be exasperated and alarmed in the highest degree. If war ensues these down-trodden members of the human family must be conquered in the end, but the whole guilt of innocent blood will surely rest on those who rejected the peaceable means of settlement provided by the law and sought it by force.

October 26, 1886.   Your obedient servant,

EDWARD CRIDGE.

[Bishop R. E. C., Resident since 1854.]

CORRECTION.

From the *Daily Colonist*, Victoria, B. C., October 29, 1886

TO THE EDITOR : Permit me to make a correction needful to the sense of my argument in my letter on the Indian troubles in this morning's issue. After my statement of the claim advanced by the Indians to rights in the land not by favor of reserves but as their patrimony, the types make me say, " The governments deny this *but* the Indians know it." The argument clearly requires, " *and* the Indians know it," that is, know that the governments so deny, and that, knowing this, they regard the surveying of the land, not as a friendly, but as a hostile act on the part of the governments.

Permit one word more. It is not, in the opinion of many thoughtful people, a just recognition and equitable adjustment of their claims that will inflame the native minds, but statements put forth by authority that they have *no rights* beyond what the rulers of the country may, in their grace and charity, be pleased to grant them. Should such statements reach their ears, and be taken seriously, there is, I think, nothing more likely to drive them to desperation.

October 28, 1886.   EDWARD CRIDGE.

_____

METLAKAHTLA.

From the *Daily Colonist*, Victoria, B. C., October 29, 1886.

TO THE EDITOR : Rev. Bishop Cridge, in a letter in your columns, has put forward views with regard to the right of the Indians to the lands of the province which are entirely at variance with law which has been recognized ever since England became a colonizing nation. And I cannot help thinking that the publication, at this juncture, of such views as are contained in that letter, is nothing more than an active encouragement to the Indians to resist a peaceable settlement of what has been a continual source of expense and trouble to the province. The Indians only act, speak, and think as they are advised, and nothing would have been heard about this claim to the lands of the province as their patrimony if it had not been pressed upon them by injudicious advising. I will quote the following extracts from the judgment of Chancellor Boyd, of Ontario :

" The colonial policy of Great Britain, as it regards the claims and treatment of the aboriginal populations in America, has been from the first uniform and well defined. Indian peoples were found scattered wide-cast over the continent, having, as a characteristic, no fixed abodes, but moving as the exigencies of living demanded. As heathens and barbarians, it was not thought that they had any proprietary title to the soil, nor any such claim thereto as to interfere with the plantations, and the general prosecution of colonization. They were treated ' justly and graciously,' as Lord Bacon advised, but no legal ownership of the land was ever attributed to them. The Attorney-General, in his argument, called my attention to a joint opinion given by a ' multitude of counsellors,' about 675, touching land in New York, while yet a province under English rule."

The opinion referred to was as follows :

" Councell's opinion concerning Coll Nicholl's patent and Indian purchases :

"The land called N. York and other parts in America now called N. East Jersey, was first discovered by Sebastian Cobbitt, a subject of England, in King Henry ye Seventh time, about 180 years since and afterwards, further by Sir Walter Raleigh, in ye reign of Queen Eliz. and after him by Henery Hudson in ye reign of King James, and also by the Lord Deleware and begun to be planted in ye year 1614 by Dutch and English   The Dutch placed a governour there, but upon complaint made by the King of England to ye states of Holland, the said states disowned ye bisness and declared it was only a private undertaking of ye West India Company, of Amsterdam, so ye King of England granted a comison to Sir Edward Laydon to plant these parts calling them New Albion and ye Dutch submitted themselves to ye English government, but in King Charles ye I's reign ye troubles in England breaking forth, the English not minding to promote these new plantations because of ye troubles, ye Dutch pretended to establish a government there again until ye year 1660, when afterwards it was reduced under ye English government and included and ratified in ye peace made between England and Holland ; then it was granted to ye Duke of York, 1664, who ye same year granted it to ye Ld Barckley and Sr George Cartrett, betwixt ye Duke's grant to ye Ld Barckley and Sr George Cartrett, and notice thereof in America several persons took grants of land from Coll Nicholls, ye Duke's govnor   Severall of ye planters have purchased of ye Indians, but refuse to pay any acknowledgement to ye King's grantees

" Q. 1st. Wither ye grants made by Coll Nicholls are

good against the assigns of ye Ld Barckley and Sr George Cartrett.

"Q. 2nd. Wither the grants from ye Indians be sufficient to any planter without a grant from ye King or his assigns.

"Ans. 1st. To ye first question the authority by which Coll Nicholls acted determined by ye Duke's grant to ye Ld Barckley and Sr George Cartrett and all grants made by him afterwards (tho according to ye comison) are void, for ye delegated power wch Coll Nicholls had of making grantes of ye land could last no longer than his master's interest who gave him ye power and ye having or not having notice of ye Duke's grant to ye Lord Barckley and Sr George Cartrett, makes no difference in ye law, but ye want of notice makes it great equity, yet ye present proprietrs should confirm such grant to ye people who will submitt to the comissions and payments of the present proprietors. Quitt rents, otherwise they may look upon them as Deceivers and treat them as such.

"Answ. To the 2nd Question by ye Law of Nations if any people make ye Discovery have ye Right of ye Soyle and Governt of yt place and no people can plant there without ye Consent of ye Prince or of such persons to whom his rights is Devoulved and conveyed. The practice of all Plantations has been according to this and no people have been Suffered to take up Land but by ye Consent and Lycence of ye govr or proprietors under ye princes title whose people made ye first discovery and upon their submition to ye laws of ye place and contribution to ye public charge of ye place and ye payment of such rent and other value for ye soile as ye proprietrs for ye time being required, and tho it hath been and still is ye usuall practice of all proprietrs to give their Indians some recompence for their land and seem to purchase it of them, yet yt is not done for want of sufficient title from ye king or prince who hath ye right of discovery, but out of prudence and Christian charity, least otherwise the Indians might have destroyed ye first planters (who are usually to few to defend themselves) or refuse all commerce and conversation with the planters and thereby all hopes of converting them to ye Christian faith would be lost. In this the common law of England and ye civill law doth agree, and if any planter be refractory and will insist on his Indian purchase and not submit to this law of plantations, ye proprietrs who have ye title under ye prince may deny them ye benefit of ye law and prohibitt commerce with them as opposers and enemys to ye public peace. Besides tis observable yt no man can goe from England to plant in an English plantation without leave from ye government, and, therefore, in all patents and grants of plantations from ye king a particular license to carry over planters is inserted, which power is prohibitting, is now in ye proprietors as ye king assigns, and therefore the same planters have purchased from ye Indians, yett having done soe without ye consent of ye proprietors for ye time being ye title is good against the Indians, but not against the proprietors without a confirmation from them upon the usuall terms of other plantations."

" WM. LEEK,	JO HOLT,
WM. WILLIAMS,	WM. THOMSON,
JO. HOLLES,	RICHD. WALLOP,
JOHN HOYLE,	HEN. POLLEXFEN.

" A true copy :
GARVIN LAURIE,
ROBT. WEST."

The above printed extract is from vol. xiii. of "Documents relating to the Colonial History of the State of New York," p. 486.

I think it accurately states the constitutional law in these words ·

" Though it hath been and still is the usual practice of all proprietors to give their Indians some recompense for their

land, and *so seem to purchase it of them.* Yet that is not
done for want of sufficient title from the king or prince who
hath the right of discovery, but out of prudence and Christian charity, least otherwise the Indians might have destroyed the first planters (who are usually too few to defend
themselves), or refuse all commerce and conversation with
the planters, and thereby all hopes of converting them to the
Christian faith would be lost. In this the common law of
England and the civil law doth agree. . . . Though some
planters have purchased from Indians, yet having done so
without the consent of the proprietors for the time being the
title is good against the Indians but not against the proprietors without a confirmation from them upon the usual terms
of other plantations? (Vol. xiii., " Documents relating to
Colonial History of the State of New York," p. 486.)

Of the six counsel who sign this opinion, one (Richard
Wallop) became Cursitor Baron of the Exchequer, another
(Henry Pollexsea) became Chief Justice of the Common
Pleas, and a third (Holt) was afterward Chief Justice of
England.

In a classical judgment, Marshall, C. J., has concisely
stated the same law of the mother country, which the United
States inherited and applied, with such modifications as were
necessitated by the change of government, to their late dealings with the Indians. I quote passages from Johnson and
McIntosh, 8 Wheat., p. 595, etc.

" According to the theory of the British constitution, all
vacant lands are vested in the crown, as representing the
nation; and the exclusive power to grant them is admitted
to reside in the crown as a branch of the royal prerogative.
. . . This principle was as fully recognized in America
as in the land of Great Britain. So far as respected the authority of the crown, no distinction was taken between vacant
lands and lands occupied by Indians. The title, subject to
the right of occupancy by the Indians, was admitted to be in

the king, as was his right to grant that title." At p. 588 :
"All our institutions recognize the absolute title of the crown,
subject only to the Indian right of occupancy, and recognize
the absolute title of the crown to extinguish that right."

Again   The relations between the government and the
Indians charge upon the establishment of reserves.   While
in the nomadic state they may or may not choose to treat
with the crown for the extraction of their primitive right of
occupancy.   If they refuse, the government is not hampered, but has perfect liberty to proceed with the settlement
and development of the country, and so sooner or later dis-
place them.   If, however, they elect to treat, they then become, in a special sense, wards of the state, are surrounded
by its protection while under pupilage, and have their rights
assured in perpetuity to the usual land-reserve.   In regard
to this reserve the tribe enjoy practically all the advantages
and safeguards of private resident proprietors.

BEFORE THE APPROPRIATION OF RESERVES THE IND-
IANS HAVE NO CLAIM EXCEPT UPON THE BOUNTY AND
BENEVOLENCE OF THE CROWN.   After the appropriation
they become invested with a legally recognized tenure of
defined lands, in which they have a present right as to the
exclusive and absolute contract, and a potential right of becoming individual owners in fee after enfranchisement.

It follows that land ungranted, upon which Indians are
living at large in their primitive state within any province,
form part of the public lands, and are held as before Confederation by that province under various sections of the B.
N. A. Act.   M. W. T. DRAKE.

____

RIGHTS OF ABORIGINES.

From the *Daily Colonist*, Victoria, B. C., October 30, 1886.

TO THE EDITOR : No one, I imagine, who considers
the human necessity to the *de facto* governments of the

world, entertains for a moment the wild idea that the rights of aborigines in the soil occupied by their fathers are to be placed on a level with civilized tenures. In no case, that I am aware of, has such a notion been entertained, even by the natives themselves. The Indians perfectly understand that the land is not of the same value to them as it is to the civilized community, and that they cannot make it so ; and they are therefore ever found content with fair and equitable reserves and capitation grants (non-interceptible), coupled with the protection of the law, and adjustment of claims in certain limited localities whereon their livelihood depends. This, I apprehend, is the whole science of dealing with Indian rights, the fundamental principle of which is natural justice, or that unwritten law which the most barbarous governments cannot afford wholly to despise.

I discern this principle underlying Mr. Drake's quotations, veiled as it is by a species of lofty grandiloquence, which reads rather strangely in our day, from which, however, that gentleman appears to draw conclusions which are neither just nor accordant with facts.

There is no risk, as there ought to be no disdain, in treating with the Indians with the extinction of their claims. This, however, our governments, so far as the northern tribes are concerned, have, if I am not mistaken, stiffly refused to do, preferring apparently the Alexandrian method of cutting the knot which—one cannot but fear—they are too haughty to stoop down to unloose, therein, also, uniquely departing from the almost universal method pursued in the States, in Canada, and in other parts of this province, and, in fact, laid down as law, in Mr. Drake's own chosen authorities.

Without wishing to use strong language, truth and a deep sense of the public weal compel me to express my conviction that the governments have been, and still are, sadly and fatally going astray over this very simple matter. The track of blood which in the Northwest has marked, and in this province now threatens to mark, the executive path, I pray God may not be laid to the charge of our rulers, but that they may be shown the better way of peace.

I may, in conclusion, add my belief that after the unqualified declaration alleged to have been made by the highest legal authority of the province in this very case, that the Indians have *no rights* in the land—a declaration which, for the sake of majesty, must be received with awe, if not with conviction—the Metlakahtlans will see the futility of prosecuting their rights by civil process ; the matter being already, by anticipation, decided against them ; and as I am well persuaded that they will not resort to violence (I speak not of the uncultivated tribes beyond), my counsel to this troubled community, whose temper and forbearance the highest in the land might do well to imitate, is to bow to the storm ; appeal to God and the Queen, as a people hemmed in by the sword but not conquered ; reserve their contributions ; pursue their industries ; and wait for the day. The day will surely come, and I would call upon all Christian people to pray the King of kings, and Judge among judges, to give wisdom to the rulers, peace to the realm, and glory to His own great name.

October 29, 1886.   EDWARD CRIDGE.

BELLIGERENT INDIANS.

From the *Daily Colonist*, Victoria, B. C , October 30, 1886

TO THE EDITOR : An article published in the *Weekly Times* of the 17th ult., headed " Belligerent Indians," condemned our action in preventing Mr. Tuck, the surveyor, from taking off a piece of our land to be a reserve   May I ask you kindly to allow me to say a few words in your paper, that your readers may see why trouble is still existing, and increasing among us. This trouble, which began nearly five years ago, could easily have been settled if it had been only treated in a civilized way in the commencement, for " a stitch in time saves nine."

When we knew that our case was a severe one, and the wound was deep, we at once laid it before the government authorities, and pointed out to them where the sore was. The men in authority acknowledged that the wound was a painful one, and expressed their wish to see it cured. The only remedy they tried to cure it with was speaking to us of government power or soothing us with promises of justice.

The one-sided Government Commission of Inquiry, in " Micawber's " style, pretended to examine into the cause of this trouble ; but, like " Micawber," failed to make any satisfactory settlement. But instead, they recommended the government to take off two acres of our village site, against our written protest, to be government land held in trust by the government for the exclusive use of the Church Missionary Society.

When we found out that all this work was not meant to settle our trouble but was mere pretension, we sent three of our native brethren as delegates to " Ottawa," who conveyed complaints, especially about the " two acres," to the Dominion Government. Sir John Macdonald, the Premier, listened to our complaints and told our representatives he would write to the Church Missionary Society advising them to remove from the " two acres " and that he would consider the other matters we had told him of. He also wrote us a letter, dated July 29, 1885, in which he says : " On receipt of a reply from that society I will write you regarding said matter and in respect to the other subjects brought before me in the papers filed by you."

Up to this date we have not received his promised letter ; but instead of writing to us he sent up Mr. Tuck on August 24th last, to scratch the old sore with a surveying instrument.

Sir, it may be the $60,000 sale of the Songeesh village made the Dominion Government forget the promise they made to us about settling our land troubles. Possibly they are looking forward to another lucky sale of our land when it is surveyed into a " reserve," and to transport us, the lawful owners, to another " ten-mile point," for " what man has done man can do again."

I ask by what right the Dominion Government own the money that Mr. Dunsmuir paid for that property ? Is honest and strict John Bull aware of these " semi-civilized " ways of doing business ? The *Times* railed at us as a set of lawless people warring against government power because we say that the land of our forefathers, which we have inherited, belongs to us and not to the government, and recommended that a gun-boat should be sent up again to settle this trouble, as if it could be cleared by grape-shot. This " semi-civilized " talker knows not that Her Majesty's ships are protectors of the lives and property of all those who are under the British flag, and not oppressors.

The game of trying to cure our complaints with gun-boats was played on us several times, and several times we have been falsely accused in the Queen's name as law-breakers, and unlawfully punished. But every time when our case was tried in a court of law we were treated not as lawbreakers but as law-abiding people.

If we are again to be maliciously punished in the name of our Queen, for being land-owners, we will submit to such punishment as before , but to be as squatters on our own land, we cannot submit to that. The Queen's own representative, Lord Dufferin, acknowledged our right to this land, and did not claim it to be the Queen's land without a treaty having first been made with us. His civilized words are still ringing in our ears. Cannon balls will not kill them. The *Times* recommends a gun-boat to " bring us to our senses." Is it the way of civilized people to recommend punishment to persons before they are known to have broken the law?

And are we out of our senses and warring against England's law because we hold fast our title to our inheritance? Is not the love of a bird for its nest a natural feeling given to it by the Creator? Does it need a " white teacher " to implant this feeling in its breast? In the Tsimshean heart just the same love for their "nest" (nest is the word by which the Tsimsheans used to call their land) has existed for generations before the " white teacher " came. Mr. Duncan did not put this feeling into our hearts. Before he came our people fought and killed those who tried to rob them of their land; and since he came he has shown us a better way of defending it. The *Times* falsely says that Mr. Duncan has taught us to be lawless, and trouble-makers; instead of this he has taught us to appeal to the laws of our Queen as our protection. Is this a crime? Mr. Duncan's work among Tsimsheans for the past twenty-nine years speaks for itself.

Cheating and underhand dealing with Tsimsheans is now too late. That game would have answered thirty years ago when European fur-dealers paid for a prime black bear-skin with a lacquered tin cup. What is wanted nowadays in dealing with our fellow-men is a civilized way of doing business, " a just balance, just weights, a just ephah, and a just hin."

Sir, I must confess that I do not believe our inheritance will be taken away from us by oppression by our Christian Queen, whose righteous laws are from God's book, the Bible, and were made for the benefit of all. It is written, " The prince shall not take of the people's inheritance by oppression to thrust them out of their possession; but he shall give his sons inheritance out of his own possession; that my people be not scattered every man from his possession " (Ezekiel xlvi. 18).

Let the world know that we are upholding the just laws of our Queen. Oppression and robbery are contrary to the laws both of God and the Queen.

Y. D. DETERMIN.
[DAVID LEASK].
Native of Metlakahtla.

METLAKAHTLA, B. C., October 8, 1886.

THE INDIAN QUESTION.

From the *Daily Colonist*, Victoria, B C., October 31, 1886.

TO THE EDITOR : Bishop Cridge, in a letter to your journal, has expressed his opinion as to the right of the Indians to the soil they have occupied for centuries, an opinion not intended to be an exposition of the law of England with regard to the Indian title and the old policy, but an opinion founded on common-sense and principles of justice. The nations of Europe by superior force, and not by right, have made a law unto themselves with reference to the rights of the inhabitants of lands they have discovered. England and other nations discover an island or a continent inhabited by a people they, from their stand-point, call barbarians, and by reason of their superior force and the weakness of the so-called barbarians, they take possession of their country, and out of *Christian charity* they allow them to occupy a part of it. Where does the Christian charity commence? Is it in first knocking a man down and robbing him because you are civilized and Christian, and your victim is not, and then out of Christian charity giving him back the smallest possible portion of his own goods—which were taken by force? This is the law of England as expounded by eminent counsel, as quoted by Mr. Drake in his letter of yesterday, in which he censures Bishop Cridge for his opinions and says, ' That he cannot help thinking that the publication, at this juncture, of such views as are contained in that letter, is nothing more than an active encouragement to the Indians to resist a peaceable settlement of what has been a continual source of expense and trouble to the province.' Now, sir, I would like to ask which is most likely to engender feelings of discontent and revenge in the Indian mind—to be told by Bishop Cridge that they have rights in and to the country which they and their ancestors have occupied for centuries, or to be told by Mr. Drake on the authority of counsel, however eminent, that they have no right or title, and that the portions of their own country set apart for them by those who took possession of their country is theirs only by charity and clemency and not by a shadow of right?

I am not a lawyer and I therefore ask the question, Is not the law in very many cases founded on custom? And although European nations in their colonial policy made unto themselves a law for claiming and holding discovered inhabited lands by force if necessary, yet what has been the custom even in the (now antiquated) legal opinions quoted by Mr. Drake, in support of the exclusive right of title in the crown, the following will be found: 'Though it hath been, and still is, the *usual* practice of all proprietors (sovereigns) to give their Indians some recompense for *their land* (it will be seen that the land is here called *their land*—inadvertently, no doubt, those words of truth slipped in), and so seem to purchase it from them, yet that is not done for want of sufficient title from the king or prince who hath the right of discovery, but out of prudence and Christian charity, least otherwise the Indians might have destroyed the first planters, who are usually too few to defend themselves, or refuse all commerce or conversation with the planters, and thereby all hopes of converting them to the Christian faith would be lost.' I say, then, if recompense has been the usual custom for 200 years, is it not now the law?

I ask any common person to imagine what the effect must

be, and what evils have taken place in trying to enforce a law founded on the principle of might here laid down.

We are told that out of prudence and charity they are paid for *their land.* " Their land " must mean the Indian's own land. The charity, it will be observed, was not for the Indians but for the planters who might be too few to defend themselves—and lest the Indians should refuse to trade—so that Christian rulers, from the actual fear that the Indians were too powerful for the early colonists and that the gains of the colonists or planters should be lessened by the Indians not trading with them, have of their Christian bounty paid them for their own lands—and on these noble and disinterested principles of justice is founded the law of England affecting the colonial policy.

I think I am correct in stating that the law quoted by Mr. Drake is unwritten so far as being enacted by any imperial statute, and is entirely the outcome of ignorant and arbitrary expediency of past ages. Since the colonies took in hand the management of their own affairs, the governments of nearly every colony and territory have come to the conclusion, whether from motives of fear or honesty, that the original occupiers of the soil must be dealt with, and their rights to those portions of the country not requisite for their actual use they should be invited to surrender by treaty for a substantial consideration In the United States all the Indian nations have been settled with by treaty, and in lieu of the domain surrendered they receive an annual allowance in food, clothing, and perhaps money—the government of that country fully recognizing that if the food-supply of the Indians is lessened by the settlement of the whites on their former hunting grounds, that it is the duty of the government to provide for their wants. Such a policy as this has been enjoined by imperial recommendation or proclamation on the older provinces of Canada, to which they have in nearly every case given effect. We have only to look at the Indian

policy of the Dominion Government in the Northwest Territory to be satisfied that Indians have some right and title to
the soil they occupy, and that the opinions quoted by Mr.
Drake, although law, have through custom become inopera-
tive in the light of the nineteenth century. The Dominion
Government has so fully and freely acknowledged the claims
of Indians to the soil over which they roamed that they have
been most anxious that such claims should be surrendered
by legal treaty, as being necessary in the interests of peace,
good government, and the settlement of the country, and all
the tribes who have "taken treaty" receive subsidies in
money, food, and clothing. Such a policy is in perfect harmony with Bishop Cridge's views, because they are humane
and just.   W. J. MACDONALD.

[Life Senator of Dominion Parliament of Canada from British Columbia.]

THE METLAKAHTLANS.

From the *Daily Colonist*, Victoria, B. C., November 2, 1886.

TO THE EDITOR: The Metlakahtla "fizgig" is occasioned by the endeavor and intention of the provincial
government to define the boundaries of a tract of land
seventy thousand acres in extent attached to and surrounding the Indian village at Metlakahtla and for the benefit of
the Indians and no one else. The Indians, through their
white misleaders, prevent by violence the surveyors appointed by the government performing this duty. They
openly oppose the government, but thus far—chiefly through
the forbearance of the surveyors—no grievous bodily harm
has been done to anyone. The Metlakahtla question is *not
one of pseudo-christianity or pseudo-philanthropy; but*
whether Indians shall be allowed at the instigation of their
misleaders to set the rule of the province at their defiance.
There can be but one answer to this question. Neither
the Indian policy of the United States nor that of Eastern

Canada has ever been adopted by British Columbia, so their practice has nothing to do with that of this province. Some five and thirty years ago Vancouver Island had a government of its own, and in dealing with the Indian question had to make a policy suitable to the Indians and to local conditions.

It was determined that the Indians should not be disturbed in their villages, but that a tract of land surrounding each village should be marked off for the inhabitants thereof for their use and benefit. It was determined not to remove them from their villages and huddle them into one or more general pen or pens for various reasons, such as that, being fish-eating Indians, they could sustain themselves better in several localities than in one ; that the tribes, being perpetually at variance with each other, nothing but murders would ensue if hostile tribes were huddled together, that the sentimental feelings of the Indians with regard to their village sites and graveyards should be respected ; that by segregation and living near or among the whites they would follow their example—learn to work—to become farmers and so forth—to become civilized and ultimately to be merged—when they know civilized ideas of right and wrong, as equals in the body politic. Such has been the Indian policy of Vancouver Island for the past thirty-five years, almost as long as the foundation of the colony. During this period Vancouver Island and the mainland became united into one colony. The Indian policy of Vancouver Island was put in force on the mainland also, when the united colonies became part and parcel of Canada This system was unaltered, and to-day is the rule and policy of British Columbia, and must be submitted to by Metlakahtlans and their misleaders, as well as by other Indian tribes. It is a system suitable generally to the province and to the aborigines.

During the past forty years, too, the province has had

many and every variety of governors—imperial and otherwise, but the policy was never altered on their account; in fact, they probably did not even recommend it. That this policy has been beneficial to the Indians—look at results—they are patent to all. A few years ago the tribes were perpetually at war, and the Indians lived ever, night and day, in dread. Now they live in peace and quiet. A few years ago they murdered each other; now they do not. A few years ago they were comparatively naked; now they are well clothed, and, instead of being poor, they are rich, rich in various ways and in money, and the misleaders had better ask themselves whose superscription is the current coin. A few years ago the strangers drove, when they could, tribes from their lands and appropriated them; even this was the case on the Northern coast and at Metlakahtla. These conquerers did not give the conquered anything but death or slavery. Talk of compensation for land! Why, the Indians have been compensated a thousand-fold, and are still continuing to be compensated, by having had and still having, a civilized people among them. A civilized people who have induced the Indians to become civilized, to leave off murder, leave off stealing, leave off wars, and leave off quasi-cannibalism at their " medicine feasts." The civilized give them employment and pay them therefor, give them the knowledge of bettering their condition, of which they avail themselves to a considerable degree; in fact, owing to the presence of the whites, the Indians are now better off than myriads of people in Great Britain, inland, and other large and civilized communities. And yet their misleaders ask for compensation. Shame!

British Columbia has not, during the past thirty-five years, acknowledged any Indian title to land, save that given them by, may I say, their conquerors—not by the sword, but by civilization and commerce. Do these misleaders want this policy altered for the sake of the Metlakahtlans? Do they want to reduce the Metlakahtlans to a lot of beggars—begging a small pittance of blankets and molasses, for what? Will not the Metlakahtlans disdain to ask, and be ashamed to receive, charity? They are not paupers and would be ashamed to be considered such. They are able-bodied and intelligent—can work for themselves, get their own living and become rich, as many of them are, and be like white men—but to be mendicants—surely never!

The British Columbian Indian policy has never deprived the Indians of anything. They have their liberty. They have justice equally with the whites—no obstruction to their fishing and hunting. They have a larger number of people to buy their produce—in fact, they are a thousand times better off than ever before—and they know it! Land they never made use of—the sea afforded them their means of subsistence. Do the misleaders not make a mistake in not asking compensation for the sea instead of for useless land? The Indians have the benefit of the sale of land as well as the white men. The government make roads and a host of other things with the money, which are as useful to the Indians as whites. Do the Indians contribute anything to the provincial revenue? If they held what their misleaders term their land—would they not have to pay five cents per acre upon "wild land?"

Teach the Indians to work, and work with advantage; this is the chief way of civilizing them and enabling them to become part and parcel of ourselves, but to teach them to rebel is against the law and must not be tolerated. Many agitators have lost their heads, metaphorically and really, before to-day.

Dulce et decorum est pro patria mori, but the misleaders take good care to keep away from the conflict—bide and hide in safety. "Prudence is the better part of valor."

J. S. HELMCKEN.

The name of Dr. Helmcken is not new in British Columbian history; his name will long be remembered in connection with the subjoining case of high-minded justice. Bancroft in descanting on the treatment of the Aborigines under the combined rule of the Hudson's Bay Co. and Colonial Government writes:

" From one of the Company's vessels then lying at Victoria, three men deserted to the *"England"* which then continued her way to Fort Rupert. Meanwhile notice was sent to Rupert of the deserters, who thereupon became frightened, left the " *England*" and took to the woods, intending to join the vessel at another port. Indians were sent in pursuit with orders from Blenkinsop, then acting for the Company at Fort Rupert, to bring the deserters dead or alive. Four days afterward the Indians returned and claimed the reward saying that they had killed them all. It was true. The sailors had been shot down in the forest by savages set upon them by an officer of the Hudson's Bay Co.

" Now mark the course of justice pursued by the officers of the imperial government. Instead of proceeding against the instigators of the murder, and arresting the officers of the Hudson's Bay Company, as they should have done, they direct the full force of their vengeance against the natives. *Helmcken, the newly fledged magistrate, cognizant of the whole affair, and well knowing who were the guilty persons, and what hand he himself had in it,* goes to the Newittee camp, twelve miles distant, and loudly demands the surrender of the murderers. The savages acknowledge the murder, but plead that they were only executing orders. Truer to themselves and to the right than were the white men, they refused to give up the perpetrators of the deed, but offered to give up the property paid them by the white men for the commission of the crime. This did not satisfy the European justice-dealers. Servants of the Hudson's Bay Company. Some one must be punished ; and as they did not wish to hang themselves, they must find victims among their instruments. As the magistrate was unable to accomplish their purpose, Wellesley sent a force under Lieutenant Burton, in three boats of the " *Dædalus*," against the Newittees. Finding their camp deserted, Burton destroyed the village, and made a bonfire of all the property he could find. The following summer, H. M S. " *Daphne*," Captain Fanshawe arrived. Meanwhile the Newittees had rebuilt their village, supposing the white men satisfied with the injury already inflicted. One day while holding a potlach, and being at peace, as they believed, with the white men, the " *Daphne's*" boats, under Lieutenant Lacy, crept into their harbor, and announced their arrival by a discharge of musketry. Men, women, and children were mercilessly cut down, persons innocent of any thought of wrong against their murderers, and their village again destroyed. Then the " *Daphne*" sailed away. Justice was satisfied ; and Blenkinsop and the rest of them went about their work as usual."

Who now will question, the propriety of Dr. Helmcken's, sitting in judgment upon the rights of the Natives ?

———

RIGHTS OF ABORIGINES.

From the *Daily Colonist*, Victoria, B. C , November 2, 1886.

To THE EDITOR . Bishop Cridge's letter in the *Colonist's* issue of the 28th inst. is, I apprehend, not likely to promote the cause of peace and good will, but the contrary, should it reach the recusant Metlakahtlans ere they have been shown the error of their ways. And here, parenthetically, let me state that before Mr. Duncan's settling at Muhki-tli-kaatla (the Indian name of the place), no sept of the Tsimshean speakers went by that name. That it had been an ancient village site for one of these septs I perceived when there very early in 1866, and utilized by Mr. Duncan, then, by his desire visiting the sick throughout the modern settlement of his forming. Several erroneous positions are assumed in the worthy bishop's letter, to be duly dealt with, no doubt, when the Metlakahtla case, if ever, comes into court.

Practically, this Western Canada of ours became a British possession so soon as fur-traders from Montreal and Hudson's Bay, working toward the setting sun, had, much to the satisfaction of the savage natives, reached the shores of the Pacific Ocean. These white men, in pursuit of the still too mighty dollar, and not without their due share of human infirmities, from which, alas! neither clergyman nor missionaries are exempt, were nevertheless chiefly, but not altogether in furtherance of their commercial pursuits, great civilizers of the untutored red men, whom from Southern Alaska to Southern Oregon they tamed into peaceable reception of the immigrating white man, who, mainly through his own, perhaps inevitable, blundering, and necessarily after fur-trading influence for peace, much weakened, had no trouble with the Indians.

On our own northwest coast, from Nisqually, W. T., to the Canadian Alaskan boundary, influences for peace for more than twenty years before Mr. Duncan, as a guest at Fort Simpson (H. B. Co.'s post), began his *then* useful teachings, had been greatly increased by the equalization of distribution of Hudson's Bay guns and ammunition, by the regular visits of the Hudson's Bay Company's steamer Beaver to every nook and corner of the very large sea-frontage of our mainland, wherever furs could be purchased. Thus, in due time, kidnapping and plundering, murderous raids, executed with the greatest treachery and secrecy, were terminated; and all found it advantageous to meet peaceably, to sell, buy, and barter at the white man's trading post, or at the appointed rendezvous of his trading steamer. Be it also remembered that at Hudson's Bay posts, in a measure, doubtless, in the interests of trade, it was a rule to discountenance the marauder and murderer, and to encourage, by kindly treatment, the peaceable and industrious. The murderer of a white man was pursued relentlessly and in the end punished as he deserved, or made an outcast of.

I had got thus far, when in the *Colonist* of to-day, October 30th, I observed my friend Bishop Cridge's second letter under the heading "Rights of Aborigines," which I gladly adopt as the title or caption of "these presents." I have only to say particularly of the bishop's second letter, and I say it emphatically, that the bloodguiltiness, if any should anywhere ensue, from present recusancy of a very small portion of the Tsimshean wide-spread nation, will be directly chargeable against the *mal-advisers* for the last five years of those previously peaceable, and for good ends eminently tractable people. Next, I cordially appeal to the sense of natural justice, to the unwritten laws mentioned in my friend's second letter. I call a halt, I urge a truce between the present contending parties, and invite them jointly with "all Christian people" (to quote my friend's words) and other humane men and women, within the province and throughout the Dominion, to combine with us in an immediate and urgent effort to induce our worthy Dominion Premier and his able, right-minded Cabinet to give to the Tsimshean now at Metlakahtla, with their tribes-men, and to the Songeesh and Swhymal Indians, conjointly, of our own near neighborhood—all on suitable reservations—able teachers of English, spoken and written, instructors in the most needed useful arts, a boarding-house for scholars from a distance, a hospital for the infirm and for her foundlings, and such other aid as would fit the Indians middle-aged and young for voting and for earning a livelihood as, and among, the white occupants of their country, of their wonted use of which they, in certain parts, but not on the Northwest coast, have been greatly deprived by our pastoral claims, enclosures, flocks, herds, etc.

Surely, Mr. Editor, sectarian divisions, weakening as the years roll on, should not prevent all religionists, churched or unchurched, or humane people, if unhappily without religion, from joining in this suggested good work, so urgently required at this critical moment.

As people claiming to be in the van of civilization we Columbians, Midland and Eastern Canadians, owe to our Indians a very kind, liberal, and judicious management, *as from wise guardian to helpless ward.* It is painful, sir, to know, as I do from frequent inquiry at Indians in Victoria streets, how very few of their children outlive infancy.

W. F. TOLMIE.

_____

"MISLEADERS" OF THE INDIANS.

From the *Daily Colonist*, Victoria, B. C., November 3, 1886.

TO THE EDITOR : The attention of the public is again being directed to the Indian land question, and well will it be for the province if the subject is met, discussed, and settled honestly, dispassionately, and equitably.

The question of land interests is confessedly just now a knotty and vital one for more countries than British Columbia. No question of modern times is engrossing so much time and taxing the talents of our statesmen. And it is notorious that most of the troubles of this generation are the outcome of blundering and injustice in years gone by, in reference to land matters.

British Columbia is called upon to settle the question squarely and justly. It is not a matter to be settled by abusing individuals or talking of generalities. If British Columbia is to be exempt from the errors and sad experience of older countries the rights of the Indians in the land must be ascertained, defined, enforced, and as sacredly defended as the rights of white men are.

Unfortunately, the question is hampered at the outset by the fact that the Indians are the weak, the poor, and the despised ones In asserting their claims they are, therefore, ever in danger of arousing the enmity and greed of their powerful neighbors. Those of us who dare befriend them or interpret their words or views are denounced as conspirators. Be it so. History is ever repeating itself, because the conditions of life remain unchanged. The struggle of right with wrong inevitably must go on to the disadvantage of right till the tune on the organ of the present dispensation is finished and the stop is changed by the hand of the Omnipotent and All-wise.

For the purpose of throwing new light on the subject at issue, it may not be inopportune at this juncture to place before the public the statements of persons in authority now living, and leave readers to decide for themselves whether those persons who deal with facts are misleaders or not in Indian affairs The Superintendent-General of Indian Affairs occupying the same position as Sir John Macdonald does now toward the Indians, in a communication to the provincial government, dated Ottawa, November 2, 1874, says : "A cursory glance at these documents is enough to show that the present state of the Indian land question in our territory west of the Rocky Mountains is most unsatisfactory, and that it is the occasion not only of great discontent among the aboriginal tribes, but also of serious alarm to the white settlers. The guaranteeing the aborigines of British Columbia the continuance of a policy as liberal as was pursued by the local government seems little short of a mockery of their claims.

" If there has not been an Indian war, it is not because there has been no injustice to the Indians, but because the Indians have not been sufficiently united."

Again, in a communication from the Department of Justice, dated Ottawa, January 19, 1875, occur the following :

" No surrenders of lands in British Columbia Province has ever been obtained from the Indian tribes with one exception. . . . Any reservations which have been made have been arbitrary on the part of the government, and without the assent of the Indians themselves.

" There is not a shadow of doubt that from the earliest times England has always felt it imperative to meet the Indians in council, and to obtain surrenders of tracts of Canada as from time to time such were required for the purposes of settlement. . . .

" It is sufficient for the present purpose to ascertain the policy of England in respect to the acquisition of the Indian territorial rights, and how entirely that policy has been followed to the present time except in the instance of British Columbia."

I think it unnecessary to quote further from these authoritative documents, but surely such words from such men ought to have weight with every honest mind.

The words and views on this subject of that great statesman Lord Dufferin, when occupying the highest position in the Dominion of Canada, are well known. I will remind the public only of a line or two. He said : " Most unfortunately, as I think, there has been an initial error ever since Sir James Douglas quitted office, in the government of British Columbia neglecting to recognize what is known as the Indian title."

In conclusion, I would ask, can it be right to characterize such persons whose views I have quoted as misleaders of the Indians, and is it not startling to hear from the lips of the chief justice in a court room—that the words of the Governor-General of Canada on this subject, spoken before " the leading men " of this province in Victoria, were only " blarney for the mob ? "

If the editor of the *Colonist* will permit me, I propose publishing copies of the documents which were filed last summer on Indian affairs when the Tsimshean delegates visited Ottawa. From these documents it will be seen, I think, that the Indians ask for nothing unreasonable and certainly for nothing in the direction of presents, which some suppose they ask for.   WILLIAM DUNCAN.

INDIAN TITLE.

From the *Daily Colonist*, Victoria, B C , November 4, 1886.

TO THE EDITOR : Does not Mr. Duncan see that in writing, " Lord Dufferin considered the Indians to have a title to the land," and then immediately afterward writing '· that the chief justice ridiculed the assertion," that the one assertion at least neutralizes the other ? The chief justice's opinion, indeed, does away with Lord Dufferin's fancy altogether, and so destroys Mr. Duncan's contention.

With regard to the ideas of the Superintendent-General of Indian Affairs, in 1874, relative to the supposed Indian rights, he only knew, at this early period after " confederation," what he had been told probably by interested parties, and judged according to his ideas of the policy pursued by his government on the east side of the mountains He is wiser now. The truth is, the position of our coast tribes— the amphibiæ—is vastly different to that of the plain Indians on the eastern side—the one wants sea-water, the other land The plain Indians were removed from their homes, huddled together in hordes, and thus their means of subsistence (hunting, etc.) more or less thus taken away and also destroyed by " sportsmen " foreign to them. They therefore required food, implements, and so forth, from the government, and annually got them.

The case of the coast Indian is entirely different. He has not been removed from his home, and the sea and all therein is have not been taken away from him. His means of subsistence remains in full, and he has an abundance of land for his purpose given him (reserves) into the bargain. The Indian policy of one government must necessarily differ from that of the other—and one may be suited to the condition of things.

With regard to the Superintendent-General's ideas of Indian troubles likely to arise (quoted by Mr. Duncan) with the Indians, about the " Indian title," there would be no danger of anything of the kind if misleaders and agitators did not put their own cranky, socialistic, untenable, impracticable, and unlawful notions into Indian heads. As it is, which has had an Indian war first, Eastern Canada or British Columbia? Judging by this, whose " policy " is the better?

Can anything more explicitly point out the desirability of extending the Nanaimo railway to the north end of the island. Such extension would render access to the Indians quick and safe in times of trouble with them. More of these communicative cranks and teachers will appear among the Indians, for " history repeats itself."

J. S. HELMCKEN.

VICTORIA, B. C., November 3, 1886.

THE INDIAN QUESTION.

From the *Daily Colonist*, Victoria, B C., November 4, 1886.

TO THE EDITOR : I think it is quite possible for a person to come to the discussion of any important public question without any bitter feelings, or saying hard things of a per-

sonal character, especially when nothing is to be gained by
either party and the discussion is intended only to ventilate
important subjects. Calling persons who may express an
opinion misleaders, instigators, agitators, and cowards is
no argument, and will not carry conviction to the mind, although it may tickle the ear of some parties. The opinions
on either side of this Indian title to land is not going to settle the question as if carrying the force of a " pragmatic
sanction," and it is therefore as well to take it in a good-
natured way

It is a matter of fact that a large reserve surrounding
Metlakahtla has been made for the Tsimshean tribe, but
only after much pleading and exhorting of the government
by Mr Duncan to that end, at a time when the intention of
the government was to give ten acres only to each family,
regardless of the quality of the soil or the character of the
country.

To my knowledge there are no white misleaders of the
Metlakahtlans, but quite the contrary. White friends of
theirs have advised them to keep within the law, and to conduct themselves with forbearance and moderation This is
not a mere assertion I can bring the proof, and I am convinced that in this direction Mr. Duncan has always advised
them. " Shame! " might indeed be cried, and Mr. Duncan
or anybody else might well be called a coward " in hiding,"
did he or they not stand up manfully for the rights of the
Indians whenever an attempt is made to ignore those rights.
No white man has instigated them to set the rule of the province at defiance. Those Indians have very good ideas of
right and wrong, which have been instilled into their minds
by white traders. It is true that British Columbia has not
adopted an Indian policy similar to that of Eastern Canada,
that does not put her in an impregnable position, but the
reverse, and the sooner she deals with the Indian question
the easier and cheaper will it be for her. It is true that the

village sites in Vancouver Island were set apart for the Indians, but there was no policy for civilizing them, for bettering their condition, or training them to anything good. No government of British Columbia attempted to establish a school, church, farm, or factory for their instruction. Nothing was done to elevate the Indians. Not until missionaries took up the question of instruction and civilizing was anything done for their temporal or spiritual improvement.

On the other hand, the Government of Canada has some consideration for the Indians—they aid the missionary with money grants for educational purposes, and in the Northwest instruct them in farming and other pursuits, but I am afraid that in their sincere efforts to benefit the red man that their aims are thwarted by the selfish indifference of subordinate agents, who may be too much occupied with their private business to attend to that for which they are paid. Many of the people of Victoria will remember the great speech delivered by Lord Dufferin to our best citizens, in which he alluded in a very emphatic way to the unsatisfactory condition of the Indian title in British Columbia. This subject was not brought to his notice by Victorians; he evidently felt it to be a pressing and important question, or he would not have mentioned it at a time when other questions demanded more immediate attention. He said : " That there could be no doubt that the Indians had a title to the land over which they roamed and which ought to be extinguished." Although those words have not the force of law, yet they are those of an eminent, clear-sighted, and astute statesman, and not " blarney for a Victoria mob," who were not thinking of Indians then. We were afflicted with a railway mania, and the Governor-General's words on the Indian question could not be intended to conciliate us. The improved condition of the Indians cannot be due to the B. C. Indian policy—there was none, beyond that of " masterly inactivity "

No doubt the white men with whom they first came into contact sharpened their appetites for commerce, and if commerce helped to civilize them it was unintentional on the part of the white man.   His advent, however, showed them that the results of exertion and labor were of some value ; they could see that inter-tribal war was not conducive to hunting and trade, and that it was more profitable to slay wild animals than human beings.   Next came the missionary influence and example, and first and foremost among the savage tribes of the North were the labors of Mr. Duncan, who made the first attempt to christianize and civilize them, who first broke down their heathen customs, who first built schools and churches in that part of the country, who first taught them to respect the laws of the country, who first taught them to live in some degree of comfort, and who first made them taste the benefits of living a settled, and civilized life.   Few, very few, whites gave the Indians work for the sake of benefiting them, but Mr. Duncan did, and with much anxiety planned and schemed how he could find remunerative employment for them.   If they are well off to-day it is not because the white man tried to make them so, but because he wanted their services and their furs, for which he paid the smallest price possible.   The Indians indirectly contribute largely to the provincial revenue, and in a large degree directly to the federal revenue, but I never knew the government do the smallest thing to benefit them ; trails formerly used would be as useful to them as the roads of the white man.   When they become voters no doubt sidewalks and roads will be made to their doors.

In conclusion, I maintain that the Indians have rights to the soil, and that in saying so I am misleading no one.

W. J. MACDONALD.

DR. HELMCKEN'S LETTERS.

From the *Daily Colonist*, Victoria, B C , November 25, 1886.

To the Editor · Several statements made by Dr. Helmcken in his correspondence on the Indian question in your columns, if taken in the usual significance of such language and read in the light of the original documents, will place the doctor in the front rank of "misleaders." In your weekly issue, November 5th, he says : " Some five and thirty years ago, Vancouver Island had a government of its own, and in dealing with the Indian question, had to make a policy suited to the Indians and local conditions." He then proceeds to give what can only be called a caricature of said policy, leaving out all reference to the Indian title—the very matter now in issue—and adds : " Such has been the Indian policy for the past thirty-five years, almost from the foundation of the colony. During this period, Vancouver Island and the mainland became united in one colony. The Indian policy of Vancouver Island was put in force on the mainland also, when the united colonies became part and parcel of Canada. This system was unaltered and to-day is the ruling policy of British Columbia, and must be submitted to by Metlakahtlans and their misleaders as well as by other Indian tribes. British Columbia has not, during the past thirty-five years, acknowledged any Indian title to land save that given them by, may I say, their conquerors—not by the sword, but by civilization and commerce." Again, in the weekly issue of November 12th : " Please remember the Indian policy of British Columbia is not an accident—it was formulated by that 'great and good man, Sir James Douglas,' and put into practice with the knowledge of Her Majesty's Government, and the whole system explained to them in a number of despatches." Speaking of the acquisition of the land in Victoria district, the doctor says : " Sir James Douglas made what he termed a treaty of amity and friendship with the Indians, in order to put the earliest settlers on an amicable footing with the Indians. The 'buying out,' as Mr. Duncan terms it, consisted in giving the Indians a quantity of blankets and other *iktas* —they had no further claims. Although Sir James Douglas continued governor for many years after this transaction, he never repeated it—never gave any other tribe a potlatch on this account. The Indians were not averse to the settlement of white people among them, so potlatches, being unnecessary, were discouraged and not resorted to. This very case, then, goes to show that Sir James Douglas was of opinion that the Indians had not any legal rights—thus agreeing with the judges and jurists."

In reply to the above, permit me to call attention to the following from original documents, as showing the views and *true* Indian policy of the home government, Sir James Douglas, and the colonial House of Assembly of Vancouver Island.

Governor Douglas to the Secretary of State for the Colonies.

VICTORIA, March 25, 1861.

MY LORD DUKE: I have the honor of transmitting a petition from the House of Assembly of Vancouver Island to your grace, praying for the aid of Her Majesty's Government in extinguishing the Indian title to the public lands in this colony ; and setting forth with much force and truth the evils that may arise from the neglect of that very necessary precaution. 2. As the native Indian population of Vancouver Island have distinct ideas of property in land, and mutually recognize their several exclusive and possessory rights in certain districts, they would not fail to regard the occupation of such portions of the colony as the white settlers, unless with the full consent of the proprietary tribes, as national wrongs ; and the sense of injury might produce a feeling of irritation against the settlers, and perhaps disaffection to the government that would endanger the peace of the country. 3. Knowing their feelings on that subject, I made it a practice, up to the year 1859, to purchase the native rights in the land, in every case, prior to the settlement of any district ; but since that time, in consequence of the termination of the Hudson's Bay Company's charter, and the want of funds, it has not been in my power to continue it. Your grace must, indeed, be well aware that I have, since then, had the utmost difficulty in raising money enough to defray the most indispensable wants of the government. 4. All the settled districts of the colony, with the exception of Cowichan, Chemainus, and Barclay Sound, have been already bought from the Indians at a cost in no case exceeding £2. 10s. sterling for each family. As the land has, since then, increased in value, the expense would be relatively somewhat greater now, but I think that their claims might be satisfied with a payment of £3 to each family ; so that, taking the native population of those districts at 1,000 families, the sum of £3,000 would meet the whole charge. 5. It would be improper to conceal from your grace the importance of carrying that vital measure into effect without delay. I have, etc.,

(Signed) JAMES DOUGLAS.

The Secretary of State for the Colonies to Governor Douglas, C.B.

DOWNING STREET, October 19, 1861.

SIR : I have had under my consideration your despatch No. 24, of the 25th of March last, transmitting an address from the House of Assembly of Vancouver Island, in which they pray for the assistance of Her Majesty's Government in extinguishing the Indian title to the public lands in the colony, and set forth the evils that may result from a neglect of this precaution.   I am fully sensible of the great importance of purchasing without loss of time the native title to the soil of Vancouver Island , but the acquisition of the title is a purely colonial interest, and the legislature must not entertain any expectation that the British taxpayer will be burthened to supply the funds or British credit pledged for the purpose.   I would earnestly recommend therefore to the house of assembly, that they should enable you to procure the requisite means, but if they should not think proper to do so, Her Majesty's Government cannot undertake to supply the money requisite for an object which, while it is essential to the interests of the people of Vancouver Island, is at the same time purely colonial in its character and trifling in the charge that it would entail.   I have, etc.,

(Signed,)   NEWCASTLE."

It should be here mentioned, that in previous despatches, dated July 31, 1858, and April 11, 1859, respectively, the Secretary of State for the Colonies had written : " Let me not omit to observe, that it should be an invariable condition in all bargains or treaties with the natives, for the cession of lands possessed by them, that subsistence should be supplied to them in some other shape."   " In the case of the Indians at Vancouver Island and British Columbia, Her Majesty's Government earnestly wish that when the advancing requirements of colonization press upon lands occupied by members of that race, measures of liberality and justice may be adopted for compensating them for the surrender of the territory which they have been taught to regard as their own.

From these official documents the following conclusions will probably be reached by impartial readers ·

1. The Indian policy of Sir James Douglas recognized in

a most specific and distinct manner the proprietary title of the Indians to the lands in the different districts which they inhabited. This is still further apparent by the wording of the documentary instruments by which that title was conveyed to Sir James Douglas as representative and agent of the H. B. Co., in respect to the lands from Sooke to Saanich (inclusive) and also Nanaimo and Fort Rupert Copies of these documents, thirteen in number, are now before me, and are denominated " Conveyance of land to Hudson's Bay Company by Indian tribes." In the body of each document it is called a *deed*, and the transaction is called a *sale*. The price in pounds, shillings, and pence is in each case stated, and conditions carefully noted. Signatures of Indian chiefs and heads of families are affixed, as also those of witnesses, with date and place of execution.

2. That the government of Her Majesty enjoined such a policy and warmly approved Sir James Douglas' efforts to carry it out.

3. That the House of Assembly for Vancouver Island just as clearly recognized the Indian title, and the necessity for purchasing it before the settlement of the various districts by the whites, and asked for aid in continuing this policy.

4. That the reason why this humane, British, and Christian policy was not continued, was not that Sir James Douglas, or the local house, or the home government, had ascertained the policy to be unwise, or wrong, or that they had changed their minds in reference to its wisdom and justice; but simply and solely that a depleted colonial exchequer would not supply the requisite funds, and the home government were unwilling to use British funds for colonial purposes. From that date the " policy " of Sir James, indorsed by the local house, the home government, and later the Dominion Government, has been held in abeyance. The evil effects of this condition of things has shown itself from year to year in dissatisfaction and difficulty among the

Indians where the whites have settled without the Indian title having first been dealt with. This appears from the official correspondence of government agents and surveyors, and is not confined to the northwest coast of the mainland, much less to Metlakahtla.

5. As the titles or claims in question do not cancel themselves by the lapse of years, it may be affirmed to-day, in the language of Mr. Nind (then government agent at Lytton), under date July 17, 1865 : " They (the Indians) are jealous of their possessory rights, and are not likely to permit settlers to challenge them with impunity , nor, such is their spirit and unanimity, would many settlers think it worth while to encounter their undisguised opposition. . . . I believe the only method of settling this matter satisfactorily, and with equity to both Indians and whites, will be for the government to extinguish the Indian claims, paying them what is proper for so doing, and giving them certain reservations for their sole use " It is to be hoped, in the interest of justice and British fair play, to say nothing of humanity and religion, that the government will take hold of this skeleton, kept in the official cupboard for so many years, which " will not down " any longer, and deal with it in a fair, equitable, and statesman-like manner. And I may be permitted to suggest, as my humble opinion, that it can best be done by taking up the matter where it was left when the above-quoted reply of the Duke of Newcastle to the address of the local house was received at Victoria. It will no doubt cost more to settle these claims by treaty now than it would have done then ; but not so much as some people suppose, and besides, its being right and in accordance with the golden rule (which, it is to be feared, some who think more of the *gold* than of the *rule*, care little about), it is after all the most economical way in which the matter will ever be settled. Enough has already been spent in utterly abortive efforts at settlement upon a *wrong basis* to have extinguished

quite a number of these claims—and the end is not yet! When General Sherman was sent to settle the Cheyennes, he spent $15,000,000 in killing thirty Indians. A word to the wise is sufficient. E. ROBSON.

NANAIMO, November 19, 1886.

————

THE GOVERNMENT AND THE TSIMSHEAN IN-DIANS.

From the *Daily Colonist*, Victoria, B. C., December 19, 1886

TO THE EDITOR : Since the relations between both the Dominion and Provincial Governments with the Tsimshean and surrounding tribes have become so strained that a collision of some sort seems imminent, I feel sure that you will find space in your paper for the following remarks on the present position of affairs. And first of all let me say that it is not my intention to go over the story of the troubles which have existed here for more than five years, but to endeavor to show how matters stand at the present moment—the position taken by the governments—the position assumed by the Indians and their teachers—the policy adopted by the governments to maintain their position—the present effects of this policy and, finally, to make some suggestions toward the adoption of a policy which would avert the threatened collision and benefit the province. The subject is a large one, and your space is limited, so my remarks must of necessity be short and to the point—but no disrespect is intended thereby.

The provincial government assumes that the fee simple of all the lands of this province is in the crown and that the Indians, as the original inhabitants, have no title or rights in any portion of these lands. In support of this claim Mr. Drake, entirely ignoring later opinions and proclamations,

as also the actual practice of the British Government in
dealing with native tribes, not only in Canada but the other
dependencies, has quoted in his letter to your paper some
opinions which, though antiquated, might have some weight
from the high legal standing of those who gave them if the
condition of the natives referred to in them was similar to
that of these Tsimshean Indians, but, unfortunately for his
argument, this is not so. The natives then referred to were
nomad tribes without any fixed habitation, while these Indians have not only fixed abodes, but hereditary, defined
tracts for hunting, fruit-gathering, and fishing. The provincial government, moreover, relies on the thirteenth section
of the terms of union to support them, forgetting that since
the union the terms of this section as the basis of an Indian
policy have been officially condemned by both governments,
and as may be seen in the blue-book of 1875, the then attorney-general of the province sketched a policy which included
the recognition of the very claim which these Indians are
now making about their hunting grounds. The Dominion
Government, too, though in 1875 they considered the adoption of the thirteenth section for an Indian policy would be
" little short of a mockery of the Indian claims," now seem
willing to sanction and aid the provincial government in the
adoption of such a policy.

Thus the government claims the right to deal arbitrarily
with all the lands—to decide the size and nature of the reserves—to dispose of, whenever they wish, all land outside
of the reserves now used by the Indians for hunting or fruit-
gathering (even where these are within defined limits and
have been hereditary in particular families) without granting
any remuneration or acknowledging any claim or right of
the occupiers of these special tracts. In fact, the Indians
are dependent upon the charity of the government for the
very ground on which they set their feet.

The Dominion Government, in recognizing this claim by

the provincial government, is permitting a mode of dealing with the Indians in this province which is at direct variance with that adopted in all other parts of Canada and which puts the Indians on a very different footing, and yet the government assume the right to enforce a special act (the Indian Act), though this act presupposes that treaties have already been made with the Indians and the lands surrendered. The position assumed by the government, then, is : 1, Power to deal with all Indian lands without regarding the interests of the Indians in them ; 2, the right to bring the Indians under a special act which puts them entirely and helplessly in the power of the Indian Department and deprives them of their freedom and power to advance themselves.

And now let us turn to the position assumed by these Indians, but before doing so, let us first take a glance at the position held by the Indians at Metlakahtla and its immediate neighborhood at the time the care of the Indians was handed over by the provincial government to the Dominion. At that time these Indians were the most advanced of any in the province. Metlakahtla was not only the seat of order but the centre from which an influence had radiated throughout the surrounding district, which was powerful enough to establish peace and order among all the tribes for more than one hundred miles around. These Indians had received the approval of the highest government officials—had been spoken to and recognized as free British subjects and encouraged to advance ; had obtained redress whenever their rights were endangered, while they had shown consideration for the claims of white men coming to reside in their neighborhood, because they felt that there was room for both the white men and themselves, while they fully trusted the government to protect their interests.

Both government and Indians were acting out the golden rule ; thus there was general peace and prosperity, and a more loyal, contented, and peaceable community did not exist in the province.

Now let us inquire, What is the present position of these Indians? Disheartened at the frequent rebuffs they have received, and the favor shown to those who would overthrow the very foundation of their prosperity; disgusted with the disregard of its pledged word which the government has shown; believing and knowing that in all right and equity they have a title to the lands and ought to be consulted regarding them; that the arbitrarily apportioning of reserves before their homes are secured and their hunting and other claims settled, and the forcible taking of all lands by the government; but, above all, their being placed under a law and rule which relegate them to the position of wild, illiterate tribes, will render it impossible for them to maintain their position, much less advance. Therefore, it is that they have combined to prevent the infliction of this intolerable yoke, but in thus combining they have not forgotten that they are Christians and owe allegiance to the King of kings.

The combination is not against law and order, nor does it spring from a spirit of disloyalty or any objection to bear the burdens of citizenship. It is a combination against the infliction of a cruel and uncalled-for injury, an injury, they have good reason to believe, which will, if inflicted prove the death-blow to their retaining their individuality in face of advancing civilization. The means they would use are such as good men need not be ashamed of, but they are heavily burdened. Around them are tribes having the same interests, but without the same principles to guide them, and whom they have to restrain while at the same time they fully sympathize with them. Then, on the other hand, the apparently harsh and uncalled-for action of the government from the beginning of these troubles is exasperating and makes it still more difficult for them to maintain this position. What the Indians are asking for may be summed up thus:

1. That, as in the case of all other Indians in Canada, treaties be entered into with them in respect of their general and particular land claims before the reserves are set apart.

2. That if the Indian Act is to be put in force among them, such changes should be made in the act as their special circumstances call for and which will make it a help and not a hinderance to their advancement.

In other words, they are asking to be dealt with as reasonable and reasoning beings, and not as wild and uncivilized savages whose only weapon is brute force, and who must be restrained by force. This is the position assumed, and we feel that in upholding them in this position we are not only *not* exciting them to disorder but, on the contrary, helping to obtain for them that simple justice which is the privilege of even the poorest who dwells beneath the shadow of a Christian government. And this leads me to speak of the policy hitherto adopted toward these Indians, and its results so far. This policy is based upon the fallacy that the Indians are a set of irresponsible beings, ignorant alike of what is good for them and how they can obtain this good; that the government without consulting them or listening to their appeals know exactly what is best, and that the Indians should simply acquiesce in these measures and thank the government for proposing them; that any attempt on the part of the Indians to show the government that the proposed measures are sure to prove detrimental to their welfare is to be looked upon as an attempt to rebel, and must be repressed with force and even the sword if necessary; and that any white man who would endeavor to support the claims of the Indians is, *ipso facto*, exciting them against the government. In one word, it is a policy of "coercion," and as the Indians have not acquiesced in it we have had the exhibition of force on the part of the government, together with the threat of more severe measures if those already used have failed. Now what are the results so far? As regards the government . 1. An expenditure of public funds of over $30,000—if my calculation be correct—with a worse than negative result. 2. The government have shown themselves as ready to use force against those who have laid aside all force and are merely seeking redress for a real grievance, and have thus destroyed every vestige of trust in their good will.

Third, they have succeeded in raising from a little matter, which might easily have been settled at first, a question which affects nearly every Indian in the province, and, finally, they have so shaken faith in the justice of English rule as cannot fail to affect the loyalty of even the most loyal. In fact, such have been the results that there seems to be good reason for the question, Are the Dominion and Provincial Governments combining to excite an Indian rising, and thereby secure an opportunity to take by force from the Indians the land which they refuse to acquire by treaty?

As regards the Indians, the results so far seem to be even more disastrous to the government, for this last attempt to overawe and frighten them and to treat as guilty felons those who were merely endeavoring to prevent, what to them seemed an irreparable injury being inflicted on them, has stirred the people to the heart. The lukewarm are becoming whole-hearted ; subscriptions are flowing in , sorrow is expressed by those at Fort Simpson and elsewhere that none from their places were among those sent to jail. It has made this question *the* question of the hour, and its consideration is the one absorbing thought. It must not, however, be understood that there is the smallest idea on the minds of these people that they can, or even wish to oppose force to force. These christianized coast Indians know better, though no one at all acquainted with the tribes at the head-waters of the Naas and Skeena would, for a moment, doubt, that if the question is raised while they are still in their wild and un-

christianized state it would become probably a war of extermination, with all its attendant horrors. With the coast
Indians recourse to arms would only be as a last and desperate resort. Meanwhile they are strengthening themselves
in their trust in their God and waiting on him, for they feel
and know they have right on their side, and well they know
that he can laugh at the most powerful armaments of nations,
and in his own way and time help and protect even the
poorest and weakest.

Living among these Indians and hearing and seeing what
goes on, such is the picture, as I see it, of the present state
of affairs, and sad I am to have to tell the tale, and little did
I once dream that I should have to disclose such a state of
things There are, I think, two questions that every thoughtful mind in the province will ask : " Are the government justified in continuing to act on a policy which has so far proved
worse than useless? and, secondly, is there no alternative
policy?" To the second of these questions I answer, that it
seems to me to be quite possible to frame a policy free from
the evils attending the present one—less expensive in opera-
tion and securing the settling up of the country in a peaceable
way. Of course, after the past, the Indians will naturally look
with suspicion on any proposal, and patience and tact in
dealing with them will be needed ; but since the government
would gain the aid and influence of every true friend of the
Indians their task would be facilitated and a bond of union
re-established between the government and the Indians.
The basis of such a policy should be *justice*, and it should
be so framed as to show that it emanated from the government as a voluntary effort and not as if wrung from them.
Then, again, it must be so framed as not to be made a precedent to unsettle Indians whose claims have already been
dealt with and who are satisfied. And again, it should so
deal with the question of the general land claims as to take
away its significance and absorb it in secondary matters,

and thus while extinguishing it not direct attention to it.   I
believe it to be quite practicable to frame such a policy, and
I feel sure that every right-minded citizen will agree with me
in saying, that if such is possible now is the time to make
the attempt, and if the government will meet in a fair and
friendly spirit those who know these Indians and who have
thought the matter over in all its bearings they will find them
ready to give them such information as will enable them to
satisfy the Indians, maintain the interests of the province,
and support the honor of the government.

ROBERT TOMLINSON.

METLAKAHTLA, November 26, 1886.

———

METLAKAHTLA.

From the *Daily Colonist*, Victoria, B. C, December 19, 1886.

BELOW will be found a letter from J. W. Powell, Indian
Superintendent, to Mr. Duncan, which speaks for itself :

BRITISH COLUMBIA INDIAN OFFICE,
VICTORIA, August, 1879.

SIR : Referring to my recent visit to the village of Metlakahtla, may I beg to convey to you my acknowledgments
for the kindness, courtesy, and co-operation with official
duties you were good enough to extend to me while at the
mission.   I cannot conclude without heartily congratulating
you on the wonderful effects of your arduous mission labors
among the Tsimsheans for the last twenty years.   I consider that you have performed a great and noble work in
reclaiming from ignorance and barbarism a most *useful, contented*, and law-abiding community, the effects of which are
not confined to your own locality, but is felt and highly appreciated by all the Northern tribes

At Queen Charlotte's Island, . . . I found your

name highly respected, and an ardent desire generally prevalent among the Hydahs to participate in the great reforms you have been chiefly instrumental in creating among the Tsimshean Indians.

Personally, I wish you every success, and I shall not fail to acquaint the Honorable Superintendent-General with the *loyal* feeling and great progress in civilization I saw so fully exhibited among the Indians during my brief and pleasant sojourn at Metlakahtla. I have the honor to be, sir, your obedient servant, (Signed,) J. W. POWELL,
Indian Superintendent.
—*Com.*

THE INDIAN QUESTION.

From the *Daily Colonist*, Victoria, B. C., 1886.

TO THE EDITOR : On examining the length of the documents I submitted to the Indian Department last year, at Ottawa, on Indian affairs, I feel it would be unfair to ask you to publish them *in extenso*. But at the request of friends, and by your kind permission, I will, instead, lay before the public a brief review of the questions at issue. First, a few words on Indian land interests. The matter stands thus. Either the aborigines have rights in the land, or they have not. All British provinces, we are told, with the exception of British Columbia—the latest born—have unmistakably settled the question in favor of the aborigines. Treaties, we know, have been made, and do now exist, between several governments and Indians. These treaties are confessedly for the extinguishing of Indian claims on lands, and therefore imply that the Indians have rights to extinguish. For governments to make treaties with Indians to extinguish their rights—if rights they had none—would be absurd.

British Columbia, by refusing to make treaties with Ind-

ians, is undoubtedly marking out for itself a new and un-
tried experience, and virtually ignoring the constitutional
laws and usages which bind all other provinces of the British empire on this subject. In the meantime the Indians
regard their rights in the soil of British Columbia to be as
valid as are the Indians' rights in other provinces ; nor will
they be easily persuaded that their foothold in the country
which their forefathers discovered and inhabited ages ago
rests solely upon the bounty of the English crown   If the
Indians are, however, entertaining a fallacy, based upon
their natural instincts, then I would ask why were they not
corrected by the Governor-General, a colonial governor, a
lieutenant-governor, and the Superintendent of Indian Affairs
on their several official visits to the North, in years gone by ?
And why did that great and good man, Sir James Douglas,
as governor, meet the Indians of Victoria and neighboring
tribes, and buy out their right to a large tract of land, including the site of this city ?

Next, as to the Indian policy adopted by British Columbia.
The Indians, by the terms of Union, were to have an allowance of ten acres of land to each family of five persons, and
Indian agencies were to be established and paid for by the
Dominion Government.   When, however, the Mackenzie
Government came into power at Ottawa, exception was
taken to the position assumed by the British Columbia Government in reference to the Indian land question, and a
stout resistance was offered to the ten-acre allowance to Indians as " being little better than a mockery of their claims."
The result of the struggle between the two governments was
that British Columbia gave way, and the ten-acre policy
was abandoned as untenable.

The facts are before the public as evidence of the foolish
and selfish policy which obtained on Indian matters when
the province was incorporated in the Dominion.   It may be
that some of the " misleaders " of the province at that time

are still in this city, and may possibly feel aggrieved at being reminded of the failure of their scheme.

Then as to the Indian agencies. What have they done for the Indians, even for those few who have been favored for many years by being the nearest to headquarters? Are the results in any sense commensurate with the expense of the machinery? Is it not proverbial that the system of Indian management is a burlesque, and an outrage on common-sense? Would such a system of mismanagement be allowed to continue if white men's interests were involved? I believe not. But the Indians have no voice in Parliament, and therefore no means of correcting abuses in the management of their affairs. They are but wards of the government, and have only the right to be silent. If they dared to complain they must travel two or three thousand miles at their own expense, wait a month before their grievances are heard, and be sent back with promises which are never fulfilled.

This brings me to notice the *requests* the Indians made through their deputation at Ottawa. *First:* They asked for their reserves to be readjusted in a few particulars before being surveyed. They complained that, not having been notified of the reserve commissioner's visit, many of their people were away when he came, and that thus it was impossible for them to give that due consideration to his business which their interest demanded. They begged, therefore, for the reserve commissioner to pay them a second visit.

A second request was that a treaty should be made with them for the lands they were to surrender, as had been done with other Indians of the Dominion. They did not ask for presents, but only that a portion of the money voted yearly for the Indians of British Columbia might reach their community, and help them in public improvements.

A third request was that the two acres of their village site at Metlakahtla known as Mission Point should not be taken from them. And Sir John Macdonald undertook to write to the Church Missionary Society to advise them to withdraw their agents from the occupancy of the land in question.

Further—the Indian deputation assured the Deputy Minister of Indian Affairs that their·brethren would gladly enrol themselves as *free men* under the British flag—but the position of slaves or paupers they could not accept. I wish here to add that, at the request of the deputy minister, I wrote a letter on the subject of Indian management, with a view to assisting the government in effectually removing all causes of complaint among the Indians

To the present time I have not made known to the Indians the terms of my letter; but, moderate as they were (and the deputy minister acknowledged they were moderate), I have reason to believe that the Indians would be willing to accept them, and if they did so, disloyalty would effectually be removed and peace restored.

In conclusion, I would urge upon all who have an interest in the province, that Indian management is demanding patient and dispassionate hearing before it is too late. It is for the people, through their representatives, to put things right. There has been enough of blundering, the Northwest rebellion being a proof of that—a rebellion which, it is said, has cost the country as much money as would suffice to support all the Indians of the Northwest in a first class hotel for their natural lives.

The Indian troubles are no new thing, nor are they due to seditious teachers. The government has been too eager to listen to false reports, emanating from persons who had their own hypocritical ends to serve. Warlike armaments are not the remedy for Indian complaints. but patience and just dealing are. It may be in the memory of some of your readers that, when an Indian village on the Skeena was burned down some years ago, through the carelessness of some miners, the Indians closed the river. The intention of the government to force the river by armed men was only abandoned through the counsel and help of the missionary. Thus a disaster and expenditure of blood and treasure were averted, and by a patient hearing and equitable arrangement the good will of the Indians was restored.

On my arrival in Victoria at the present juncture, I lost no time in beseeching the government to refrain from sending a ship of war to Metlakahtla. I offered to go up in the coast steamer with any gentleman the government might depute and use my best efforts to bring about an amicable settlement. I pointed out that the most suitable person to go was the reserve commissioner, and Mr. O'Reilly offered to go if he received orders. The peaceful measures I proposed were, however, rejected and the ship of war has gone.

W. DUNCAN.

THE END.

LaVergne, TN USA
14 September 2010
196952LV00003B/28/P

9 781177 000093